# PARALLEL MONEY MARKETS – VOLUME ONE

*By the same author*

The Case Against Floating Exchanges

The Case Against Joining the
Common Market

Decline and Fall? Britain's Crises in the Sixties

A Dynamic Theory of Forward Exchange

The Euro-Dollar System: Practice and Theory of
International Interest Rates

The Euro-Bond Market

Foreign Exchange Crises

The History of Foreign Exchange

Leads and Lags: The Main Cause of Devaluation

A Textbook on Foreign Exchange

# PARALLEL MONEY MARKETS

PAUL EINZIG

VOLUME ONE
THE NEW MARKETS IN LONDON

MACMILLAN
ST MARTIN'S PRESS

First published 1971 by
THE MACMILLAN PRESS LTD
London and Basingstoke
Associated companies in New York Toronto
Dublin Melbourne Johannesburg and Madras

SBN 333 11369 1 (hard cover)

Library of Congress catalog card no. 75-143999

Printed in Great Britain by
R. & R. CLARK LTD
Edinburgh

# Contents

# Preface

THE main object of this book is to provide in an easily accessible form much-needed factual information about the new money markets that have come into existence during the last decade or two. Although a number of good books have been added to the extensive literature on money markets, most of them cover mainly the traditional markets and deal only very cursorily with the 'parallel' markets – as the new money markets have come to be called. This in spite of the fact that while there is relatively little to be said about the traditional markets that is new – apart from the impact of the parallel markets on them – there is ample scope for originality in describing the evolution, organisation and activities of the new markets and analysing their broader significance. Many interesting articles and booklets have appeared on the subject in recent years, but they do not obviate the necessity for an attempt to publish the material in greater detail and within the covers of a book.

The present volume – the first of two volumes dealing with money markets in London and in other centres – aims to fill this gap in monetary literature, in particular as far as the provision of factual material is concerned. I have included in it detailed accounts of the way the various new markets work, on which I was able to collect much material in the course of my prolonged field research in the City and in other quarters. I feel justified in claiming that in this respect I have covered some new ground. Apart from the markets in Euro-dollars and in Certificates of Deposits, with which I have been familiar ever since their inception, I had to familiarise myself with the other markets. Some of them are at the time of writing still at an early stage of their evolution, but I feel justified in producing an interim report on them which will be, I hope, of some use both to those interested in the new markets for practical reasons and to those who are concerned with the broader theoretical implications of the institutional changes we have witnessed and are still witnessing.

I have tried to cover briefly these broader aspects too, but, to forestall critics, I readily admit that I am myself far from being satisfied with the result of my efforts in that sphere. In trying to deal with the metaphysical aspects of my subject – in the sense of Professor Gaston Jèze's definition: 'Je comprends par mèta-physique tout ce que je ne comprends pas' – I have found myself from time to time quite candidly out of my depth. I could have, and perhaps should have, spent more time trying to follow up all the broader implications of my factual material. But to do so would have delayed its publication, and the sands are running out. I felt, rightly or wrongly, that it was more important and more urgent to make that material available for others than to attempt to provide a more profound analysis of it. So I have confined myself to indicating some of the lines on which such analysis could usefully proceed.

I hope that my observations on some theoretical aspects of the parallel money markets, inadequate as they admittedly must be, will help those who will undertake the task of processing my factual material. But I also hope that when performing that task they will not divorce their analysis altogether from the realities on which all sound theoretical speculation must surely be based. I feel the need to stress this, because of the growing tendency of monetary theory to become a sheer intellectual exercise at its best and a pseudo-intellectual parlour-game at its worst, for the exclusive benefit of a mutual admiration society to which it is addressed.

Let me illustrate what I mean. A reviewer of my book *The Case Against Floating Exchanges*, Professor Walters, took me to task for criticising economists who favour floating exchange rates on the fallacious assumption that the rates would float to the level at which imports and exports would balance automatically, and who ignore the fact that capital transactions and other non-commercial transactions would always divert exchange rates from their trade equilibrium level. My critic contends that economic models disregard capital transactions only in order to isolate a particular problem as 'a stepping stone to solutions of practical problems'.

But the trouble is that, having produced an unrealistic model as a stepping stone, too many economists present it as the *complete* answer to a practical problem, in total disregard of its other facets calling for other stepping stones that lead in different directions. Because they believe that in an imaginary world where all foreign exchange transactions originate from trade freely floating rates would necessarily settle around their trade equilibrium level – even that contention is subject to important reservations – they apply their conclusions with an enviable degree of cocksureness to our real world in which foreign exchange transactions originate from several other sources as well as from trade.

This argument may appear irrelevant from the point of view of my present subject. But there is ample scope for those who will process my material to become guilty of fallacies similar to the one I denounce above. That is why I deem it necessary to raise a voice of protest against such misuse of my material, even though I am aware that in all probability my protest will be ignored.

I am greatly indebted to the large number of specialists in the various money markets who have contributed towards my factual material. They include executives and dealers in banks, discount houses, firms of brokers and finance houses, and also officials of the Public Works Loans Board, the Institute of Municipal Treasurers and Accountants and the Finance Houses Association. They gave me generously their time when answering my long lists of questions. I also had opportunity to familiarise myself with the official attitude towards the new markets. The list of names of those but for whom this book could not have been written runs into three figures, but I am sure most of them would prefer to remain anonymous.

I am also indebted to H.M. Stationery Office for authorisation to reprint official material published in the *Board of Trade Journal* and in *Financial Statistics*, to the Bank of England for permission to use statistics published in its *Quarterly Review*, to the Finance Houses Association for permission to reprint the table first published in *Credit* showing total finance house deposits and those borrowed by members of that Association, and to the *Midland Bank Review* for permission to reprint its table of interest rates.

120 Clifford's Inn,                                              P. E.
  London, E.C.4
    *February 1971*

# CHAPTER ONE

# Introduction

PROGRESS means that everything in our life becomes infinitely more complicated, both in the sphere of theory and in the sphere of practice. Einstein's theories were incomparably more complicated than those of Newton, but they were simplicity itself compared with present-day physics. Industrial equipment, military weapons, the legal system, medicine, and so on and so forth, have all become extremely involved within the lifetime of the present generation. In the sphere of economics, the teachings of Marshall and Keynes appear to be elementary compared with present-day theory.

There is no reason why the monetary system should provide an exception to the general trend of increasing complexity. There are now many more money markets, some local and some international. Transactions within them and between them have become more complicated. There is a wider variety of techniques, a wider range of practices, a wider choice between alternative borrowing and lending facilities. Most of these changes have occurred before our very eyes. There have been more institutional changes in the monetary sphere during the last quarter-century than between the end of the Napoleonic Wars and the end of the Second World War. More institutional changes are pending or are under consideration.

The money market is one of the spheres in which there have been a large number of important changes during the past decade or two. Large and increasing numbers of parallel money markets have developed. The term 'parallel' should not be interpreted in the geometric sense in which parallel lines mean lines that, according to the definition of the *Oxford Dictionary*, are continuously equidistant, lines which never meet and may continue infinitely without coming into contact. In the various money markets which are included under the description 'parallel money markets', rates are not equidistant from each other. Differentials may tend to be steady in normal conditions, but even then they are liable to fluctuate, albeit within narrow limits. In abnormal conditions the lines represented by the rates quoted in the various markets tend to diverge from each other or converge towards each other materially. Indeed occasionally they contact each other and they even cross each other.

Nevertheless the term 'parallel' is substantially correct. The markets are parallel, not in the geometric sense that their rates are equidistant – like the Bank rate and the deposit rates allowed by clearing banks – but in the metaphorical sense that they offer to borrowers and lenders alternative facilities to those obtainable in the traditional markets. Both borrowers and lenders have a wider choice than in the traditional markets. The terms allowed in the parallel markets are more flexible and more adaptable to changing requirements.

Although, as we shall see in Volume 2 of this book, parallel markets exist also in some continental financial centres, they exist mainly in London, in New York and in Canada. The London financial market in particular has developed a wide range of parallel markets, mostly in sterling but also in dollars and, to an incomparably smaller degree, in other foreign currencies. Although some other financial centres are very advanced and sophisticated in most respects, they have failed so far to produce facilities for short-term and medium-term borrowing and lending similar to those obtainable in London.

The time has come to produce a systematic detailed description of these markets. So long as there was reason to believe that the new markets were mere passing phenomena there might have been an excuse for neglecting their technical and theoretical implications. But now it is evident that most if not all of these markets have come to stay. They have become an integral part of the British monetary system and, in their international aspects, of the international monetary system.

With the sole exception of the Euro-dollar market, which received ample attention during the 'sixties, the broader aspects of the other parallel markets have been virtually ignored by most theoretical monetary economists. This may be due in part to the inadequacy of factual material on these markets, for which I, among others who have access to such material, must plead guilty. But possibly theoretical economists are inclined to underrate the importance of these institutional changes, as most of them underrated for a long time the importance of Euro-dollars and, before that, the importance of forward exchange. Yet the parallel markets have some very far-reaching theoretical implications which provide ample scope for academic economists to explore new ground.

Factual information about the inter-bank sterling market is far from adequate. While there is now ample literature about the Euro-dollar market and there is, thanks largely to the Bank for International Settlements, also ample statistical material available, the market for inter-bank sterling deposits is still largely *terra incognita*. Dependable statistical material is completely lacking and such calculations as are made can hardly be regarded as being more than mere 'guesstimates'. The descriptive material on practices and techniques of this market, as of the other parallel money markets in London, and the literature concerning the origin of inter-bank deposits and the use made of them, are confined almost entirely to pamphlets published by various firms of discount houses or brokers operating in the market.

My foremost task was therefore to provide as detailed descriptive material as possible on the inter-bank deposit market. It is by far the longest chapter in this book, owing to the considerable importance of this market. I tried to examine the influences operating in the market and its inter-relations with other markets.

Next in importance is the description and examination of the market in sterling Certificates of Deposits. Although it is much smaller than the inter-bank sterling market, having only been in existence since October 1968, it is expanding rapidly and it has considerable potentialities, especially after the removal or relaxation of the credit squeeze.

The markets in deposits for Local Authorities and for hire-purchase finance houses, too, deserve much attention, even though their development is handicapped by the fact that they are both 'one-way streets'. Their deposit receipts are non-transferable and there is therefore no secondary market in them. Even so, they are of considerable importance both from the point of view of the local money market and of international movements of funds.

There is a brief chapter on the inter-corporation market, in which business firms lend to each other their liquid surpluses, with or without bank guarantees. At the time of writing this market is still of moderate size, but should the credit restrictions continue for very long it is liable to assume noteworthy dimensions.

The markets in deposits in dollar denominations, the Euro-dollar market and the market in London dollar Certificates of Deposits form part of the system of London parallel money markets even though they transact business in terms of foreign currencies. Their size exceeds that of the corresponding two parallel sterling markets, the inter-bank sterling market and the market in sterling Certificates of Deposits. Their creation pre-dates that of the latter, and the increased use of dollars as an international currency has also helped them to expand. Owing to a change of official policy in respect of authorising U.K. residents to borrow in terms of foreign currencies, the local importance of the Euro-currency markets declined temporarily. A third parallel dollar market in London, the market in dollar commercial paper or promissory notes, was still in its initial stage at the time of writing.

Before embarking on the task of dealing with the parallel markets, I have devoted some brief chapters to the traditional markets, just to complete the picture. Their inter-relationship with the parallel markets is covered in greater detail in the chapters dealing with the parallel markets themselves, indicating in outline the broader aspects of the new system. The effect of the advent and expansion of parallel markets and of their trends on the volume of credit, on the velocity of credit and on interest rates is examined. I am aware that, having regard to the relative brevity of experience with the new markets and to the inadequacy of statistical material relating to some of them, I am skating on thin ice when inferring broad conclusions from insufficient evidence. But the questions have to be raised and answered provisionally, if only to indicate the theoretical problems which arise from the operation of the new markets.

Perhaps the most important aspect of the subject is only too familiar to us all – the extent of the risk involved in the spectacular expansion of unsecured credits. The commercial risk for lenders in accepting the names of borrowers and the limits applied to that risk are dealt with in the various chapters on the particular parallel markets. What needs careful consideration is the overall risk for the entire community – the extent to which the new system, while assisting individual borrowers and lenders, carries the possibility of a major crisis. The question which calls for answer is whether, as a result of the expansion of unsecured credits to a multiple of the amount of fully secured Wall Street loans in 1929, the world is not in an even more vulnerable position than it was on the eve of the Wall Street slump.

# CHAPTER TWO

# The Traditional Markets

## (1) AN EFFICIENT MECHANISM

BEFORE embarking on the investigation of parallel money markets it is necessary to summarise briefly the organisation and functioning of the traditional money markets. So much has been written ever since Walter Bagehot's epoch-making classic, *Lombard Street*, about the discount market and the market in short credits, and also about the more recent traditional markets in Treasury bills and short bonds, that it would be difficult to try to write anything original about them. The aim of this chapter and of the subsequent three chapters is less ambitious than that of the subsequent chapters, which do try to break new ground – it is mainly to summarise the well-known facts about the traditional markets. Although occasional reference will be made to the way in which they have been affected by the emergence and development of the parallel markets, the detailed treatment of that subject will of course be reserved for later chapters.

The London discount market, around which the other traditional markets have developed, is an institution of which the City has been rightly proud and which is the object of admiration and envy in other financial centres. It is a highly efficient mechanism which acts as intermediary between the banks and the Bank of England on the one hand and between the banks themselves on the other. To some extent it also acts as intermediary between non-banking clients and banks. This was its original function when it first came into existence in its modern form in the early 19th century. The relative importance of that function declined towards the end of the century, but was recently revived once more. Its main function is, however, to act as a clearing house through which the banks' surpluses and deficiencies of liquid funds are offset against each other. At the same time it provides the mechanism through which the Bank of England seeks to apply its policy measures aiming at the regulation of the volume of liquid funds and through which the management of the Treasury's floating debts can be run smoothly.

## (2) TRADITIONS OF THE TRADITIONAL MARKETS

The markets dealt with in this chapter are called 'traditional' not only because they have been in existence for a great many years – actually the market in short bonds is of relatively recent origin and the market in trade bills was only revived to any noteworthy extent relatively recently – but also because their methods of operation conform to certain traditions which are not followed to any extent in the parallel markets.

1. In the traditional markets loans must be fully secured, while in the parallel markets they are unsecured.
2. In the traditional markets loans are supposed to be self-liquidating, while in the parallel markets they need not be self-liquidating.
3. In the traditional markets there is a lender of last resort – the Bank of England – while in the parallel markets there is no such lender.
4. In the traditional markets the authorities often take the initiative to regulate the flow of funds, while the parallel markets are left to their own devices.
5. In the traditional markets the need for conforming to well-established rules slows down business to some extent, while in the parallel markets business is more informal and therefore more expeditious.
6. In the traditional market it is sought to uphold the traditional method of transacting business through personal calls – even if only in the mornings – while most business in the parallel market is transacted by telephone.

In reality the above comparison between the two sets of markets is rather oversimplified and, like all oversimplifications, it is subject to exceptions. Loans in the parallel markets are not all unsecured. In the market for Local Authorities mortgages are traded marketwise and other loans are a general charge on the rates. Nor are all loans in parallel markets non-self-liquidating. Deposits lent to finance houses, in so far as they are used for financing hire-purchase credits, are self-liquidating, even if the pace of their self-liquidation is slower than that of commercial bills. On the other hand, Treasury bills need not be self-liquidating unless they are issued for the sole purpose for which they were originally invented – to anticipate revenue or proceeds of loans due to be collected. In the market for Local Authorities there is a lender of last resort, the Public Works Loans Board, and in the Euro-dollar market the Federal Reserve is the lender of last resort for the deposits borrowed by American banks.

Likewise, the Euro-dollar market – and to a less extent the market in London dollar Certificates of Deposits – is not left entirely to its own devices, as the Bank for International Settlements intervenes from time to time. Routine business in Lombard Street is quite expeditious in spite of having to shift bundles of securities between discount houses and clearing banks and the Bank of England. Finally, the bulk of the business in the traditional markets is now also transacted by telephone, even though the morning visits of top-hatted representatives of the discount market to banks continue. Incidentally, although their main object is to deal with business relating to the traditional markets, they often take the opportunity to pick up orders from banks for Certificates of Deposits and other business transacted in the parallel markets, especially since some discount houses have come to combine that function with the functions of deposit brokers and money brokers through acquiring control over broker firms. In any case, discount houses may also deal in parallel markets on their own account.

The view is still widely held that the tradition of morning visits by top-hatted brokers and dealers is more than just one of the quaint City customs which die hard. Survivors of the old generation are convinced that daily personal contact with clients is a help in running the money markets, traditional and parallel, in the correct spirit. They may well be right, and members of the new generation who regard the daily visits as a time-wasting anachronistic ritual – like the brief sessions many continental foreign exchange markets have at the *Bourse* – are inclined to underrate the importance of the personal element in conducting business in money.

'Traditional markets' are often looked upon as being synonymous with the discount market and are often referred to by the traditional name of 'Lombard Street' – a name which has survived in spite of the fact that only two out of twelve discount houses now have their premises in the famous street which has witnessed dealing in money since medieval times. In a memorandum addressed to Elizabeth I and attributed to Sir Thomas Gresham, it was stated that 'the way to rayse sterling' was 'by making money scaunt in Lumbard Strete' – a rule which our monetary authorities still seek to apply, and which is the basic principle of the 'money school'.

Whenever we talk about the London discount market we have two distinct but closely related markets in mind – the market in bills and the market in short-term credits. The two markets are so closely interwoven that it would be difficult to deal with the one without overlapping with the sphere of the other. Bills are 'bought' largely for the purpose of employing liquid funds more profitably, and they are 'sold' mainly for the purpose of gaining possession of liquid funds which, unless required immediately, are employed in the market for short-term loans. Conversion of short-term loans into bills and *vice versa* are usually two aspects of the same transaction. Just as purchases and sales of goods have two aspects – the money side and the goods side – transactions in bills usually have two aspects – the bills side and the credits side.

Institutions participating in the discount market in the broader sense of the term belong to the following categories:

(1) *Discount houses.* They are the centre of the discount market. Clearing banks and banks of every kind lend them their surplus funds, mostly in the form of loans overnight or at call or at very short notice. They withdraw their funds whenever they require cash. It is to them that banks offer their bills or those of their customers for sale, and it is from them that they buy bills for their portfolio or for their customers. Their role in respect of short loans is a one-way street – they only borrow but do not lend to banks. It is because of their two-way role as buyers and sellers of bills that discount houses can maintain their function as the clearing house for the banks' surpluses and deficiencies in liquid funds. Since the development of the inter-bank sterling market, non-clearing banks can employ their liquid funds more profitably in that market, but they feel under obligation to provide the means which enable discount houses to buy their bills. There are twelve members of the Discount Houses Association and a number of other firms – including running brokers – which, without being members, transact similar business on a smaller scale and form part of the market. It is the privilege of the discount houses to borrow from the Bank of England and it is because the latter acts for them as lender of last resort that funds borrowed by them may

safely be considered as being virtually as liquid as cash or balances with the Bank of England.

Discount houses combine the role of brokers with that of principals as far as transactions in bills and in short-term funds are concerned. They deal on their own account as well as on account of their clients inside or outside the market. They act as intermediaries between non-banking clients and banks. We shall see in later chapters that they play an increasingly active part in parallel markets, but their principal function is still, and is likely to remain, to absorb and release liquid funds of banks and to provide a market for commercial bills – whteher bank bills or trade bills – and for Treasury bills and short bonds.

(2) *Clearing banks.* The discount houses exist largely for the convenience of the clearing banks (and of the Scottish banks, which play a role similar to that of clearing banks). It is mainly through the intermediary of discount houses that clearing banks employ their surplus cash in a highly liquid form, in a form in which it can be re-converted into cash at any time. From this point of view the advent and expansion of the inter-bank sterling market has not made any direct difference to the clearing banks. For although their affiliates operate in that market and in other parallel money markets very actively, the clearing banks themselves keep aloof from them. This is because under their traditional rules, by which they have to maintain a minimum of 8 per cent of cash reserve and of 28 per cent of liquidity ratio, they could not include in their liquidity ratio moneys lent to parallel markets.

Moreover, under their cartel arrangement clearing banks are precluded from paying higher deposit rates than 2 per cent below the Bank rate of the day. They still depend, therefore, on the discount market for balancing their cash position by disposing of unwanted surpluses and recovering the funds they need for meeting requirements, either through increasing or reducing their short credits, or through buying or selling their bills.

Clearing banks are the principal participants in the money market. Their relative importance in the traditional markets has increased since the development of the inter-bank sterling market, because non-clearing banks are now in a position to use that market as an alternative clearing house for liquid funds. It is lendings and withdrawals by clearing banks that determine more than ever the trend in the traditional money market.

Clearing banks also participate actively in the bill market both as buyers and sellers on their own account or on account of their customers. Although they prefer to finance their domestic customers by means of overdrafts, they grant acceptance credits to foreign customers and to some extent also to domestic customers.

(3) *Non-clearing banks*. This category includes accepting houses, merchant banks, overseas banks with London head offices, London branches and affiliates of overseas banks, etc. Until the emergence of the inter-bank sterling market all these banks depended largely on the traditional market as the clearing house for employing their surpluses and covering their deficiencies in liquid funds, in the same way as clearing banks still depend on it. As already remarked, the inter-bank sterling market now provides these banks with facilities for placing their surpluses on terms more favourable than those obtainable in the discount market. It also enables them to attract funds through borrowing inter-bank deposits, as an alternative to selling bills in the discount market. Nevertheless, since they need the discount market for placing bills they have remained participants in that market, though to a more limited degree than before, also as lenders of short-term funds.

In particular on days when money is easy in the parallel markets, lenders may be able to obtain better rates in the traditional market, where a minimum call money rate is fixed by the clearing banks. In any case non-clearing banks may feel that at least part of their liquid resources should be employed in the traditional market. Accepting houses in particular consider it to be of vital importance that a good market for fine bank bills should remain in existence. Of course all non-clearing banks have accounts with at least one clearing bank and they are granted overdrafts on those accounts. But the rate on such overdrafts is usually costly and non-clearing banks only resort to such facilities if they have no means of drawing on those of the traditional market, by withdrawing short loans or by selling bills, and if the facilities available on parallel markets are even more expensive.

(4) *Borrowers and lenders outside the market*. A wide variety of big firms outside the market lend their liquid funds to discount houses, and smaller firms borrow from banks through their intermediary, in the form of acceptance credits. The former include financial institutions of various types – insurance companies, building societies, finance houses, all kinds of trusts, pension funds. The latter include industrial and commercial firms.

As we shall see in Chapter 4, discount houses and bill brokers have revived during recent years their original function of touring the country to acquire industrial and commercial customers whose bills they may keep in their portfolios, or place in the market. More recently, however, they have also begun to act as intermediaries between foreign clients and parallel money markets, especially through selling abroad CDs and LA deposits.

(5) *Borrowers and lenders abroad.* Discount houses have many clients outside the United Kingdom – banks, business firms and others with liquid funds at their disposal. Owing to the competition of the parallel markets with the traditional markets, some discount houses go out of their way to attract foreign clientèle. While in the old days they were almost entirely local institutions, more recently they have become distinctly more international. Their representatives travel abroad to introduce new business.

(6) *The Bank of England.* It is because the Central Bank is willing to act as lender of last resort for the discount market that discount houses are in a position to provide the highest degree of security and the maximum of liquidity for moneys lent to them. Ever since the early beginnings of the market, the firms engaged in it with the Bank of England's approval have the privilege of borrowing from the Bank against the deposition of eligible security, and of rediscounting with it bills held in their portfolio.

No bank or other financial institution, however big, has this privilege. For this reason lending in the discount market is an absolutely safe way of ensuring that the loans can always be turned into cash – subject only to the terms accepted by the lender. Although clearing banks and other banks have current accounts with the Bank of England, those accounts cannot be overdrawn, and the only way in which these banks can obtain money from the Bank in addition to drawing on their balances is indirectly through selling bills to discount houses, or calling loans from them, thereby making it necessary for them to fall back upon the Bank.

So while in the last resort it is the Bank itself that performs the task of equalising net surpluses and net deficiencies of the banking community, this is done through the intermediary of the discount houses. Conditions on which the latter may borrow from the Bank are extremely strict. They can only borrow against eligible collateral securities amounting to 105 per cent of the loans in the case of short-term Government bonds and to 100 per cent plus 25 per cent of the amount of the discount when the security consists of bills. If the securities should depreciate, discount houses have to provide additional securities to bring their amount up to the prescribed limits. Discount houses must possess sufficient capital resources to provide the required securities and to increase them if necessary. Only bills and bonds that are nearing maturity are eligible. Discount houses can also borrow from clearing banks against security with the same provisions regarding margins, but clearing banks are less strict concerning the range of eligible securities.

The discount market still has a large turnover in spite of the competition of the parallel markets, but the volume of its resources and of its turnover is now overshadowed by the latter, especially by the inter-bank sterling market and by the Euro-dollar market. One of the reasons why many banks like to employ part of their resources in the traditional market is that, thanks to the existence of a lender of last resort and also to the Bank's policy to intervene systematically to iron out fluctuations, its rates for overnight loans and money at call are not subject to such violent ups and downs as the corresponding inter-bank sterling rates.

In any of the parallel markets which have no lenders of last resort, supply and demand have to balance at rates at which a counterpart is forthcoming for the excess supply or for the excess demand. To attract the necessary counterpart rates may have to be adjusted very considerably. In the discount market, on the other hand, the Bank usually helps one way or another to prevent excessive fluctuations of short money rates. It does so on its own initiative if it deems this expedient. The other side of the picture is that from time to time official policy aims at creating artificial tendencies in the traditional market, which alone is used as the mechanism for applying official policies in the money market. But official intervention is also liable to affect the parallel markets to some extent indirectly.

(7) *The Treasury*. Treasury bill issues are a very important factor – indeed very often the most important factor – among the influences determining the trend in the traditional market. They first assumed such importance in the discount market in the First World War, when acceptance business came to a halt and public expenditure came to be financed partly through Treasury bill issues. Again from 1931, when the circulation of bank bills came to be virtually confined to those issued under Standstill Agreements, Treasury bills became practically the bread-and-butter of the market. Clearing banks agreed not to tender for them, so as

to give the discount houses a fair chance to obtain reasonably large allocations at Friday's tenders. Nor do they buy Treasury bills until after they have run for at least seven days.

As competition reduced Treasury bill rates to an unprofitable level the discount houses agreed in 1935 to tender jointly at a fixed price for the whole amount offered. Under this system, which is still in force, the amounts allotted are divided among the discount houses in proportion to their capital resources.

The discount market plays an important part in Treasury financing also by providing an active market for short-dated bonds. Discount houses are buyers of bonds approaching maturity and this role makes redemption or re-financing operations easier. Clearing banks are prepared to accept short-dated bonds as collaterals up to 10 per cent of the total since no securities are required in the inter-bank market. It is difficult to imagine the latter market, or any parallel market, taking the place of the traditional market in that respect.

From the above it is evident that in spite of the development of the parallel markets the traditional markets continue to play a very important role and are in some respects very useful and in other respects even indispensable. It is therefore entirely mistaken to believe that as a result of the expansion of the parallel markets the days of the traditional markets are numbered. It is argued in some quarters that the discount houses only had a *raison d'être* so long as banks felt inhibited from dealing in deposits directly with each other. But even if this were so, that inhibition still exists as far as clearing banks are concerned, in spite of its removal in respect of their affiliates. And the development of parallel markets has not affected the role played by discount houses as intermediate institutions between the banks and the Bank of England. So long as the Bank of England chooses to retain this system the traditional market continues to remain indispensable, in spite of any expansion of the parallel markets.

The view is held in Leftish quarters that it is quite unnecessary to maintain a set of middlemen between the Central Bank and the banking community, and that they perform no socially useful function. The same quarters do not seem to worry about the untold thousands of trade unionists who watch their fellow-workers working in shipyards and factories under inter-union arrangements arising from borderline disputes, but are concerned about the few hundreds of people employed by the discount market. Since some of them believe that on the same grounds the Stock Exchange and even Lloyd's are also superfluous, they are obviously divorced from practical realities. As far as the discount market is concerned the smooth functioning of its highly skilled mechanism is an advantage which can hardly be expected to be understood by politicians or politically minded economists. It is well worth while to employ some hundreds of people and to allow discount houses to earn a few million pounds' worth of profits every year for the sake of keeping this unique mechanism in being. In any case discount houses and bill brokers are now actively engaged also in various parallel money markets.

The Bank of England is most unlikely to sacrifice the advantages it derives from the operation of the discount market. For this reason alone the question whether the traditional markets should be supplanted by the new markets simply does not arise. It is of course conceivable that a Left-wing Government might listen to those who would like to eliminate the discount market, in which case the Chancellor of the Exchequer would have full power to instruct the Bank of England to make the required changes to that end. But any intelligent Chancellor of the Exchequer would put up a strong fight against being forced to take such a decision, which would be highly detrimental not only to London's standing as a banking centre but also to the smooth management of the floating debt.

It is well to recall that the disappearance of the discount market has been freely predicted on a number of occasions during its history. As the leading historian of that market, Wilfred King, pointed out in a remark quoted in the Institute of Bankers publication *The London Discount Market Today* (1969), at every stage of the evolution of the discount market 'there have always been people to predict that it was about to die, even that its demise was imminent, on the ground that its supposedly basic functions had ceased to exist'. But all that happened on each occasion was that the market adapted its activities to the changed requirements. To some degree it has already adapted itself to the new conditions created by the development of the parallel markets and further progress is likely in that direction. But such is its international prestige and its technical skill that if it did not exist it ought to have been invented, instead of giving serious thought to its deliberate elimination.

Apart from any other reasons, the continued existence of one section of the British banking mechanism which maintains London's traditions for sound finance to the extent of 100 per cent (indeed to the extent of 105 per cent, allowing for the safety margin of collaterals securing loans to discount houses) amidst the billions of unsecured credits in the parallel markets must surely be psychologically reassuring. The value of this market might come to be realised more widely than it is at present if and when the parallel markets should ever come to be affected by serious difficulties. Situations are liable to arise – though let us hope that they never actually will arise – in which the existence of a secure island amidst an ocean of uncertainties might prove to be of immense value.

# CHAPTER THREE

# Short-term Money

MOST countries, even some very advanced ones, have no market in short-term money. Banks abroad have to keep adequate cash reserves or balances with their Central Banks, erring if anything on the cautious side. They may have some easily marketable securities, but first and foremost they rely on their rediscount facilities with their Central Banks for supplementing their cash supplies required to meet any unexpected withdrawals. British banks, on the other hand, rely largely on their ability to offset each other's cash surpluses and deficiencies through the money market. Until comparatively recently this meant the traditional money market. Today that task is shared between the traditional money market and the inter-bank sterling market. In spite of the development of the latter, the former continues to play a very important part as far as clearing banks are concerned, though a considerably less important part as far as non-clearing banks are concerned.

One of the reasons why a money market stands a good chance of operating smoothly in Britain is that the banking habit among the public is more widespread than in most other countries. There is very little hoarding of notes. Whenever one of the clearing banks loses deposits through excess of withdrawals of deposits over new deposits, the chances are that its loss is the gain of some other clearing bank or clearing banks. It is true that many millions of wage-earners and others have no bank account, and everybody keeps some cash for spending. But the moment the cash is spent the chances are that it finds its way into one or other of the clearing banks, directly or indirectly.

The total resources of all clearing banks are of course subject to basic long-term influences, but in the short run they fluctuate within relatively narrow limits, even though they are subject to seasonal and other temporary influences. On the assumption that by and large one bank's loss is some other bank's gain, the clearing of surpluses against deficiencies is a much simpler operation than it would be if the British public, like people in France and many other countries, were in the habit of hoarding on a large scale and to a fluctuating degree.

By and large, British clearing banks are able to offset changes in each other's cash position to a high degree. It is the object of the money market to provide an efficient mechanism for that purpose. The money market is a kind of clearing house, at any rate to the extent to which there is no net surplus or net deficiency for the entire banking system. All clearing banks have funds loaned to the discount houses. Those with a surplus for the moment increase their lendings, while those with a deficiency for the moment withdraw some of their funds.

But if the sole function of the money market were a routine equalisation of surpluses and deficiencies, the same end could be achieved by direct inter-bank dealing – as indeed it is achieved to some extent between non-clearing banks in the inter-bank sterling market. The main function of the traditional money market in combination with the discount market and with the Bank of England is to provide a mechanism for offsetting net surpluses or net deficiencies of the entire banking system. In other countries this is done by direct assistance to banks by their respective Central Banks and by the reflux of net bank surpluses to these Central Banks. In Britain there is an intermediary mechanism which performs this task.

Since 1825 British banks have not borrowed direct from the Bank of England – except in emergencies such as the two World Wars, for the duration of which the Bank of England took into 'cold storage' the banks' frozen bills payable in enemy or enemy-occupied countries. In normal or comparatively normal conditions the banks cover their cash requirements through the intermediary of the discount houses. They do not borrow from discount houses but lend them a high proportion of their liquid resources, which are at their disposal whenever they need cash. If that is not sufficient, or if they prefer not to reduce their loans to the money market, they sell bills in the same market. The discount houses provide the cash required by banks which call their loans from them or sell them bills either with the aid of money lent by other banks which have unwanted cash surpluses, or by borrowing from the Bank of England or from clearing banks against securities, or by discounting bills with the Bank of England.

The basis of the absolute liquidity of discount houses lies not in their own resources – which are very modest by comparison with their turnover – nor even in their capacity to borrow from clearing banks, but in the Bank of England's willingness to act as lender of last resort by granting them loans or by discounting their bills. It is the certain knowledge that the Bank of England is always in the background, ready to supplement the resources of discount houses if necessary, that enables the banks to depend implicitly on the liquidity of their loans to discount houses, also on their ability to unload on the market bills eligible for rediscount or for serving as security for loans by the Bank or by clearing banks to discount houses. As we already observed, banks consider their loans to discount houses to be, next to cash and to balances with the Bank of England, the most liquid form of assets. Traditionally they aim at maintaining about 10 per cent of their 28 per cent of minimum liquid reserve in the form of loans to discount houses – the rest being 8 per cent in cash and 10 per cent in bills marketable in the discount market.

The money market enables clearing banks to steer halfway between the Scylla of keeping unnecessarily large cash balances which yield nothing and the Charybdis of finding themselves short of the conventional minimum cash supplies they are expected to maintain.

Giving evidence before the Radcliffe Committee in his capacity as Chief Cashier, Sir Leslie O'Brien, now Governor of the Bank of England, referred to the London money market in the following terms: 'We believe it to be the most highly flexible mechanism for looking after the needs for short-term money that there is in the world.'

But this high degree of flexibility is largely due to the part played in it by the Bank of England itself. In the inter-bank sterling market or in any of the other parallel money markets, if supply and demand for money do not balance, the rate has to move to a level at which the surplus supply or the surplus demand attracts counterparts. Sometimes counterparts are only forthcoming on very unfavourable terms. In the traditional money market the Bank of England can, and does, perform an equalising function by covering the deficiency or mopping up the surplus, on terms that are usually less drastic than those emerging from the free play of supply and demand. It thereby prevents or mitigates unwanted fluctuations of interest rates. The market is not free from disturbing fluctuations, but excessive movements can be moderated by the ability of the discount houses to borrow from the Bank, or by the initiative of the Bank. The discount houses, and the banks that lend to them, may be absolutely certain that any net deficiency of their liquid resources would be covered, even though in given circumstances the Bank performs this task on penalising terms.

The discount houses carry out their equalising functions with the aid of very modest resources of their own. Their total capital and free reserves amount to about £70 million. But they can invest in bills and short bonds anything up to thirty times their capital resources. This is because they can borrow extensively from clearing banks and from other banks, or from non-banking clients and, whenever necessary, from the Bank of England.

At the end of 1969 the total amount borrowed by the discount houses was £1,725 million, compared with £1,573 million a year earlier and £1,662 million two years earlier. Of the £1,725 million, £1,402 million was borrowed from clearing banks and Scottish banks, £214 million from non-clearing banks and £109 million from 'other sources' which included non-banking financial institutions of various kinds, business firms and overseas loans. It may be interesting to compare these latest figures with those prior to the development of the inter-bank sterling market. At the end of 1951, out of a total borrowing of £991 million the discount houses owed £624 million to clearing banks and Scottish banks and £247 million to non-clearing banks. The loans of the latter continued to increase until they reached £395 million at the end of 1953. Thereafter they declined, as a result of their transfer to the inter-bank market, to £201 million by the end of 1966, since when they have remained more or less static. The loans by clearing banks and Scottish banks, on the other hand, increased from year to year, though not without temporary setbacks. Evidently the relative share of clearing banks and Scottish banks in the activity of the traditional money market has increased considerably compared with that of non-clearing banks.

Lending by clearing banks may assume the following forms:

(1) *Basic money*. This consists of money at call and is lent practically permanently at a rate fixed by the cartel of clearing banks at $\frac{3}{8}$ per cent above deposit rate.

(2) *Overnight money*. The amount of this is much larger and the interest rate is almost always higher than the basic money rate.

Its amount fluctuates very widely according to the changing requirements of the lending banks.

(3) *Privilege money*. Clearing banks hold limited amounts at the disposal of discount houses for the sole purpose of enabling them to meet unexpected requirements arising after 2.30 p.m. when it is no longer possible to borrow from the Bank of England. Their total is estimated at £5 million for the entire market. Interest is charged at $\frac{1}{2}$ per cent above the basic rate and the loans are always repayable on the next business day.

Non-clearing banks are not bound by the cartel and their lending rates fluctuate according to market conditions. When money is easy discount houses may be able to borrow from non-clearing banks at lower rates than from clearing banks, whose basic rates are kept rigid by the cartel.

Non-banking depositors or non-resident clients may be attracted by the rates paid by discount houses. They pay the clearing banks' deposit rate for loans overnight – clearing banks only pay that rate for deposits subject to seven days' notice – and $\frac{1}{4}$ per cent above that rate for loans up to seven days.

Discount houses borrow from the Bank of England, either in the form of loans against security or by rediscounting bills. On 12 December 1969 the total of advances by the Bank to discount houses was £63·5 million. These advances are usually overnight, occasionally for two to seven days when it is necessary to tide the market over a squeeze. Applications for advances have to be made before 2.30 p.m. at the Discount Office. The Bank may take the initiative in lending to discount houses at market rates, but when it wants to tighten money it only grants advances at or even above Bank rate, or it grants them for a period of seven days, even if borrowers needed them overnight only.

The Bank may also take the initiative in intervening to make money easier or to mop up surplus funds, by means of buying or selling bills, either to discount houses or to clearing banks. Bills sold to the Bank or used as security for advances must have an average maturity of not more than three weeks. These operations by the once-mysterious 'special buyer' were surrounded with much secrecy in the old days and City Editors referred to them with bated breath. It shows the extent to which the Bank of England has relaxed its former secretive attitude – *pace* the report of the Select Committee of the House of Commons inquiring into its affairs – that its *Quarterly Review* contains detailed statistical information – quoted in Appendix 2 – about the number of interventions, the forms they assumed, and the amounts involved specified according to the form of the interventions.

The total advances to the market from the Bank are always a bare fraction of its borrowings from banks. They provide just the uncovered balance. The amount of assistance given to the market in the form of buying bills is much larger. During the period between 17 April and 21 May 1969, the amount of Treasury bills purchased by the Bank was £476·5 million, in addition to other bills of £103·6 million. During the same period funds amounting to £110·8 million were mopped up by the Bank through sales of bills. The 'special buyer' sometimes buys and sells bills on the same day, if the change in the state of the market or in the official attitude towards it calls for such change of tactics. When the Bank buys bills from the clearing banks the latter are expected to pass on the proceeds to the discount market, charging somewhat higher rates. The 'special buyer' indicates the Bank's preference for certain maturities. Although there is no legal obligation on the part of the discount houses or the banks to comply, they usually do when it is possible.

The most important factor in the market is the ebb and flow of clearing bank requirements. Although the fluctuations of the requirements of non-clearing banks are apt to be relatively wider, they are now met largely by operations in the inter-bank sterling market, so that, as we saw above, in spite of the increase in the relative importance of non-clearing banks, the importance of clearing banks in the traditional money market is now greater than before. There are systematically recurrent general trends, such as increased withdrawals for income tax payments in February and August, for purchase tax payments in February, May, August and November, and for rate payments in April and October. Clearing bank deposits tend to be highest towards the end of the year. They decline during the first quarter, mainly because of tax payments, increase in the second quarter, decline in the third quarter and increase again in the last quarter.

During the course of a week, the trend on Mondays is variable, on Tuesdays there are withdrawals, Wednesdays tend to be more or less evenly balanced, on Thursdays the tone is apt to be easier because of Government disbursements, while on Fridays wage payments and cash requirements for weekend shopping result in heavy withdrawals of funds. Part of the cash that leaves the banking system on Friday returns by Monday or by Tuesday at the latest. The requirements of non-clearing banks are incalculable and do not obey any definite recurrent trends, since they depend mainly on movements of large individual deposits which do not tend to offset each other as the multitude of small clearing bank deposits do.

The day in the money market begins with the visit by discount house representatives to banks referred to in some detail in the last chapter. They take place at 10 a.m. or soon after. The banks inform the discount houses about their withdrawals or new lendings. All arrangement is made by word of mouth and no contracts are exchanged on the spot, though subsequently the discount houses send written confirmation. Transactions subsequent to the morning visits are made by telephone, mostly on private lines. On the occasion of the morning visits the discount houses also collect buying or selling orders for bills, sterling or dollar CDs, and LA or finance house deposits. But all this is incidental: the main object of the call is to make arrangements for balancing the banks' cash positions in good time to enable the discount houses to make any necessary arrangements with the Bank of England.

The money market is in close touch with the Bank of England even on days when it does not have to apply for advances or have bills discounted. Representatives of discount houses pay daily calls to senior officials of the Discount Office to keep them informed about the prevailing trend and to obtain information about the Bank's views on the line the authorities would like them to take.

# CHAPTER FOUR

# Commercial Bills

THE purpose of commercial bills is to finance self-liquidating short-term commercial transactions, as an alternative to financing by means of overdrafts. In the London market there are two kinds of commercial bills – trade bills and bank bills, according to whether the bills bear the signature of a bank. Trade bills are drawn by a business firm and are accepted by another business firm. Bank bills are drawn by a business firm and accepted or endorsed by a bank. Every commercial bill must bear two signatures. Promissory notes which only bear one signature are often used in business transactions and have a large market in New York under the name of 'commercial papers'. Until recently they had no market in London.

Trade bills are drawn by a seller of goods and accepted by a buyer of goods. They must state the amount payable and the date on which it is payable, the purpose for which the bill is drawn and the name of the bank at which it is payable. Once the drawer accepts the bill it becomes his absolute liability, but in case of default the holder has recourse on the drawer and on any endorser if the bill changed hands before he acquired it. Trade bills may finance domestic transactions between producers and buyers of their goods. They may finance exports if exporters draw the bills on the U.K. representative of foreign importers. They can finance imports if foreign exporters draw the bills on U.K. importers.

Bank bills may be drawn by foreign firms – with or without a guarantee by foreign banks – and are accepted by a U.K. bank. Historically there is no rigid line of distinction between trade bills and bank bills. Ever since medieval days many business firms combined the function of a merchant with that of a banker. Hence the name of merchant banker. Italian merchant bankers dominated the London bill market during the late medieval period and for some time after the Renaissance. Hence the name of Lombard Street where they had their premises. But British firms too took

an increasingly active part in the bill market. In the 16th century
Sir Thomas Gresham built the Royal Exchange largely for the
purpose of dealing in bills, and that building, rebuilt in the 19th
century, performed the same function right until 1920.

Markets in commercial bills have existed in various financial
centres all over Europe ever since the late medieval period, but
until comparatively recently the bills dealt in were overwhelmingly in terms of foreign currencies. This was originally due to the
medieval church law against 'usury', under which it was forbidden
to charge interest on loans. This law was circumvented by disguising domestic loan transactions in the form of foreign exchange
transactions and disguising interest charges in the form of exchange
rate differentials.

In modern times a market in domestic bills in terms of sterling
developed in London gradually during the 19th century, thanks
largely to the activities of bill brokers who acted as intermediaries
between the provincial industrial and commercial firms on the one
hand and between the London banks and the Bank of England on
the other. This business in commercial bills changed in character
during the second half of the century when, as a result of the
expansion of the branch network of the London joint stock banks,
domestic business came to be financed largely by means of bank
overdrafts. Activities in trade bills declined in consequence,
though in certain produce trades, especially in the timber trade,
they remained the principal device for financing current transactions. But generally speaking, accepting houses lost interest in
domestic bills.

During the second half of the 19th century an increasingly
active business developed in sterling bills financing not only
British imports and exports but also international trade between
foreign countries. This business largely assumed the form of
acceptance credits, under which a London accepting house
accepted the bill drawn by the foreign exporter on the foreign
importer's agent or by the importer on his bank. As a result of the
acceptance of such bills by a London banking house of first-class
standing, they became marketable at the favourable rate quoted
for 'fine bank bills'.

Until recently the bank bill in London was an international
currency. Its supremacy was for a century virtually unchallenged.
A very high proportion of non-British foreign trade – not only
with countries of the Sterling Area but also between non-sterling

countries – was financed with sterling acceptance credits. The sterling bills drawn on those credits were the favourite short-term investments of banks and of non-banking holders all over the five continents.

This was largely the result of the soundness of the British banking system, a subject to which we shall return in Chapter 6, which deals with inter-bank sterling deposits. But the soundness of the British banks – especially of deposit banks – was, and still is, based on the proverbial *sang-froid* that is inherent in the British character. The mass of British depositors are not given to panicking in crises. There is no deposit insurance in Britain and, as far as the great mass of depositors are concerned, there is no need for it. They simply trust their banks.

This is the main reason why the names of first-class London banks command respect all over the world. Until the series of sterling crises between 1964 and 1967, culminating in the devaluation of 1967, sterling bills remained a favourite investment, even though the devaluation risk was covered by forward exchange operations. Although sterling ceased to be trusted under the Labour Government the name of leading British banks remained above suspicion. Many wealthy investors abroad who wanted to spread their risk deemed it expedient to entrust a proportion of their assets to British banks, whether as depositors or as holders of their acceptances.

Although this line of business was interrupted by the First World War it was resumed after the war and developed considerably during the 'twenties. To a large extent it came to assume the form of acceptance credits granted to foreign firms under the guarantee of banks in their own countries. Clearing banks, too, came to take a keen interest in such business and as a result of competition the commission was reduced to ½ per cent p.a. The character of bills also changed. Most of them were no longer accompanied by shipping documents and there was reason to believe that a high proportion of them was simply finance paper in the guise of trade bills, used by German and other banks for financing long-term credits by means of replacing the bills when they matured.

This system broke down in 1931 when most of the acceptance credits became frozen. Under standstill agreements renewed every year maturing bills were met out of the proceeds of replacement bills sent by the debtors, bills which abandoned any pretence of being anything but finance paper. These bills were easily market-able until the outbreak of the war in 1939, when they were taken into 'cold storage' by the Bank of England.

As a result of this experience it was some time after the Second World War before acceptance credits for financing foreign trade were resumed on an appreciable scale. Already during the last few pre-war years some acceptance houses had reverted to granting acceptance credits to British firms to finance domestic trade. This business was gradually expanded after the war in the absence of an adequate volume of international business, which had been the bread-and-butter of the commercial bill market until 1939. But during the 'fifties acceptance credits to foreign firms came to be resumed once more on an increasing scale, and they were once more used extensively for financing trade between non-British countries. In 1957 a ban was placed on such use of acceptance credits and on the use of acceptance credits for re-financing. As a result the volume of international bank acceptances declined and the relative proportion of trade bills and domestic acceptances increased.

Throughout that period Treasury bills played an increasingly important role in the discount market. Their amount and their relative importance came to exceed those of commercial bills considerably. But commercial bills remained in demand because clearing banks readily discounted them on the strength of their acceptance by some banks of first-rate standing. Even so, Treasury bills reigned supreme and changed hands at more favourable rates than fine bank bills, the rates of which were before the war almost at par with those of Treasury bills. Until the late 'sixties fine bank bills were usually quoted some $\frac{3}{16}$ per cent above Treasury bills for the corresponding maturities, but more recently the differential has widened quite considerably. In June 1970 it was as much as $1\frac{1}{4}$ per cent, presumably because of the decline in the volume of Treasury bills, but mainly because the amount of commercial bills that the discount houses and banks are entitled to hold came to be limited by the credit ceiling.

There was a time when it was widely believed that the market for commercial bills was doomed to disappear or at any rate shrink into insignificance. But, as we said in Chapter 2, their use increased considerably during the 'sixties, thanks to the initiative taken by discount houses and bill brokers who went out of their way to acquire new clients among manufacturers and merchants.

They offered credit lines to business firms at first in competition with the overdraft facilities provided by clearing banks at a slightly lower cost. Later on the acceptance credits were welcomed by business firms over and above their credit limits with clearing banks, during the frequently recurrent credit squeeze. This additional source of credit was a great attraction even when the cost of such facilities rose above that of overdrafts.

Brokers and discount houses introduced the firms to accepting houses which granted them acceptance credits. Alternatively, discount houses discounted bills drawn by the seller on the buyer and accepted by the latter. Later ceilings were imposed on acceptance credits also, and trade bills were brought under the bank's ceiling if they were acquired by a bank. But until the ceiling on acceptance credit was imposed this supplementation of credit facilities went a long way towards easing the credit squeeze. The ceiling was raised somewhat later.

The rate for fine bank bills applies only to bills accepted by clearing banks, by members of the Accepting House Committee and by other first-rate non-clearing banks. Rates for trade bills are of course higher and necessarily vary widely according to the prospects of the trade concerned, the standing of the firm that issues them and that of the firm that accepts them. Discount houses and bill brokers are in a good position to ascertain the standing of business firms whose bills they discount or which they introduce to banks. Some of them specialise in certain trades or in certain areas.

Trade bills are often accompanied by shipping documents or by warehouse receipts. The presence of such documents is liable to affect favourably the rates at which they are discounted, though the standing of the firm concerned is more important. While rates for fine bank bills are virtually uniform for all first-class names, rates for trade bills are apt to differ widely and the spread between them is apt to fluctuate. The minimum rate is the Bank rate for firms of first-rate standing, though competition for the business of the largest firms is apt to reduce the rates for their bills below the Bank rate. Indeed the bills of giant international firms are taken at, or very close to, rates for fine bank bills. Trade bills of good-class firms are usually quoted at about 1 to $1\frac{1}{2}$ per cent above Bank rate for three to four months and at about $1\frac{1}{2}$ to 2 per cent above Bank rate for four to six months.

If trade bills are endorsed by a bank of good standing they can be marketed at a much lower rate, but they do not quite rank with bank acceptances. This apparently absurd difference according to whether a bank signs the bill across its face or on its back is due to the fact that the accepting bank itself assumes direct obligation to meet the bill on maturity, while if a bank endorses the bill it only becomes liable for its payment if the holder produces evidence that the drawer or the acceptor has defaulted on its payment.

The Bank of England encourages the use of trade bills because they are self-liquidating. From 1966 the official buyer has from time to time purchased small parcels of trade bills to enable the Bank to check their quality.

As part of the credit squeeze the Bank of England placed a limit on holdings of commercial bills by discount houses, so that they were only able to buy bills to replace those which matured or were sold. It was permitted to raise the limit by 5 per cent by March 1966. In November 1968 it was fixed at 102 per cent of the level in force before the devaluation of 1967.

Bank bills usually represent a high proportion of the banks' bill portfolios. The overwhelming majority are issued for three months. They are usually acquired by discount houses in the first instance and are seldom sold to banks until at least a week after their issue. On Thursdays, when discount houses meet to decide on the weekly Treasury bill tender of their syndicate, they also fix the minimum rate below which they will not buy fine bank bills. There is a narrow spread between the rates for fine bank bills and eligible bank bills which do not qualify for that category.

As a general rule the rates for both bank bills and trade bills are lower the nearer they are to maturity. One of the reasons for this is that the Bank of England prefers to rediscount bills that are near their maturity. The average maturity of batches of bills rediscounted with the Bank is twenty-one days.

The acceptance commission, which was $\frac{1}{2}$ per cent p.a. during the 'twenties, is now at a more realistic level of $1\frac{1}{4}$ to $1\frac{1}{2}$ per cent for first-class borrowers. It may be as high as 3 per cent or even higher for smaller firms.

During periods when sterling was under a cloud the high acceptance commission and the high bill rates did not deter foreign demand for sterling acceptance credits, because the discount on forward sterling reduced the net cost. Many borrowers left the exchange risk open in the hope of benefiting by a devaluation.

In addition to trade bills and bank bills the market also deals in finance papers. These are bills which do not represent automatically self-liquidating commercial transactions but serve the purpose of raising short-term credits for financing transactions, usually for longer terms. Bills issued by finance houses may be classed in that category, because the average maturity of hire-purchase debts which they finance is usually eighteen months.

There has been a great expansion in the volume of commercial bills held by banks during the late 'sixties. This is largely the result of the expansion of world trade. Even though an increased proportion of international trade is now financed in dollars the requirements of trade for sterling bills are still on the increase.

During the late 'sixties acceptance credits in terms of dollars were introduced in London. The market in dollar bills drawn on these credits is not very wide, but it has distinct possibilities. This method of financing foreign trade in terms of dollars has much to recommend it compared with financing by means of Euro-dollar credits.

# CHAPTER FIVE

# Treasury Bills

THE market in Treasury bills is one of the most important traditional markets in London. It provides facilities for market dealing and for dealing between banks and non-banking customers in short-term negotiable credit instruments whose security is entirely above suspicion and which are absolutely liquid, being easily marketable. The absence of adequate money markets in several countries which are sufficiently advanced financially to be able to develop such markets is often attributed to the absence of transferable short-term Government bills, on the assumption that the development of a market in such bills would encourage the emergence of markets in other forms of short-term credit.

Treasury bills are bearer securities issued by H.M. Treasury, which undertakes to repay their amount out of the Consolidated Fund on the date of their maturity. They are repayable mostly in ninety-one days, but occasionally bills for sixty-three days are also issued.

Exchequer bills of a similar kind were issued in the 17th century but Treasury bills in their present form and under their present name were first introduced in 1877, in response to Walter Bagehot's suggestion. There are two methods by which Treasury bills are issued – by tenders or by tap. Each Friday the *London Gazette* invites tenders for the following week's issue of Treasury bills, stating the amount and maturity of the bills to be offered. Payment may be made on any day of the week following the week in which the bills are issued, and maturity is reckoned on the basis of the dates on which the bills are actually issued and paid for.

The minimum amount of a Treasury bill is £5,000 and the maximum amount is £250,000. The minimum amount for which tenders can be submitted is £50,000. They must be submitted through a bank, broker or discount house by 1 p.m. each Friday, and the result is announced by 2 p.m. Those who submit tenders must state the amount they are prepared to pay per £100 of the bills, and the Bank of England, acting on behalf of the Treasury, allots the bills to the applicants who offer the most favourable price.

Another method of issuing Treasury bills is through their allocation to various Public Departments to meet their respective requirements or to employ their funds temporarily pending their eventual use after the sale of the bulls. Interest rates allowed on such bills need not bear any relationship to market rates. But if the bills are issued to the market by tap, that is, through sale by the Bank of England on any day that is convenient to the authorities, they are sold at current market rates. The Bank of England itself tenders for bills on account of foreign Central Banks and other customers.

Originally Treasury bills served only the purpose of temporary financing in anticipation of impending taxation receipts or the issue of Government loans. But during the First World War and again during the Second World War the issue of Treasury bills became a more or less permanent method of financing part of the floating Public Debt, whenever this appeared to be a cheaper or more convenient form of borrowing, and to the extent to which the increase of the amount outstanding was in accordance with the requirements of monetary policy.

As already stated in Chapter 2, during the two World Wars, and also after the crisis of 1931 when the volume of commercial bills declined, and again for some time after the Second World War Treasury bills were the bread-and-butter of the discount market. In order to give discount houses a chance to keep the market going during the lean years of the 'thirties, clearing banks agreed in 1935 not to tender for Treasury bills and to acquire them in the market only when they were at least one week old. At the same time discount houses formed a syndicate to prevent cut-throat competition, and this syndicate applies every week for the whole amount offered. The proportion allotted to the syndicate depends on the volume of outside tendering and on the respective prices offered. The amount obtained is allotted to individual discount houses in proportion to their respective capital resources.

Between 1939 and 1951 profit margins on Treasury bills, which were issued at a fixed rate, were negligible. Flexible rates were restored after the advent of the Conservative Government. There is from time to time a great deal of outside tendering and the relative proportion of the allocations to the market fluctuates widely. In addition to the bills that come to the market directly or indirectly out of allocations through tenders, there are also 'tap bills' allotted originally to Government Departments, the Exchange Equalisation Account, the National Debt Commissioners, the Public Trustee and the Bank of England. They too may find their way into the market when the Bank of England deems it necessary to mop up money by selling bills to the discount houses or to clearing banks.

For a long time dealing in Treasury bills issued either through tenders or through tap constituted the main activity of the discount market. The Treasury bill issue was also considered to be the main monetary policy device by which the authorities sought to influence the volume of liquid resources of the clearing banks and, through it, the volume of credit supply. But the Treasury is not entirely free in determining the amount of its bill issues, which is influenced among other things by seasonal taxation receipts and by Exchange Equalisation Account operations.

In the late 'sixties there was an unexpected revival of commercial bills, the volume of which has been expanding ever since. Nevertheless, Treasury bills remain an important element in the traditional market. Although a parallel market in Treasury short-term deposits on the lines of the LA deposit market is conceivable, it would not be nearly as satisfactory as the present system of financing.

In addition to the discount houses and the Bank of England, non-clearing banks, various other types of institutional investors, business firms, non-resident customers of banks, etc., may tender.

Exchange Equalisation Account operations affect the volume of tap bills, in that purchases of gold or foreign exchanges are financed by such means, while the proceeds of sales of gold or foreign exchanges in support of sterling can be used for the reduction of the volume of tap bills issued. But such changes need not necessarily affect the volume of bills in the market to a corresponding extent, if at all. Likewise the ups and downs of Budgetary deficits or surpluses need not have a direct bearing on the volume of Treasury bills issued, which depends on the debt management policy of the authorities who decide in what form the deficit is to be financed, having regard to the state of the Gilt-edged market and the money market. By and large it is however, correct to say that Budgetary deficits and purchases of gold and foreign exchange holdings tend to increase the volume of bills in the market while Budgetary surpluses and sales of gold and foreign exchanges tend to reduce it.

Clearing banks acquire and hold Treasury bills as an essential part of their liquid resources. Treasury bills are always marketable and, owing to their large turnover, it is always possible to obtain quotations in accordance with the market position. For these reasons, next to actual cash, and to balances with the Bank of England and money at call with the discount houses, Treasury bill holdings are considered the most liquid form of assets.

One of the reasons why clearing banks agreed voluntarily to abstain from tendering for Treasury bills is that when tendering they would have had to fix in advance the dates on which they would have to pay for the bills allotted to them. This is often not convenient for, apart from the uncertainty regarding the amount of bills that would be allotted, it is difficult for the banks to foresee in advance their cash requirements on any particular day the following week. It is more convenient, therefore, to decide each day if they require Treasury bills and to cover their requirements in the market.

Expectations of Bank rate changes are among the strongest influences – indeed in most instances *the* strongest influence – affecting Treasury bill rates. From this point of view discount houses, by undertaking to tender for the whole amount regardless of Bank rate prospects, assume a risk that is not compensated by a corresponding chance of making a profit. For when a Bank rate increase is expected, outside tenderers abstain from tendering so that practically the entire amount is allotted to the market, while when a Bank rate reduction is expected, there is very heavy outside tendering so that the amount allotted to the market on which it could make a profit is very small. It is true, expectations of Bank rate changes are very often mistaken. But to the extent to which these are more or less predictable it is a case of 'heads I don't win tails I lose' as far as discount houses are concerned.

Before the emergence of the parallel markets Treasury bills were the favourite form of short-term investment in which to employ foreign balances, official and unofficial, apart from other reasons because the volume of fine bank bills available was relatively limited. Even now leading foreign Central Banks employ their holdings of sterling very largely in the form of Treasury bills. But since the late 'sixties the decline in the volume of Treasury bills, the increase in the volume of commercial bills and the availability of alternative facilities in the parallel markets have diverted a high proportion of foreign demand from Treasury bills, both at tenders and in the market.

Notwithstanding the decline in Treasury bill issues at the time of writing, the discount market continues to render the Treasury invaluable service by taking over week after week the entire amount of its Treasury bill issues if no other buyer is available, and by ensuring the smooth working of the market in Treasury bills. It is for this reason among others that the authorities are in favour of safeguarding the traditional market from being driven out of existence by the parallel money markets with their higher yields and more flexible facilities. Moreover, the services of discount houses to the Treasury are not confined to the sphere of Treasury bills.

During the late 'thirties the discount houses developed a very active business in short-dated bonds or in bonds approaching maturity. They buy such bonds and keep them in their own portfolios. This makes re-financing of maturing debts much easier. Thanks to the discount houses the market in short-dated Government bonds has improved considerably. Although discount houses began to deal in bonds soon after the First World War, it was the lean period of the 'thirties that induced them to expand this sphere of their activity. Clearing banks agreed in 1934 to lend to discount houses against the security of bonds.

The portfolios of discount houses in short bonds are not confined to Government issues. They deal in Commonwealth and Colonial issues, and in bonds of Local Authorities. The Bank of England encourages the practice of buying short-dated Government bonds by discount houses, enabling them to register changes in ownership one day after the transactions. Normally the registration might take some three weeks. The main market for Government issues remains of course the Gilt-edged market, but the additional market for short-dated loans created by the discount houses has been found very helpful. The high turnover in short bonds and loans approaching maturity has created convenient facilities for buyers and sellers alike.

Admittedly the extension of the activities of discount houses to cover short-term Government loans involves additional risk as well as additional profit possibilities. On about half a dozen major occasions during the two decades since the return to flexible interest rates, most discount houses suffered grievous losses on their bond portfolios. This experience raises the question in the City whether the authorities are altogether fair to the institutions which serve them faithfully as the instruments of their monetary and debt management policy.

Again and again it has been observed that Bank rate changes have been timed in such a way as to ensure that they are not made when the market expects them. This would never be admitted in official circles, which contend that the changes are made when they are called for by the prevailing situation, regardless of whether the market expects them or not. And yet on innumerable occasions when the trend has pointed towards a Bank rate increase or restriction, Thursday after Thursday passes without the much-expected change, which then takes place after the market has given up expecting it.

While there is every justification for trying to mislead the foreign exchange market where those whom the Bank tries to catch out are its enemies, there would be incomparably less justification for playing the same game in the money market where those who pay the price of these curious tactics are the Bank's closest friends and allies. As pointed out earlier in this chapter, the system under which the syndicate of discount houses applies every Friday for the entire weekly issue of Treasury bills loads the dice against the discount houses. This cannot be helped, it is inherent in the system. But it would be unfair on the part of the authorities to go out of their way to inflict losses on the discount houses by timing Bank rate changes so often in such a way as to ensure that they should come unexpectedly. At times this might be inevitable. But there have been many recent instances in which the circumstances conveyed an impression that it was deliberate. Such suspicions must not be taken seriously. Conceivably the authorities are anxious to prevent the recurrence of the experience of 1957 when allegations of a leakage of information about the impending increase in the Bank rates led to a judicial inquiry. Even though it completely cleared the authorities and the banks concerned, not unnaturally the authorities are anxious to avoid the recurrence of that experience.

After each Bank rate increase the discount houses are confronted with a choice between cutting their losses or financing their holdings with the aid of costlier short-term borrowing. While this kind of risk is unavoidable it is inconceivable that the authorities would increase it deliberately, just for the sake of avoiding any suspicion of a Bank rate leak.

# CHAPTER SIX

# Inter-Bank Sterling Deposits

## (1) AN IMPORTANT MARKET

AMONG the institutional changes in the monetary and banking system that occurred during the 'sixties, the emergence of the inter-bank sterling market is of outstanding importance as far as the London market and the British banking system are concerned. It is true that the amount of inter-bank sterling deposits is much smaller than that of Euro-dollar deposits. But the market in the latter is primarily an international market and its impact on the British economy and on the British monetary and banking system is less pronounced than that of the inter-bank sterling market. Possibly the market in sterling Certificates of Deposits might prove to be potentially more important, judging by the success of the American experience with that device. But at the time of writing the amount of CDs and the turnover in their market is considerably short of the amount of inter-bank sterling and the turnover in its market. Moreover, the latter market, too, has considerable potential for further expansion, even though its present outstanding volume is already well above that of the traditional money market.

The importance of the new market lies partly in the fact that it has lent greater flexibility to the British credit system and partly in the fact that through its development British banks have rid themselves of an inhibition which had hitherto handicapped their freedom of action – their self-imposed rule against borrowing from each other marketwise in terms of sterling. The principle that inter-bank borrowing is admissible had already been conceded by the development of inter-bank dealings in Euro-dollar deposits in the late 'fifties – even though banks strongly object to the description of a transfer of a deposit from one bank to another as a loan transaction. According to the terminology of the market, the deposits are 'given' and 'taken', they are not 'lent' and 'borrowed'. Nevertheless, for years after the emergence of increasingly active Euro-currency markets inter-bank transactions between British banks in London in sterling deposits were still considered taboo.

## (2) AN INHIBITION OVERCOME

The unwillingness of British banks to borrow from and lend to each other in terms of sterling through a money market is difficult to explain. There was much inter-bank dealing in Euro-sterling deposits in foreign financial centres, but under the provisions of exchange control in the U.K. this was not possible in London, except between non-resident holders, through the intermediary of a broker or of a bank. This inhibition was not confined to British banks. Even in the absence of exchange control there was, and is, no inter-bank market in bank deposits in the United States for instance – apart from the market in Federal Funds – or inter-bank dealing in Swiss franc deposits in Switzerland.

Even if there was some logic in the self-imposed rule before the emergence of inter-bank dealings in Euro-dollars and other Euro-currencies after the development of the Euro-currency markets, it then became illogical to abstain from engaging in similar trans-actions in our own domestic currency. After all, inter-bank sterling deposits have the same characteristics as inter-bank dollar deposits – as Euro-dollars could and perhaps should be called. Both are unsecured credits, transacted in large individual items between banks. The risk for the lending London bank in an inter-bank sterling deal with another London bank is less than in an inter-bank dollar transaction, for delivery of the dollars on maturity might conceivably be prevented by exchange control measures, while no such risk exists as far as transactions in inter-bank sterling between banks in the U.K. are concerned.

The diminution and cessation of the inhibition British banks had felt about dealing with each other in sterling deposits was a gradual process, and it is impossible to ascertain even approxim-ately when the change occurred. As we shall see in Chapter 11, the emergence of the Euro-dollar market was also a gradual process and individual instances could be traced back to the early 'fifties and even earlier. But its development into a factor of importance in the international monetary and banking system dates from 1957, when exchange restrictions imposed on certain types of sterling acceptance credits made it necessary to find alternative facilities. There is no such dateline as far as the emergence of the inter-bank sterling market is concerned. Its early development has attracted even less attention outside the market than that of the Euro-dollar market in its early stages. Inter-bank sterling rates did not come to be quoted systematically in the financial Press until the late 'sixties and information on the market was until recently quite inadequate. Comment on the trends in the new market in the financial Press was also very scant until the late 'sixties.

### (3) HOW THE MARKET CAME INTO EXISTENCE

The inhibition which prevented British banks from borrowing from each other delayed not only the development of the inter-bank sterling market but also the publicising of such dealings for a long time after the development of the market. Inter-bank dealings in loans between banks which belonged to the same group or which had special relationships with each other had always existed but naturally received no publicity.

Possibly inter-bank dealings in sterling between banks without any such special relationships may have originated in the 'fifties in the following way. The reserve bank of one of the Commonwealth countries is said to have considerably reduced its sterling balances with London branches of commercial banks of that country. The manager of one of the banks concerned happened to mention this to the London branch manager of a commercial bank of another Commonwealth country, which happened to have had a surplus of sterling balances transferred to it by the reserve bank of its country. As he had no profitable use for these funds he suggested to his colleague that they might kill two birds with one stone by depositing his bank's surplus sterling with the other bank on the understanding that the latter would do the same if and when the situation should become reversed. This device came to be followed by other Commonwealth banks. Later it spread gradually to other types of non-clearing banks.

Another explanation attributes the development of inter-bank sterling dealings to the practice of treasurers of many banks of charging, for bookkeeping purposes, too high interest rates on extra funds allocated to their foreign exchange departments for outward arbitrage. This was a perennial grievance of all foreign exchange dealers who had felt handicapped by it in their endeavours to work profitably. Some of them came to agree among themselves that in future they would lend each other their surplus funds at live-and-let-live interest rates. The practice spread unobtrusively and gradually, and for a long time it is supposed to have been exercised without the knowledge and approval of the managements concerned. Later on it came to be regarded as part of the routine activities of foreign exchange departments. Possibly this was why the inter-bank sterling market developed in many instances in the foreign exchange departments rather than between the money market departments of banks.

Conceivably inter-bank dealings in sterling existed even before the expansion of the Euro-dollar market in London. But the example of that market must have been largely responsible for inspiring the creation of a systematic active market in inter-bank sterling on a large scale. Not until the early 'sixties was the existence of the inter-bank sterling market realised outside those directly concerned and, as already observed, it was given virtually no publicity until the late 'sixties.

Needless to say, the expansion of the inter-bank sterling market was much less spectacular than that of the Euro-dollar market. At the early stages inter-bank sterling was less important even than Euro-sterling. But by 1969 inter-bank sterling came to exceed Euro-sterling in importance, although its volume was still much smaller than that of Euro-dollars.

## (4) THE VOLUME OF INTER-BANK STERLING

It is even more difficult to compile reliable figures about the volume of inter-bank sterling than about that of Euro-dollars. The Bank for International Settlements publishes much statistical material in its annual report about the latter, but even those figures must be regarded with much reservation. There is no dependable statistical material on the outstanding amount of turnover of inter-bank sterling. The most popular assumption is that the amount of non-clearing bank deposits with other U.K. banks gives some indication of the size of the outstanding amount. The figures are published in the *Bank of England Quarterly Bulletin* and they show that at the end of 1969 the amount of current account balances and deposits of accepting houses, overseas banks and other banks in the U.K. with other U.K. banks was £1,566·9 million. But to assume that this amount necessarily indicates the grand total of inter-bank sterling deposits would be a grossly misleading oversimplification of a highly complicated statistical problem.

That figure includes important items which are not inter-bank deposits. A high proportion of them must represent current account balances of non-clearing banks with clearing banks. For all non-clearing banks have such balances with at least one of the clearing banks and they may also have current accounts with other non-clearing banks. Although such balances are usually kept at a minimum because no interest is paid on them, their aggregate must be a considerable sum and it would have to be deducted from the figure of £1,566·9 million.

When an inter-bank deposit is re-lent in the market its amount is transferred from the lending non-clearing bank's account with a clearing bank to the borrowing non-clearing bank's account with a clearing bank, pending its use by the borrower for lending in one of the parallel markets or for lending to some customer outside the market. If it is re-lent outside the market or if it is invested in LA deposits or in finance house deposits, the amount appears in the borrower's current account with one of the clearing banks. When any of the borrowers spends the proceeds, the amounts involved appear in the recipient's account with a clearing bank. A large part of the non-bank deposits held by clearing banks originates from inter-bank deposits lent by non-clearing banks outside the market.

In other words, while a large part of the figure of £1,566·9 million does not constitute inter-bank deposits, transactions in such deposits are liable to give rise to large amounts of non-banking current account balances on deposits with clearing banks. Considering the extent to which inter-bank deposits are re-invested outside the market or are lent to customers, it seems probable that the amount which has to be added to the figure of non-clearing bank deposits exceeds considerably the amount which has to be deducted from it. It seems reasonable to assume, therefore, that at the end of 1969 the total of inter-bank sterling was considerably higher than £1,566 million, possibly in the neighbourhood of £2,000 million, or perhaps even above it. The highest estimate I encountered was £3,000 million but £2,000 million was the most widely accepted estimate of the figure in the market – which does not necessarily mean that it is correct. Whenever some item is quantified by someone with a degree of self-assurance, everybody else is inclined to regard the figure as authentic.

## (5) PARTICIPANTS IN THE MARKET

One of the many reasons why a further expansion in the volume of inter-bank sterling is probable is the increase in the relative importance of non-clearing banks compared with that of clearing banks. This seems to be a basic trend which is liable to continue. To a large extent it is due to the increase in the number and importance of clearing bank affiliates which are technically non-clearing banks for statistical purposes. They take a most active part in inter-bank dealing and are likely to increase in importance. The increase in the number of new foreign bank branches in London is another reason why inter-bank sterling dealing is likely to increase.

The market in inter-bank sterling includes many banks – their number is estimated at about 160 at the time of writing – and a number of brokers. Most new foreign bank branches operate in inter-bank sterling deposits, especially the American branches. Even though they came to London mainly for the purpose of having direct access to the Euro-dollar market, they are anxious to supplement and diversify their activities and increase their earnings by taking a hand in other markets. If their parent institutions are of high standing their names are taken for considerable amounts for inter-bank sterling deposits. On the other hand, the extent to which the names of smaller banks are taken is usually limited. Of course the names of affiliates of clearing banks, or of banks jointly controlled by clearing banks and foreign banks, are taken for very substantial amounts and account for a high proportion of the turnover. More will be said below about the extent to which various names are taken in the inter-bank sterling market.

Other participants in the market besides clearing bank affiliates are accepting houses, merchant banks, overseas banks of every kind, Commonwealth and foreign branches and affiliates, provincial, Scottish and Northern Irish banks, Channel Island banks, etc. Discount houses, too, act as principals, while the broker firms they control act as brokers for inter-bank sterling transactions. They can hold inter-bank deposits among their assets, but to the extent to which they are in a position to provide eligible security as collaterals for loans it is to their advantage to borrow in the traditional market, because rates are lower.

There are ten active deposit brokers. Nine of them belong to the

Foreign Exchange and Deposit Brokers' Association. All these brokers have private telephone lines with a large number of banks. In addition, many firms act as brokers on a smaller scale, usually as a sideline. Their number is believed to be around thirty-five, which also includes some firms for which deposit business is just incidental. For instance two Stock Exchange firms operate mainly in order to finance their clients' security transactions or to employ temporarily their clients' idle funds pending reinvestment. The turnover of most of these smaller brokers does not justify private telephone lines with banks. There are four foreign exchange brokers which between them transact the bulk of inter-bank deposit business. They all have three sections dealing with foreign exchanges, Euro-currencies and inter-bank sterling respectively. Some have a section for medium-term credits.

While all local foreign exchange business and a high proportion of Euro-currency business goes through brokers there is a fair amount of direct dealing in sterling deposits between banks. Some of the banks have private telephone lines with other banks with which they have a special relationship, and also with some other banks with which they are usually in frequeht communication. But the number of such direct lines between banks is relatively small and the volume of business done without the intermediary of brokers is not thought to exceed one-quarter of the total on average. Direct dealings are liable to increase if, as a result of the advent of more stable conditions with narrower fluctuations and narrower spreads, brokers' commissions should come to represent too high a proportion of the spreads and the potential profit margins. That commission is at present $\frac{1}{32}$ per cent for both parties, making $\frac{1}{16}$ per cent out of a normal spread of $\frac{1}{8}$ to $\frac{1}{4}$ per cent.

### (6) HOW THE MARKET OPERATES

Deals are concluded in the same way as in foreign exchanges and Euro-currencies, with the essential difference that they are implemented on the same day instead of being implemented after two clear days. Dealers register the amounts and maturities on slips which are passed on to their increasingly mechanised accounts departments. The latter dispatch the confirmatory note to the party by messenger. The lending bank encloses with the confirmatory note the payment in the form of a cheque drawn on a clearing bank. But deals which are concluded after 2 p.m. are implemented on the following morning only, unless otherwise stipulated.

The inter-bank deposit market, like the foreign exchange market and the Euro-currency market, has become highly mechanised. Some of the more active banks have computers with whose aid they are in a position to know every evening or the following morning the accumulated interest on each deposit lent or borrowed, right up to that day. The computers also calculate the average interest rates paid and received on the outstanding totals or deposits borrowed and lent.

The inter-bank sterling market has assumed to some degree the function of a clearing house of liquid funds, a function hitherto performed by the traditional market. It offsets surpluses of cash of some banks against the deficiencies of cash of other banks. The bulk of overnight deposits and deposits at call and a great deal of deposits up to seven days or deposits subject to short notice not exceeding seven days are transacted between banks within the market. But the market also provides facilities for employing surplus cash and for raising short-term money for insurance companies and other financial institutions, large investors, Stock Exchange firms, etc. Sophisticated treasurers of industrial and commercial firms are familiar with its operations and they too take advantage of the more favourable rates quoted for short deposits.

Many treasurers are still old-fashioned and do not go out of their way to use their firm's liquid funds to the best advantage. But the number of firms which take advantage of the higher rates obtainable in the parallel money markets in general and in the inter-bank sterling market in particular – even though they have no direct access to the latter – is on the increase. Some of the large corporations have engaged the services of a former foreign exchange dealer or a retired money market operator with specialised experience in such transactions.

By far the larger part of the turnover consists of short-term transactions. But it would be a mistake to generalise in this respect, as indeed in most other respects, as far as this market is concerned, for the proportion of short-term transactions varies widely according to the policies pursued by the various banks. Those banks which need the deposits to meet some specific requirement of their clients usually borrow for three months or longer. Those which use the market mainly for adjusting their cash positions usually borrow or lend overnight or for very short periods, or the deposits lent or borrowed are subject to very short notice. Others engage in time arbitrage, which normally means lending long deposits and financing the transactions at lower rates with short deposits renewed again and again, though from time to time it may appear to be profitable to borrow long deposits and to re-lend the proceeds at the prevailing high short rates, in the hope that short rates will remain high. When expectations of lower interest rates stimulate the demand for long maturities, their rates decline below those of short deposits.

## (7) VARIOUS PRACTICES AND TECHNIQUES

Profit margins of $\frac{1}{16}$ per cent are usually considered adequate by banks which job in and out of the market and match maturities without taking any risk on changes in interest rates. But banks which take a view on the prospects of interest rates and assume a certain amount of calculated risk naturally expect a higher profit. Likewise there is, or should be, a wider profit margin on switching the proceeds of deposits into the market for Local Authorities and even more profit from investing in finance house deposits. Re-lending to customers is usually the most profitable method of employing the deposits.

New banks are inclined to be content for a short time with receiving slightly less favourable rates as lenders of deposits, in order to establish themselves in the market as active dealers. They would be ill-advised, however, to try to make their presence felt by bidding perceptibly above the prevailing market rates when borrowing deposits, because that would be a false start. It would convey the impression that they badly need the cash. While in the foreign exchange market and in the Euro-dollar markets even well-established banks operate occasionally without a profit in order to 'show the flag', to create goodwill and to attract other business, this practice is not prevalent in the inter-bank sterling market.

Nor are the tactics – applied by some banks in Euro-dollars before the market assumed its present size – of trying to mislead the market by initial lending in order to reduce the rate, or initial borrowing in order to raise the rate, for the sake of following it up by larger transactions in the opposite direction, encountered nowadays. This is because the turnover has become so large that on most days only very big initial transactions would be able to move the rate, and the operator could never be certain of bringing off his bluff.

Very often deposits at call or subject to short notice are left with the borrower for long periods if the lender, while wanting to ensure that he can recover his money at short notice, has no reason for excercising his right. Long deposits, too, are often renewed for the same periods over and over again. The rates are re-negotiated whenever deposits are renewed. Some depositors in this highly sophisticated market have subconsciously revived the custom that prevailed among depositors with village saving banks in backward countries in the 19th century – withdrawing their deposits just to make sure their money is still there and then re-depositing the money immediately.

## (8) THE MARKET'S ROUTINE

Although some of the most active banks dealing in inter-bank sterling are prepared to quote dealing rates both ways, this practice is not nearly as widespread as in the foreign exchange market or even in the Euro-dollar market. Only some of those banks which synchronise the two transactions and match maturities and are content with a narrow margin of profit without having to take any risk are in the habit of quoting both ways. The spread between their quotations is at times inclined to be relatively wide. It is often wider when they quote to brokers than when they deal direct with other banks, so as to make room for the brokerage.

Early in the morning brokers contact the banks to ask for their quotations, which at that stage are more often than not purely tentative and unbinding. Lists of rates are communicated for information only. Brokers may suggest rates at which they expect it might be possible to do business. If banks are interested in some of the tentative quotations the brokers try to find a counterpart. Only a few dealers are at their tables at 9 a.m. sharp, and active dealing seldom begins much before 10 a.m. By then the market is fairly familiar with the range of quotations for various maturities and also has some idea of the prevailing trend. Active 'value today' transactions continue till about 3.15 p.m. – the time limit for London clearing – but it is possible to deal until much later, right up to 5.30 p.m. for 'value tomorrow'.

Banks may make firm quotations to other banks or to brokers for a definite amount and for a definite date. Or they may give brokers instructions to communicate to them any quotations they receive up to a certain rate, for maturities in which they are interested.

As in the foreign exchange market and in the Euro-currency markets, it is sometimes against the interests of a bank to disclose the direction in which it intends to operate. Of course this cannot be avoided in the case of direct dealing between banks except by quoting both ways, which many banks are unwilling to do. Nor is it easy to avoid it when a bank wants to borrow even through the intermediary of a broker, because the potential lender wants to know the identity of the would-be borrower. In many instances the former is content if the broker merely describes the type of bank – clearing bank affiliate, first-class accepting house, big American branch, etc. – knowing that the would-be lender has taken that name on many previous occasions. But much more often than not the lender wants to know the borrower's name, just in case its limit for that name is exhausted.

On the other hand, the broker need not as a rule disclose the name of the potential lender to the potential borrower. He has to exercise discretion, however, not to arrange a transaction which would place a borrower under some degree of moral obligation to accept an unwanted name on a future occasion, having borrowed a deposit from the bank concerned. More will be said about limits for names later in this chapter.

### (9) WHEN ARE QUOTATIONS BINDING?

The rule about the binding nature of a quotation once it is made by a bank is the same as in other markets. If it is accepted immediately – that is, in a matter of a few seconds – it is binding for the bank which made the quotation. There is apt to be a lapse of a few seconds unless the broker happens to have a potential counterpart on another line, in which case the deal could be clinched at once. But if the time lag is unduly prolonged the quotation ceases to be binding. Time may be gained by asking for a number of rates for different maturities, even though the bank is only interested in one maturity. The length of the interval is largely a matter of reciprocity, if both parties know each other's identity and are familiar with each other's dealing method. But it also depends on the trend of the market. If rates are apt to move fast the rule about *immediate* acceptance means just that. Even a second's delay might convert a small profit on the basis of the rate quoted into an appreciable loss.

When a firm quotation is for no definite amount and is accepted immediately it is considered binding up to certain standard amounts, the size of which may depend on the size of the bank that made the quotation. If it is a clearing bank affiliate, or the branch of a big American bank, or one of the larger non-clearing banks, the standard amount is £500,000. If the bank that quotes the rate is smaller, it is £250,000. But on the basis of reciprocity leading banks are apt to regard £1,000,000 as the standard amount up to which their quotation is considered to be binding even if during the interval of a few seconds the rate they had quoted has become disadvantageous to them because rates have moved in the wrong direction.

Very often amounts of individual transactions are well above the standard amounts. A deal may cover anything up to £10,000,000 or even more. On the other hand, it is possible to deal in smaller amounts, though seldom less than £100,000. There are occasional deals in broken amounts if a bank wants to find a counterpart for some definite transaction with a customer, but even such amounts are usually multiples of £10,000 or at any rate of £5,000.

## (10) A VARIETY OF TRANSACTIONS

Brokers have a staff of specialists in inter-bank sterling. Some of them even have a specialist in forward-forward business. The market has expanded to such an extent that today the inter-bank sterling department alone may be as large as the entire dealing room was even a few years ago. In the case of smaller banks and brokers the same dealers often deal also in sterling and dollar Certificates of Deposits, about which more will be said in Chapters 8 and 13. These markets are inter-related because discount houses lend surpluses in the inter-bank market and because Certificates of Deposits often provide an alternative for inter-bank deposits. If discrepancies between the two sets of rates exceed the normal figures, either in general or for certain dates, they provide opportunities for arbitrage. For the same reason, the same departments may also deal in Local Authorities and hire-purchase deposits, about which more will be said in Chapters 8 and 13.

Inter-bank sterling deposits can be transacted for maturities varying from deposits overnight to deposits up to five years. I have even heard of negotiated transactions up to seven years. For short loans the structure of maturities is similar to that of the traditional market. The difference is that in the inter-bank deposit market it is normal to transact business for maturities up to two years, and it is possible to negotiate even longer transactions in terms of years. Moreover, the new market is better organised for dealing in broken maturities than the traditional market. Altogether its terms can be adapted more easily to changing requirements. There is business not only in deposits for fixed maturities but also in deposits subject to notice. There are deposits at call and standard periods of notice are two days for deposits up to fourteen days, one week for deposits up to a month, and one month for longer deposits. But at the time of writing there is more dealing in deposits for fixed maturities and it is easier to obtain quotations for fixed periods. The most frequent fixed maturities are deposits overnight, deposits for two days, seven days, fourteen days, one, two, three, six and twelve months. Deposits in terms of years up to five years and longer are in strong demand when a fall in interest rates is expected, but in such situations the majority of depositors prefer Certificates of Deposits and are content with a somewhat lower rate for the sake of retaining their freedom to recover their money before maturity.

## (11) INTEREST RATE DIFFERENTIALS

Interest rates on inter-bank deposits are higher than those on loans for corresponding maturities in the traditional market. This is only natural, for while the latter are fully and indeed more than fully secured, the former are entirely unsecured. An equally important reason for the difference is that in the traditional market there is a lender of last resort – the Bank of England – so that the borrower is in a position to recover his money in any conceivable circumstances. In the inter-bank sterling market, on the other hand, there is no lender of last resort, so that there is a theoretical possibility that in conditions of extremely tight money the borrower might not be able to raise the funds required to meet his liability on the date of maturity, however solvent he may prove to be in the long run. What usually happens in such emergencies is that the borrower pays fantastically high interest rates for deposits overnight and meets his liability – at a high cost. Another difference is that those who lend in the traditional money market usually have the assurance that their money is being re-lent in a self-liquidating form for essentially sound purposes, while in the inter-bank sterling market they have no idea even of the identity of the ultimate borrower let alone of the purpose for which their money is being borrowed.

For all these reasons differentials between rates overnight are apt to fluctuate wildly. There is normally a differential of up to $\frac{1}{4}$ per cent in the rates on deposits for one month or longer. Considering the difference in the relative degree of security, this may appear to be a very modest differential, and its small extent implies a very high compliment to borrowers of deposits. It also indicates the large size of the market and the resulting opportunity to deal in very large amounts for the sake of very narrow profit margins. But the main explanation is the prolonged absence of major bank failures and the resulting widespread optimism about the unlikelihood of a recurrence of the banking crises of the past. The moment the slightest doubt ever arose about this it would manifest itself in a widening of the differentials. This might attract more money from the discount market, but the Bank of England is in a position to discourage this by reducing the amount available for transfer into the inter-bank market.

The differentials are subject to fluctuations largely because official intervention is confined to the traditional market. Even though the Bank of England confines its money market operations to very short-term credits and very short bills – its intervention in the foreign exchange market and in the Gilt-edged market may of course produce incidental side-effects on traditional markets and parallel markets alike – the effect of its tactics and policies in respect of the traditional market tends to spread over longer maturities in the traditional market. There is no such effect in the inter-bank market, except very indirectly.

Profit margins are normally so narrow that banks which confine their operations to deposits with matched maturities only find it worth while to operate in large single amounts. Operations in smaller items may be considered worth while if dealers take a view on the prospects of interest rates or if they serve the purpose of covering a previous commitment. Some banks may prefer to carry out a transaction running into several millions of pounds in several instalments but others prefer to deal in one single transaction no matter how large the amount involved may be.

The size of individual amounts also depends to a large degree on the trend of the market. When the turnover is large it is often possible to lend or borrow large amounts without moving the rate perceptibly. But on the days when quotations move wildly with very little actual business, or when the market is inactive and the rates keep steady, it might be found advantageous to divide a large transaction into several smaller transactions, say, into five amounts of £2,000,000 each in preference to attempting to borrow or lend a single deposit of £10,000,000.

## (12) FORWARD-FORWARD TRANSACTIONS

There is a great deal of forward business done in the inter-bank sterling market. 'Forward-forward' is the market's term for it, because a loan is arranged to take effect at a future date, or a deferred loan is swapped against an immediate loan for a shorter period or against another deferred loan for a different period. Forward-forward business can be transacted either in one single transaction or in two separate transactions. It can be done in one immediate short-term deposit transaction and one deferred long-term deposit transaction, or in two separate deferred transactions with different maturities and with different dates at which they take effect. If it is done in a single transaction a short–long forward rate is fixed. But such swap rates are usually a matter for negotiation. The calculation of the swap rate between two deposits for standard maturities is a matter of simple arithmetic, but for broken dates it has to be done with the aid of calculators, though it is often based on the rates for the nearest standard maturities.

The most widely used standard forward-forward maturities are one month against two months or against three months, three months against six months or against twelve months, and six months against twelve months. As far as I have been able to ascertain, the longest forward-forward transaction has been one year against two years.

As we shall see in Chapters 8, 9, 10 and 13 forward-forward business is also transacted in the markets for sterling and dollar Certificates of Deposit, LA deposits and finance house deposits. It is possible to borrow or lend forward inter-bank deposits against lending or borrowing sterling CDs. It is also possible to combine forward-forward business with arbitrage between sterling and dollar deposits, or between inter-bank sterling and LA or finance house deposits, but such complicated transactions, and indeed forward-forward transactions in general, are only carried out by the most sophisticated dealers, usually during periods when the market is inactive. The majority of banks confine themselves to less complicated transactions, which is the reason why there may develop relatively wide profit margins in forward-forward transactions for the more enterprising banks.

Expectations of changes in interest rates are the main factor giving rise to forward-forward business, because various dealers hold different views of these expectations. Deviations from the normal 'yield curve' – the equilibrium line between maturities for various dates – as a result of some fortuitous influence resulting from specific transactions which alter the supply–demand relationship for particular dates, can also give rise to forward-forward business.

The normal amount of a deal in the forward-forward market is £250,000 and the largest amount I have ever heard of is £2,000,000. The volume of turnover changes, but it is never very large because of the small number of banks actively engaged in such transactions. Sometimes long intervals pass between two transactions, but there are days when a number of them are concluded in close succession.

## (13) ARBITRAGE OPPORTUNITIES

Arbitrage opportunities provided for the dealers in the inter-bank market are manifold. We have already referred to time arbitrage which becomes profitable when abnormal discrepancies arise between rates for various maturities. Apart from forward-forward transactions in the form of dealing in deposits for various standard maturities, or in deposits for broken dates, forward-forward transactions are frequently resorted to on the eve of awkward dates. Thus banks may borrow in December deposits which are to be delivered in the New Year, or lend deposits to be delivered after the turn of the year. Such operations enable banks to take advantage of the decline in deposit rates after the cessation of end-of-year pressure, speculating on the extent to which the turn of the seasonal trade is liable to affect the market.

International arbitrage is yet another sphere in which inter-bank sterling may be employed by banks which operate in the market through their foreign exchange departments. Money market departments are unfamiliar with such use of their borrowed inter-bank sterling, though foreign exchange dealers might initiate their colleagues in the art of interest arbitrage. Exchange control regulations restrict the use of inter-bank deposits for out-ward arbitrage because of the limits fixed by the Bank of England for the covered forward commitments of each bank. But circum-stances are liable to arise where inward arbitrage in the form of switching Euro-dollars or other foreign funds into inter-bank sterling becomes profitable. Shortly before devaluation in 1967 domestic arbitrage was highly profitable because of the meteoric rise in interest rates for short-term sterling credits. Fantastic profits were thus earned by arbitrageurs for a few days.

In a less spectacular way, the improvement of sterling during the early months of 1970, due mainly to tight money conditions caused by the Budgetary surplus, resulted in a reduction of the premium on forward dollars to a level at which it became profit-able to engage in inward arbitrage operations when inter-bank sterling rates were above Euro-dollar rates. In theory, it was more profitable to switch into Euro-sterling, because the latter com-manded higher rates of interest than inter-bank sterling rates. But the market for Euro-sterling in Paris, Zürich or Frankfurt was not nearly as good as the London market in inter-bank sterling, where it was easier to deal in large amounts. From the point of view of exchange control it did not make any immediate difference whether Euro-dollars were switched into Euro-sterling or inter-bank sterling. From the moment Euro-sterling is lent to a U.K. resident it becomes internal account sterling for the duration of the loan. It can be re-lent to residents but not to non-residents.

During periods when sterling is not under a cloud foreign arbitrageurs are quite willing to buy uncovered sterling and invest it in inter-bank or LA deposits. The return of confidence in sterling early in 1970 resulted therefore in an increase in the amount of uncovered foreign sterling balances. Even so, only part of them tended to come into the Euro-sterling market, because a high proportion was held on sterling current accounts with London banks or served the purpose of covering current com-mercial and financial transactions in the U.K. In any case, as we shall see in Chapter 12, such a market as exists in London in Euro-sterling is negligible although it is possible for brokers to arrange deals in it between non-resident holders. The Bank of England disapproves of the development of a market in it in London.

London banks find it from time to time worth their while to borrow Euro-currencies and swap them into inter-bank sterling even at a small loss, because in doing so they increase their authorised ceilings for covered foreign exchange commitments. The limits fixed for each authorised dealer for covered or un-covered forward exchange positions handicap the expansion of the foreign exchange business of London banks. These limits were reduced materially in 1968 and came to be enforced more severely, because the Bank of England discovered that in the intervals between return dates some banks had been in the habit of exceed-ing their limits. As a result, those guilty of this irregularity were compelled to submit daily returns. Since then all banks have come to conform to their exchange limits more strictly. The only way in which they can increase the limits is through the creation of 'negative limits' by means of inward arbitrage.

Since it is net commitments that count, the amounts committed in outward arbitrage are reduced by the amounts obtained through inward arbitrage. This practice is also known under the term 'easing operation', because it tends to relax the inconveniently tight limits imposed on the foreign exchange activities of banks. Much of the foreign exchange that flows in through such inward arbitrage is invested in inter-bank sterling, though much of it also finds its way into other parallel markets.

## (14) INTER-BANK MARKET VERSUS TRADITIONAL MARKET

Because of the direct effect of official intervention in the traditional market in overnight loans, the interest differential is apt to be very much wider for rates on such loans and for very short maturities in general. For instance at the end of February and March 1970 the rate on deposits overnight rose to 32 per cent and 35 per cent respectively, while day-to-day money in Lombard Street remained available at rates which could not exceed the Bank rate. The Bank always covers the deficiency of the traditional market, but, as already observed in Chapter 3, it may do so on terms that penalise discount houses.

Any house that is in a position to provide eligible securities is able to borrow at the Bank rate. The fact that for a few days money rates rose in the inter-bank market to more than 25 per cent above those quoted in the traditional market indicated that those unable to withdraw funds from the traditional market found themselves in a situation in which they had to cover in the inter-bank market their urgent requirements regardless of costs.

But official intervention in the traditional market is not altogether without effect on rates in the inter-bank market. After all, the possibility of withdrawing money from discount houses or of selling bills to them is a potential source of deposits available for re-lending in the inter-bank market. Many non-clearing banks possess substantial bill portfolios and their decision on whether to sell bills in the traditional market or borrow inter-bank deposits does depend to a large degree on the extent of the rate differential. If inter-bank rates are high compared with bill rates, banks unload bills in the discount market, thereby forcing discount houses to borrow either from clearing banks or, if the latter are unable or unwilling to lend, from the Bank of England. Or the resulting tight money conditions induce the Bank of England to intervene by buying bills from discount houses or from clearing banks. Tight conditions in the traditional market are liable to have a psychological effect on the inter-bank market, in addition to reducing the volume of lending, even in the absence of any actual operations affecting that market.

Above all, to the limited extent to which discount houses take an active interest as lenders in the inter-bank market and in the market in sterling CDs there is a connection between the traditional market and the inter-bank market. When conditions in Lombard Street become tight, discount houses withdraw their funds from the parallel markets, thereby contributing to some extent towards creating tighter conditions in the markets.

Having regard to all these considerations it is correct to say that the traditional market and the inter-bank market are not isolated from each other completely. But, as we saw above, wide differentials are apt to arise as far as very short maturities are concerned. In any case the two markets are subject to the same basic influences, albeit to a different degree in given circumstances. Changes in the Bank rate or in Euro-dollar rates are apt to affect the entire structure of interest rates in the traditional money market and in all parallel money markets, though of course not necessarily to the same extent.

## (15) INADEQUATE CONTACT WITH THE TRADITIONAL MARKET

Although, as pointed out above, the two markets are far from being completely isolated from each other, the contact between them leaves much to be desired. Tempting as it may be for clearing banks to withdraw their funds from the traditional market in order to re-lend them at higher rates in the inter-bank market, considerations of their liquidity ratio prevent them from doing so. Non-clearing banks may not be inhibited from making such re-arrangements to the same extent, but even they have to keep a substantial proportion of their liquid assets in the traditional market, whether in the form of short loans or in the form of bill holdings. What matters is that banks wanting to raise cash have the choice between withdrawing funds from the traditional market or borrowing in the inter-bank market.

Discount houses are unwilling to commit more than a small portion of their resources outside the traditional market even if the higher rates obtainable there make this appear tempting. For their chief clients, the clearing banks, are liable to call on their resources unexpectedly, and this might force them to fall back on the lender of last resort. The differential has to assume substantial proportions before the discount houses can be tempted to divert any noteworthy amounts from the traditional market to the inter-bank market. As we shall see in Chapter 8, they are more inclined to employ their funds in the sterling CD market.

## (16) FOREIGN EXCHANGE DEPARTMENT OR MONEY MARKET DEPARTMENT?

Opinions are divided on the question whether the inter-bank sterling market originated in the foreign exchange departments or in the money market departments of banks. We saw earlier that there are at least two theories about its origin. Both theories are probably correct. While in some banks inter-bank sterling dealing originated in the money market department, in other banks it originated in the foreign exchange department. The recent tendency seems to be to transfer the business to the money market department or to set up an independent inter-bank deposit department. In smaller banks the foreign exchange department may have one or two dealers specialising in inter-bank deposits, assisted by several clerks processing the deals they conclude. In larger banks and in big brokers' dealing rooms quite a number of dealers may specialise in inter-bank sterling. While in some establishments the same dealers may operate in inter-bank sterling and in Euro-currency deposits, in other establishments Euro-currencies are transacted by foreign exchange dealers. In either case all three branches are closely connected with each other and have to try to keep each other informed.

When the number of participants in inter-bank sterling transactions was relatively small, money market experts were familiar with the standing of the banks concerned. But with the advent of scores of new foreign bank branches in London, foreign exchange dealers are now better placed to ascertain the standing of the new participants and to follow any changes in their standing. They know much about the creditworthiness of the parent institutions abroad through their long experience in dealing with them in the foreign exchange market, where any changes in the fortunes of foreign banks are followed more closely.

The main argument in favour of leaving the money market department in charge, or for placing the department under the treasurer's direct control, lies in the importance of the inter-bank sterling market from the point of view of adjusting the non-clearing banks' liquidity. The treasurer is responsible for avoiding inadequate or excessive liquidity and he has to provide for the monetary requirements of all departments. His main channel for operations to that end is the money market department if it operates both in the traditional market and in the inter-bank market.

### (17) NEED FOR CLOSE CONTACT

What matters is that there should be the closest possible contact between the departments concerned, whichever of them is in charge of inter-bank sterling operations. Otherwise some bank might borrow inter-bank sterling from the money market department of a particular bank and swap it for dollars with the foreign exchange department of the same bank at the same moment over two different telephone lines. In so doing it could make a profit at the expense of the bank concerned, which might be avoided if the two departments were in closer contact.

The usual practice of clearing bank affiliates is to transact their foreign exchange business through the foreign exchange department of the parent institution. The parent institution, in turn, leaves the dealing in inter-bank sterling and in Euro-currencies to the affiliates. Some banks have more than one affiliate for transacting various types of inter-bank business, or for granting medium-term credits or special export credits financed with the aid of inter-bank deposits.

Even though inter-bank sterling transactions are handled in many banks by foreign exchange departments or by a separate department that is physically adjacent to the foreign exchange dealing room, inter-bank transactions are under much closer supervision by the treasurers of the banks. While working capital required for outward arbitrage transactions or for Euro-currency transactions is usually allocated by the management to the foreign exchange departments, operations in inter-bank deposits, like operations in the traditional markets, constitute a direct responsibility of the treasurers, who have to ensure a well-balanced cash position for their banks. Their supervision is not necessary if the dealers simply synchronise the borrowing and lending of deposits or if they job in and out of the market without affecting their net cash positions except temporarily between two transactions. But when it comes to time arbitrage the treasurer has to keep a watchful eye on future cash requirements. Moreover, the inter-bank sterling market has become an important channel for the adjustment of the banks' cash position. When treasurers are short of cash they might instruct their dealers to borrow whatever amount they need, provided it is obtainable on reasonable terms. It is the treasurers' task to estimate their banks' future cash requirements and to instruct their dealers to cover the required maturities accordingly.

## (18) LIMITS FOR NAMES

Because brokers are entitled to disclose the potential borrower's name there is less likelihood of complications arising over names such as are liable to arise in the foreign exchange market where brokers never disclose the name of either of the parties concerned until the deal is concluded. Thanks to the familiarity of brokers with various banks' attitudes towards certain names or towards certain types of banks, they are usually in a position to avoid exposing a would-be borrower of standing to a refusal. But the possibility that the potential lender has exhausted its limit for the would-be borrower's name is always there. Instances are known in which names of leading banks were refused by banks much smaller than themselves, because most banks have a limit even for the names of the largest banks and the smaller banks' limit for the larger banks' names had been exhausted. In many instances, however, leading banks have virtually no limits for each other's names.

Limits are usually fixed at management level and dealers have to obtain special authorisation on occasions when it would suit their interests to exceed these limits for the sake of some profitable deal. But to obtain such authorisation is apt to involve delay, as a result of which the quotation might cease to remain binding. The rate is apt to move in the meantime or the bank which has quoted the rate is apt to find a counterpart during the intervening seconds.

Since the minimum amount for individual transactions for big banks is usually £250,000, that must also be the lowest limit for which any name is taken. As for maximum limits, there are many medium-sized banks which would not take the name of even the biggest bank for more than, say, £4,000,000 or £5,000,000. Bigger banks have much higher maximum limits for names, as much as £10,000,000 or £20,000,000 or more. In practice, there are virtually no limits for commitments between banks of first-class standing such as clearing bank affiliates or London branches of leading foreign banks. Some banks differentiate according to the maturity of the deposits. They may take first-class names without limit for overnight deposits but apply limits for longer maturities. Other banks are less inclined to assume that nothing much could happen during the course of a single day, or even during the hours while London is closed.

Another consideration which plays an important part in determining limits is the availability of resources at the lender's disposal and its keenness on the proposed transaction. If it has ample idle resources which it wants to employ profitably or if the profit margin on the deal is attractive, its dealer might be able to persuade the management to relax its limit.

In theory there is a limit to the amount for which each bank is prepared to take the name of every other bank. There is a wide variety of principles on the basis of which various banks fix their limits for lending unsecured inter-bank deposits or Euro-currency deposits to any one bank. Each bank is liable to adjust the basic rules or the amount fixed on the basis of the rules, whenever the general prospects, or its own position, or the position and prospects of individual banks change.

## (19) HOW LIMITS FOR NAMES ARE FIXED

Many banks fix their limits for names on the basis of the capital resources of the banks concerned, but while some fix it as low as 10 per cent of these resources others go up to 20 or even 25 per cent. Another method of determining the limits is by some fixed proportion of the banks' total assets or of their total liquid assets. Other banks take the balance sheets as a whole into consideration, while others again simply rely on their credit information departments' judgement. In view of the possibility of the adoption or reinforcement of exchange control, different views may be taken of limits applied to sterling commitments and to foreign currency commitments. Inter-bank sterling deposits lent to a bank and sterling Certificates of Deposits issued by the same bank come under the same limit.

As a general rule limits for London branches or affiliates of American and other foreign banks are determined by the standing of their respective parent institutions. Likewise, fully owned or controlled affiliates of British banks enjoy the reflected glory derived from the high standing of parent banks. Even if a big bank owns only a minority shareholding in a smaller bank, it is assumed to be morally responsible for the latter's liabilities. There are various kinds and degrees of special relationship between banks and they are taken into consideration. Merchant banks are judged to a large extent according to whether they are members of the Accepting Houses Committee. Banks owned jointly by a number of leading banks of various nationalities are given high limits.

But on whatever basis the limits are fixed they are not likely to remain permanent. Apart from changes in the figures that serve as a basis for calculating the limits, their amounts are bound to be influenced by the nature and extent of the banks' operations in the market. If a bank becomes a borrower on an unduly large scale and operates for some time one way only, this is liable to induce banks to lower their limits for its name, or even to refuse to take it. A bank which is prepared to pay regularly higher rates than those paid by other banks of its class is also liable to come under a cloud after a while. While it is understood that smaller banks are willing to pay slightly higher rates, any evidence that they are too keen on borrowing would be taken into consideration. Banks are always on the lookout for information indicating that a bank is over-borrowing and trying to raise loans up to the limit to which a large number of banks are prepared to take its name. It is easier to ascertain this in the case of inter-bank sterling deposits than in the case of Euro-currencies, which may be borrowed in other markets besides London.

## (20) POSSIBILITIES OF DEFAULTS

Even in respect of inter-bank sterling the complete absence of any pooling of information and the almost complete absence of any exchange of information is a disadvantage. Banks are apt to be in the dark about the total extent to which any bank has drawn on the entire market's facilities. But rumours do get around. If a bank is a persistent borrower it is only a question of time before the market comes to form a fair idea about this. Brokers are in a better position to know if a bank is over-borrowing, but their lips are sealed. Nevertheless, they may become reluctant to propose to their valued clients transactions with banks which, to their own knowledge, have already borrowed too much.

As we observed above, limits to names of foreign banks are liable to be influenced by exchange control fears. Such fears are allayed in the case of London branches which balance their assets and liabilities more or less in sterling or which lend in sterling some of their foreign currency resources in addition to re-lending in sterling the amounts they have borrowed in sterling.

But banks are also liable to get into difficulties through excessive or imprudent lendings of foreign currency deposits abroad, and this possibility cannot be disregarded. It is widely assumed that, as far as first-rate banks are concerned, the monetary authorities of their countries would never place them in a position in which exchange restrictions would prevent them from meeting their liabilities. But even from this point of view it might be advisable to bear in mind that in 1966, after some failures and scares of failures affecting the Euro-dollar market, the Bank of France warned foreign banks on a semi-public occasion not to assume that French banks would be allotted as a matter of course the necessary dollars to solve the difficulties that might be caused through any defaults by their Euro-dollar debtors.

Should the London branch of a foreign bank find it difficult to meet its inter-bank sterling liabilities, exchange control in its own country might conceivably prevent its head office from coming to its rescue. The contingency is extremely remote as far as first-rate banks of advanced countries are concerned, but it should not be ignored to the extent of disregarding obviously unsound practices by a particular branch on the assumption that it would always be backed by its head office. For instance, although the speculative losses of the Brussels branch of a leading New York bank in the 'sixties, substantial as they were, were easily met by its head office, had they occurred in the middle of a major dollar crisis the possibility that the American authorities might have adopted exchange control and declined to authorise the transfer of the dollars required to cover the deficiency cannot be ignored.

## (21) DEALINGS WITH SMALLER BANKS

There are rate differentials between deposit rates paid by first-class banks and those paid by smaller banks. Many banks would only deal with first-class banks, but the fact that there are some 160 banks participating in the market – even though many of them do not operate systematically – seems to indicate that it is possible for banks of good standing to borrow deposits even if they are relatively small.

Although there are many banks which would refuse to lend to smaller banks, or would take their names for relatively small amounts only, smaller banks dealing among themselves derive much benefit from offsetting each other's surpluses and deficiencies. The rates paid on such deposits are of course somewhat higher than the standard rates quoted for first-class banks. There is a general assumption that important banks would always be helped out of a tight corner by the Bank of England or by the Central Bank of their respective countries, while in many quarters the view is held that smaller but sound banks have to rely on their own creditworthiness.

Many banks are prepared to lend small amounts to smaller banks for the sake of the interest differential and for the sake of other business that such transactions are liable to attract. There are, or were until recently, also differentials on deposits lent to first-class banks in countries which had, or were liable to have, exchange controls in operation or whose banks were systematic borrowers on a large scale. For this reason for a number of years leading Italian and Japanese banks had to pay higher rates. These differentials gradually declined – as they did in the case of Euro-dollar transactions with such banks – and by 1970 they had virtually disappeared. Even Communist State-controlled banks, which had to pay substantial differentials in earlier years, have come to insist on being charged standard rates, and very often they have their way, although many banks are still unwilling to deal with them at all.

The market is becoming increasingly sophisticated in more than one sense. In normal conditions spreads between borrowing and lending rates are now narrower. The volume of dealing has increased considerably, so that it is now often possible to transact relatively large amounts without necessarily moving the rates appreciably. A large and increasing variety of operations has developed. There is an increasing degree of specialisation by banks or, within the same bank, by dealers, in certain types of operations or practices.

## (22) PROFIT MARGINS AND RISKS

We saw earlier that a number of banks specialise in quoting both ways and being prepared to deal either way, taking good care to cover their resulting commitments by deposits with matched maturities, for the sake of such profit margins as can be secured without taking any risk if the borrowing and lending can be synchronised. The net profit on such operations is bound to be narrow. Out of this profit margin the substantial and increasing overheads have to be covered. Even an interval of a few seconds between the two operations – which is often inevitable – entails a risk, although it might, on the other hand, increase the profits if the rate should move in favour of the operator during the interval.

Such operations were very popular in the early years of the Euro-dollar market. But in 1965 the failure of the Stinnes Bank in Germany and the vegetable oil scandal in New York reminded banks that a risk quite out of proportion to the profit margins was ever-present in the case of unsecured non-self-liquidating loans. The inter-bank sterling market never witnessed such light-hearted jobbing in and out of the market as was experienced in the Euro-dollar market before the difficulties mentioned above made dealers less light-hearted. But in the prolonged absence of new banking difficulties affecting inter-bank deposits both markets drifted back into the habit of dealing in matched maturities, with the transactions synchronised, for the sake of very narrow profit margins.

## (23) TIME ARBITRAGE

Other banks specialise in time arbitrage, which necessarily involves a certain degree of risk. The extent to which chief dealers are given a free hand by their managements to rely on their judgement regarding prospective changes in interest rates varies from bank to bank and from time to time. Any bank which suffers losses through bad luck or bad judgement is liable to abandon time arbitrage or drastically curtail it, at any rate for a while.

Some banks confine themselves to fixed deposits, while others prefer to borrow deposits subject to notice, largely on the assumption that the notice will not necessarily be exercised for some time. Many banks borrow in the inter-bank sterling market mainly for the purpose of re-lending the proceeds of the deposits to Local Authorities or to finance houses for the sake of the interest differential. Other banks again specialise in time arbitrage, taking advantage of the discrepancies that frequently occur in respect of maturities that are not particularly popular – for instance maturities for two, four, seven to eleven months, which are apt to be neglected at times, the standard maturities being one, three, six and twelve months. Time arbitrage opportunities occur when supply or demand for certain maturities increases abnormally in connection with some large transaction or even through the coinciding of a number of smaller transactions. Finally, any big transaction for some broken date enables arbitrageurs to benefit by the resulting slight distortion of the yield curve.

Easily predictable readjustments of short rates distorted by seasonal or other familiar influences provide arbitrage opportunities which are relatively free of risk and, owing to the unilateral pressure that precedes the change in the tendency, reasonably profitable for those in a position to swim against the seasonal tide. Most clearing banks want to improve their cash ratio and liquidity ratio in their detailed returns for the third Wednesday of the month, and the resulting operations provide arbitrage opportunities. Banks all over the world practise window-dressing for the end of their financial year. But if their financial year does not end on 31 December they will take full advantage of the effect of operations by the majority of banks whose financial year does end on 31 December.

Some such sources of profits are essential for most banks to justify the existence of their inter-bank deposit departments. The narrow profit margins on purely routine transactions seldom suffice to cover overheads. These costs have increased considerably, partly because the sharp increase in the number of foreign branches in London has created a strong and urgent demand for experienced dealers who now command high salaries, apart altogether from the general rise in salaries, rents, telephone charges, etc. Any increase in turnover necessitates additional costly installations. The increasing mechanisation of operations in all financial markets involves a big capital outlay and often also higher running costs. Above all, rents and purchase prices for premises have risen very steeply, and any expansion or conversion of banking premises is very expensive.

## (24) VARIOUS USES OF DEPOSITS

In most instances in which banks want to retain the deposits they borrow, instead of jobbing in and out of the market or using them for arbitrage or re-investment, the proceeds of the deposits go into the banks' general pool of funds. But they may not be able to increase their credits to customers owing to the operation of a credit squeeze. When in 1969 the trend in the Gilt-edged market appeared to have turned, many banks employed the deposits to finance speculation in a further rise in Government stocks. This was done by a number of new American branches.

There are many other specific purposes for which borrowed deposits are used. They cannot of course be used for speculating on a rise in the price of gold, because gold bought in London has to be paid for in dollars. But there is no similar restriction on transactions in silver. Such operations need not be speculative. For some time it was profitable to buy cash silver and re-sell it for forward delivery. The premium on silver futures must cover the interest charge on the deposit and the cost of storage and insurance. Such operations are only profitable when expectations of a rise in the price of silver give rise to an adequate premium on forward silver. Similar operations in other commodities may also be financed by inter-bank sterling deposits.

## (25) CREDIT SQUEEZES

The credit squeeze, which prevents banks from borrowing for the purpose of increasing the amount of credits to their customers, slows down the expansion of the market. It operates very much against the interests of new foreign branches. Credit limits are based on the volume of credits granted by the banks concerned in the past, but since new branches can have no previous records the Bank of England has to fix their limits at an arbitrary figure.

It had been suggested that the Bank was inclined to fix the limits for new foreign branches deliberately low in order to encourage them to lend in terms of Euro-dollars or other Euro-currencies. This was possible during 1968–70 because licences to borrow in foreign currencies were granted more freely, even though many would-be borrowers were discouraged by the restriction on covering the exchange risk on such loans. The conversion of the proceeds of such loans into sterling yielded dollars to the authorities, at any rate for the duration of the loans. In recognition of this, the argument ran, the limits for sterling credits was raised for the benefit of those foreign branches which had earned that reward by contributing towards the increase of the official reserve. In the meantime they had to re-lend in the inter-bank market or in some other parallel market any sterling deposits borrowed in excess of their credit ceiling. They were in a position to lend to Local Authorities or to invest in Gilt-edged.

Actually, the main consideration which keeps credit ceilings for new foreign branches at a low level is probably that it would be unfair to encourage their competition with British banks when the latter are prevented by their credit ceilings from lending to industry and commerce.

## (26) DEALINGS WITH OUTSIDE DEPOSITORS

Customers outside the market usually lend overnight or for short periods, so as to employ their liquid resources, but they usually borrow for three months or longer. Even though the rate allowed on deposits to all but the largest business firms is much lower than current market rates between banks, it is higher than the rates allowed by clearing banks on deposits subject to seven days' notice, which is 2 per cent below the Bank rate under the cartel arrangement. Large corporations have acquired the habit of employing their liquid funds in inter-bank deposits overnight or in the form of other short deposits. They may deal either direct with banks or through the intermediary of brokers. They also take advantage of the higher interest rates obtainable in the market on longer deposits when they want to employ temporarily unspent proceeds of recent capital issues.

Clearing banks, since they are prevented by their cartel agreement from paying more than 2 per cent below the Bank rate, were losing large depositors as a result of the development of the inter-bank market and other parallel markets. We have already mentioned that it was largely in order to avoid this that they established affiliates which were in a position to pay higher deposit rates. As a result, when their good customers express dissatisfaction over the inadequacy of the deposit rates paid under the cartel arrangement, the banks simply suggest that they transfer their deposit accounts to the affiliate, which is in a position to pay higher rates. Even though legally the liabilities of clearing bank affiliates are not guaranteed by the clearing banks there is such a strong moral liability that many depositors unhesitatingly transfer their deposits to affiliates for the sake of the higher rates, in preference to transferring them to non-clearing banks. But many accepting houses, merchant banks and overseas banks have also come to inspire more confidence during recent years through becoming stronger as a result of amalgamations and the introduction of new capital into well-established family houses.

A number of British banks have affiliates in the Channel Islands to which large deposits are attracted for fiscal considerations. These affiliates, and also some local Guernsey and Jersey banks, and banks in other 'tax havens' actively participate in the inter-bank sterling market. Wealthy Middle East depositors are in the habit of placing some of their funds in inter-bank sterling.

## (27) LIMITS FOR TOTAL OPERATIONS

There is a ceiling, fixed by managements, for aggregate gross or net commitments by any bank in inter-bank sterling. When that ceiling is approached dealers become anxious to avoid actually reaching it, and for this reason they only operate if the profit margin is well above the minimum. The same is true if the limits in respect of particular names are approached.

Unless treasurers of banks are in direct control of inter-bank operations they usually fix a limit up to which the department concerned is authorised to lend or borrow. Sometimes such limits are exclusively in respect of inter-bank sterling, and separate limits are fixed for operations in other parallel markets, but in other instances they include Euro-currencies and funds lent or borrowed in all parallel markets. Such ceilings are often for gross lending, so as to prevent dealers from committing their banks for amounts far in excess of what the managements deem it to be safe to lend, by simply re-borrowing the amount lent in excess of the ceiling, thus keeping net commitments below the ceiling. But if treasurers consider the liquidity of their bank more than adequate they are liable to impose limits also on net borrowing, except for purely temporary operations.

The attitude of treasurers and managements towards these limits is usually flexible. Managements and the chief dealers themselves are usually much more rigid in their attitude towards limits for individual names.

In spite of the limits for names, the size of the turnover is apt to indicate from time to time that those limits must have been exceeded in a great many instances. For instance during the Euro-dollar boom in 1969 most American bank branches must have exhausted their limits with all London banks by their large-scale borrowing of Euro-dollars. Nevertheless they remained the most active operators in the inter-bank sterling market. In one known instance the London branch of one fair-sized American bank borrowed on a single day inter-bank sterling and Euro-dollars to a total exceeding £100,000,000.

The possibility of a sharp contraction of limits for names, and also of a lowering of the ceilings which managements authorise for their dealers, carries the danger of credit deflation as soon as some major default or a deterioration of general economic conditions induces banks to exercise greater care. It is presumably mainly because of this possibility that the market has the impression that the Bank of England is not enthusiastic about the expansion of the inter-bank sterling market. So long as the moderate inflationary boom continues all banks will remain solvent and profit-making. But any serious setback in business conditions is liable to lead to bank failures with chain-reactions that would result in large-scale reductions of limits for names. It is true that there has been no such crisis since the war. But we have not concluded a covenant with Providence that there will never be another crisis.

## (28) INFLUENCES AFFECTING INTEREST RATES

We saw earlier that expectations of future changes in interest rates in general are liable to affect the differentials between long and short maturities. There were periods during the early part of 1970 when rates quoted for various maturities were almost identical, because of the uncertainty of prospects and because conflicting expectations more or less offset each other. The natural trend in this market, as in other markets, in the absence of strong expectations of changes is for long maturities to be more expensive than short maturities, because lenders relinquish the use of their money for longer periods and because of the higher degree of uncertainty over a longer period. The widespread anticipation of a decline in interest rates in the long run that prevailed early in 1970 resulted in a reversal of the yield curve and for some time long maturities were actually cheaper than short maturities.

Apart altogether from basic influences, the inter-bank deposit market as well as the traditional market is exposed to technical and seasonal influences. The banks' practice of adjusting their commitments for days for which they have to submit returns to the authorities is liable to be a passing technical influence on rates. So is the customary adjustment of positions on the eve of holidays and even more on the eve of weekends which are considered, rightly or wrongly, to be critical. On Wednesdays, and even more on every third Wednesday of the month, the adjustments made by banks in the U.K. for the sake of the returns they have to submit to the Bank of England, affect short rates of every kind. So do window-dressing operations on the approach of the end of the year and, to a less extent, on the approach of the end of the half-year. Inter-bank rates are also affected by seasonal tight or easy conditions.

Even such passing influences as the heavy over-subscription of a public issue, which places issuing houses in temporary possession of large funds pending the receipt of letters of allotments by subscribers, are liable to affect inter-bank deposit rates. The ups and downs of the Gilt-edged market, and of the Stock Exchange in general, are liable to affect inter-bank sterling rates because of their effect on the volume of funds attracted or released by the Stock Exchange under the influence of changing expectations. They affect of course also the traditional market, but while the Bank of England endeavours to smooth out such temporary disturbing influences there, the inter-bank market is left to its own devices, and the influences are allowed to produce their full effect, especially on very short rates. But we must bear in mind that the ironing out of operations in the traditional market by means of intervention cannot be taken for granted, because the Bank's attitude is unpredictable. Quite conceivably in given situations when the official policy is in favour of tight money conditions it might suit the Bank to allow some temporary abnormal influences to produce their effect. Even then that effect is not likely to be as pronounced as in the inter-bank market, because the discount houses are always able to borrow from the Bank in the last resort.

## (29) FISCAL CONSIDERATIONS

The inter-bank sterling market has succeeded in achieving a high degree of popularity abroad during the brief period of its existence. After the return of confidence in sterling early in 1970 much of the former balances that returned to London came to assume the form of inter-bank sterling deposits. At any rate this was the case with deposits up to 364 days, beyond which banks in the U.K. have to pay interest net, after deducting income tax. This makes relatively little difference to depositors resident in the U.K. but it effectively deters non-residents from depositing their money in the U.K. for a period of one year or beyond. Although the tax is eventually refunded to non-resident depositors, it takes about four weeks from the end of the business year of the bank that has deducted the tax to recover the tax, provided that its business year ends in December. If its business year happens to end in March the interest is not refunded until the following January. Apart from the loss of interest involved, the inconvenience of having to reclaim the tax and the ever-present possibility of delay in refunding it is in itself sufficient to deter non-residents from depositing their money in the U.K. beyond 364 days, unless they do so against sterling CDs on which interest can be paid gross up to five years. The inter-bank sterling rate – especially for relatively long terms such as six months – is followed very closely abroad as an indicator of the trend of interest rates.

There may arise of course some major financial or political crisis which would discredit this market, as the crisis of 1931 discredited acceptances for a time. But in the absence of such a crisis the expansion of the market is likely to continue and to gather momentum once the credit squeeze is ended. Although the expansion of the inter-bank sterling market is not likely to assume proportions comparable with the expansion of the Euro-dollar market, it seems probable that the turnover and the outstanding amount will continue to grow both in terms of absolute figures and in relative terms.

## (30) WHY THE MARKET HAS COME TO STAY

In many quarters this view is not shared. Various possibilities are envisaged which would lead to a decline or even to a disappearance of the inter-bank sterling market. This frequently recurrent prophecy recalls the persistent prophecies in the late 'fifties and in the early and middle 'sixties, which confidently predicted the disappearance of the Euro-dollar market. As I recalled in the fourth edition of my *Euro-Dollar System*, many of the contingencies which had been expected to bring the market to an end did in fact materialise during the 'sixties, but this did not prevent the market from continuing to expand at a spectacular rate, even though it suffered occasional temporary reverses. There is no reason for supposing that it will be otherwise with the inter-bank sterling market.

After all, the development of both markets constitutes in a sense progress towards a more adequate monetary system. The facilities they offer fulfil genuine requirements and represent real improvements. The fact that these markets segregate wholesale banking from retail banking would be in itself sufficient justification for their existence.

The inter-bank sterling market, like the Euro-dollar market, goes a long way towards removing the rigidities imposed on banking terms or banking practices by official regulations or by banking traditions. It makes for a higher flexibility of facilities. It also makes for quicker and simpler transaction of business between lenders and borrowers. On the other hand, it sacrifices the advantage of the systematic scrutiny of securities by the lending banks – whether clearing banks or the Bank of England – thanks to which the quality of bills that circulate in the traditional market is maintained at a high level. It is mainly through this scrutiny that excessive borrowing is discovered and discouraged.

Now that the inter-bank sterling market does exist, many

people consider it strange in retrospect that it did not develop much earlier, at any rate as far as institutions of first-rate standing are concerned. Admittedly, dispensing with securities implies a degree of confidence in borrowers which has only developed in recent times. But then growth of confidence in banking conforms to the secular, indeed millenial, trend which has been progressing, temporary setbacks apart, ever since the early origins of money, credit and banking. My *History of Foreign Exchange* traces this progress over thousands of years. It is in keeping with the progress of civilisation itself. Of course the credit system and the high degree of confidence among bankers on which it rests, like civilisation itself, is liable to experience setbacks through wars or other major crises. But in the past each reverse has been followed by a resumption of progress. And unless there should be a world disaster which causes irreparable harm there is no reason why the experience should not continue to repeat itself in the future.

The new institution is in existence, for better or for worse, and those who operate it are continually gaining experience in its operation. Even if the institution should eclipse, the knowhow would remain and would become available when conditions for its application became once more favourable. Should the interval be too long, so that the generation that is familiar with the operation of the system disappeared, the system has now been described in detail and at least a future generation would not have to stumble on it once more by trial and error but could resume where its forerunners had been forced to abandon it. The eclipse of acceptance credits in the 'thirties, and of foreign exchange dealing during and immediately after the Second World War, did not mean the end of those two institutions. They were resumed as soon as conditions for their revival became favourable, even though the number of those who were familiar with their application through first-hand experience was relatively small.

## (31) INFLUENCES ACTING AGAINST MAINTENANCE OF THE MARKET

Admittedly, the inhibitions that delayed the development of the market still operate to some extent. Many banks which actively operate in the market were at the early stages of development anxious to let it be understood that they used the market solely for lending and not for borrowing. Even if that was true at that time – which is open to some doubt in at least some instances – most banks now candidly admit (albeit not necessarily on public occasions) that they borrow as well as lend inter-bank deposits. Clearing banks still operate with the aid of their affiliates and this prevents them from operating on the scale on which they could operate if the parent institutions themselves took an active hand. Their American opposite numbers are restrained by no such inhibitions and operate on a full scale through their London branches in the Euro-dollar market and, to a more moderate extent, in the inter-bank sterling market.

One of the reasons why it is still widely believed that the inter-bank sterling market has not come to stay is that its emergence and expansion coincided with a persistent high and rising level of interest rates. It is argued in many quarters that, should the adoption of the policy advocated by the 'money school' – according to which tighter credit should replace dear money permanently as a deflationary device – lead to lower interest rates it would be detrimental to the inter-bank sterling market as well as to the Euro-dollar market. But in itself a decline in interest rates need not affect either of the inter-bank markets materially, even if profit margins and turnover temporarily declined. In any case the theory that tight money could be an alternative to dear money is fallacious. If money is kept tight it is bound to be dear, and if in accordance with the principles of the 'money school' fiscal and other alternative devices of monetary policy, such as incomes policy, should be abandoned in favour of the credit squeeze, the whole credit squeeze and nothing but the credit squeeze, money would have to be kept tighter than ever and therefore it would be dearer than ever.

## (32) EFFECT OF STERLING'S IMPROVEMENT IN 1969–70

The return of confidence in sterling during most of 1969–70 helped the market because it attracted foreign balances, both covered and uncovered, through inward arbitrage. This trend would become reversed if as a result of wage inflation or other causes a new period of sterling crises developed. But such a setback would not materially affect the domestic aspects of the market – unless it were accompanied by banking difficulties, which is unlikely. A dollar crisis – which is at the time of writing quite on the cards because American industries seem to have caught the 'English disease' to an increasing degree – would mean inward arbitrage to London as a result of the depreciation of forward dollars.

The possibility of the effect of changes in British exchange control must also be envisaged. Fears of a reinforcement of control would deter inward arbitrage. On the other hand any premature relaxation of the existing controls might lead to large-scale outward arbitrage, which would cause a rise in interest rates in the inter-bank market as in other markets.

Another possibility which must be considered is an abandonment of the cartel between clearing banks. The authorities were at one time inclined to try to persuade the clearing banks to restore free competition in respect of deposit rates and credit terms, but that is not the present official attitude. This is understandable, for unless the banks are able to obtain a high proportion of their deposits at 2 per cent below the Bank rate – in addition to being able to hold current account balances free of interest – they would expect higher short-term rates for their loans to discount houses, which in turn would result in higher short-term rates on Treasury borrowing. Should deposit rates on small accounts be increased as a result of a termination of the cartel, higher Treasury bill rates would necessarily be expected to ensure a profit margin for the banks. The clearing banks themselves are most unlikely to take the initiative for the abolition of the cartel, which has worked reasonably satisfactorily, especially since they can get the best of both worlds by operating in parallel markets through their affiliates.

## (33) THE OFFICIAL ATTITUDE

If it appeared certain or even probable that the new market would drive the traditional market out of existence there could be no doubt about the direction in which the Bank would throw the considerable weight of its influence on the scales. But, as we saw in Chapter 2, it is far from being a foregone conclusion that further progress of the inter-bank market must mean the end of the traditional market. There are, moreover, other considerations for which some quarters in the Bank of England may conceivably have welcomed the new development. Admittedly it was not the inter-bank sterling market but the Euro-dollar market and the market in London dollar Certificates of Deposits that attracted a

large number of American and other foreign bank branches to
London during the late 'sixties. But as a result of any prolonged
decline in activity in Euro-dollars some of these branches might
withdraw unless they have additional spheres in which to operate.
The inter-bank sterling market constitutes one of these spheres,
and its expansion would reduce the likelihood of withdrawals of
recently opened foreign bank branches.

Even the Labour Government, which was opposed to sterling's
role as an international currency, and which was responsible for
the drastic reduction of that role, was favourably inclined towards
the inter-bank sterling market and other parallel markets. Mr
Wilson, in a speech at the Guildhall in 1968, paid a high compliment to the City for having brought the new money markets into
existence.

The Bank of England is naturally concerned about the misuse
to which the market can be put compared with its perfect control
over the traditional market. To strengthen its control the Bank
would have to change its fundamental rule not to lend to the
market without being fully secured by eligible securities, which is
inconceivable. But there is no reason why the Bank should not
borrow in the market to mop up funds.

What puzzles bankers is that the Bank of England did not
indicate any concern about the absence of security for Euro-
dollar deposits, and that the official attitude towards the development of the Euro-dollar market was one of benevolent neutrality.
It is true that the Bank's task is to look after sterling. But should
an important London bank ever default on its Euro-dollar commitments, the repercussions would be liable to be just as damaging to
sterling and to the City as if it had defaulted on inter-bank
sterling deposits. However this may be, while the Bank did
encourage the expansion of the Euro-dollar market to some
extent, it has been strictly neutral towards the growth of the inter-
bank sterling market.

It is true that the authorities have done nothing towards
actively discouraging the development of the inter-bank market,
although they are in a position to restrict its growth and even to
bring it to an end altogether. Should there be, however, indications
of over-borrowing by any individual bank or by the market as a
whole the Bank would naturally indicate its disapproval, which
no bank can afford to ignore. Official circles are believed to be
concerned not only about the absence of securities and about the

volume of the transactions but also about the absence of any assurance that the loans are self-liquidating.

It seems reasonable to assume that one of the considerations that prevent the authorities from opposing the development of the market is its desire to attract and retain the largest possible number of foreign branches, for the purpose of maintaining London's prestige as a world banking centre. Since credit ceilings prevent these branches from poaching on the British banks' preserves by lending sterling to customers, they are provided with an opportunity to operate in the inter-bank market, and through it in other parallel markets.

# CHAPTER SEVEN

# Inter-Corporation Deposits

## (1) A CONSEQUENCE OF THE CREDIT SQUEEZE

PARALLEL money markets are concerned with inter-bank dealings or with dealings between banks and institutions such as Local Authorities or finance houses. Dealings between banks and their non-banking customers are considered to be outside the market. To be logical, there should be even more reason for excluding dealings between two non-banking customers. Yet there is much to be said for including among the parallel money markets the inter-corporation market in deposits. For one thing, such transactions are very often initiated on the suggestion of banks to their clients. Brokers very often act as intermediaries between corporations requiring funds and those having liquid surpluses. Moreover, inter-corporation deposit transactions are similar in form and in substance to inter-bank deposit transactions. To the extent to which they will develop after the end of the credit squeeze, when the banks will be in a position to meet their customers' credit requirements, they will divert business from the inter-bank market in which the banks will raise the additional money.

It is the credit squeeze that has resulted in the development of this new short-term sterling deposit market. Because of the credit ceilings and other restrictive measures banks are unable to satisfy the requirements of many of their clients in full. Even though many high-class firms would be prepared to pay to their banks rates well above prime lending rates, the money is often just not available.

For this reason, in a large and increasing number of instances big corporations have drifted into the habit of lending to each other their temporary cash surpluses. This has of course always been done between firms of the same group. But existing circumstances have led to the increasing adoption of the practice even between firms unconnected with each other. In fact some banks, when they are unable to meet their clients' credit requirements themselves, suggest to them that they should approach firms which are known to be very liquid. Usually banks do not charge any commission for such services, but they hope to benefit by retaining the goodwill of their clients even though they are unable to meet their credit requirements. If the firms with a surplus are also their clients they kill two birds with one stone by doing a good turn to both clients. In so doing they lose no deposits immediately, since deposits lent by one firm to the other are merely transferred from one account to another. But the borrower is likely to make more active use of the deposit in which case it might find its way to some other bank.

## (2) THE ROLE OF BROKERS

Such inter-corporation deposit transactions are often also arranged between firms which do not keep their deposits with the same bank, through the intermediary of brokers. This constitutes another departure from the old rule according to which brokers should only act as intermediaries between banks. But such departures are morally justified because banks for their part no longer adhere strictly to the rule of using brokers as intermediaries in all transactions among themselves.

There is no means of ascertaining, or even estimating reliably, the approximate extent of inter-corporation deposit transactions. Guessing their total is even more difficult than guessing that of inter-bank transactions. What is certain is that, should the credit squeeze continue, the volume of inter-corporation sterling deposits would tend to increase considerably and this limited parallel market is likely to develop on a larger scale.

## (3) THE LEGAL POSITION

One of the reasons why the inter-corporation deposit market has not developed more extensively lies in the uncertainty of the legal position. Under the Moneylenders Act business firms, unless they are licensed moneylenders, are only permitted to grant credits in connection with genuine transactions arising from the pursuit of their own trade. Otherwise lending might contravene the Act. Opinions are divided on this legal point, but there is a sufficient degree of doubt to discourage lending to any but first-class firms who are above suspicion. The lender has to be certain that the borrower will not disclose the transactions to the authorities. For this reason the inter-corporation deposit market is essentially a 'gentlemen's market'.

The inter-corporation deposit market cannot develop on any appreciable scale unless and until the legal position is clarified and uncertainty on that account is eliminated. Whether the Government would be prepared to legislate to that end depends on its attitude towards the inter-corporation sterling market and towards the credit expansion it is liable to cause. Possibly the outcome of a legal action might remove the existing doubts by proving them to be unfounded.

Up to the time of writing the inter-corporation sterling market has not expanded sufficiently to cause concern in official circles. But a spectacular increase might well be looked upon with misgivings, for inter-corporation sterling is even further outside official control than inter-bank sterling. So long as the official monetary policy is against a credit expansion this circumvention of the ceilings imposed on bank credits to trade can hardly be looked on with favourable eyes.

### (4) FIRMS BECOME LESS DEPENDENT ON BANKS

While inter-bank sterling is liable to be influenced both psychologically and materially by official policy in the parallel market, there is no reason for business firms to adapt their attitude towards inter-corporation transactions to official policies. In so far as they possess liquid surpluses it is entirely for them to decide whether to deposit them with their banks – or with other borrowers offering a higher rate – or to lend them to some other business firm. Nor has the latter any reason for abstaining from borrowing from another firm if bank loans are unobtainable. It is, therefore, conceivable in theory that during a period when the official policy favours tight money an expansion of inter-corporation deposits might reduce the effectiveness of official efforts to that end. But in order to be able to produce a perceptible effect in that direction, the inter-corporation deposit market would have to increase to several times what is believed to be its present size.

Bankers certainly would not welcome such developments. Inter-corporation lending might well survive the credit squeeze once the clients have got into the habit of dealing with each other instead of dealing with their banks. But so long as banks are unable to satisfy the credit requirements of their clients they have no actual ground for complaints. In any case the deposits which change hands between corporations remain if not within the same bank, at any rate within the banking system as a whole.

## (5) GUARANTEED INTER-CORPORATION DEPOSITS

Some banks actually assist in the development of the inter-corporation market, not only by putting firms with unsatisfied credit requirements in touch with firms possessing surplus liquidity but also by guaranteeing such lending of inter-corporation deposits. It is believed that such guaranteed deposits form a high proportion of the inter-corporation deposits. This practice has been for some time quite prevalent in some foreign countries.

Needless to say, when banks play such an active part in the transaction they charge a commission which is apt to be on the high side. The banks are in a position to assist their customer at the same time as earning a profit by such means, because guarantees do not come under the credit ceiling unless they lead to lending to industry by another bank. This is yet another reason why the inter-corporation deposit market might conceivably develop into a sizeable loophole through which the credit squeeze could be evaded. The authorities would then have some reason for viewing this practice with concern. But the remedy lies in their own hands.

## (6) HOW INTER-CORPORATION BUSINESS IS TRANSACTED

The amounts of inter-corporation deposits range from £25,000 to several millions. Standard maturities are similar to those of the inter-bank deposit market. It has been said that even medium-term deposits up to five years are at times arranged, but the great majority is overnight money or very short loans.

There are no established rules whatsoever in this most recently developed market, which is an additional reason for lenders to select eligible borrowers with particular care – unless of course they get a bank guarantee. It is said that London branches of some smaller American banks which have as yet no regular clientèle and whose credit ceiling has been fixed very low are keen to try and earn their overheads by granting such guarantees, much to the dismay of their well-established rivals, with higher credit ceilings, which might lose business as a result.

Insignificant as the market may be at the time of writing, its development is well worth watching. After all, some of the present-day gigantic parallel markets, too, had a very modest beginning.

It is quite impossible to estimate the amount of inter-corporation deposits, among other reasons because much of the business is not done through any of the well-known City deposit brokers. Firms in the West End and even private individuals with good personal connections among businessmen act as intermediaries, charging a commission well above the $\frac{1}{8}$ per cent charged by brokers on inter-bank transactions. Some of these intermediaries have advertised for business in the financial Press. The transactions are usually in large individual amounts, and the range of maturities is the same as in the inter-bank market. Inter-corporation transactions are arranged at times in clubs, on golf courses and at cocktail parties where business executives meet.

# CHAPTER EIGHT

# Sterling Certificates of Deposits

## (1) AMERICAN INITIATIVE

THE British banking community is rightly proud of being able to adapt its practices to changing requirements. Although fundamentally conservative, paradoxically enough it is at the same time highly progressive. As pointed out in Chapter 1, its ability to move with the times has been amply proved by the initiative it took in creating the Euro-dollar market and other Euro-currency markets, the Euro-bond market, the markets in Local Authorities deposits and finance house deposits, and the inter-bank sterling market, all within the brief space of a few years. The delay in the creation of a market in Certificates of Deposits, long after such a market had come into being and proved to be an outstanding success in the United States was, therefore, out of character and it calls for an explanation.

Certificates of Deposits originated in New York in 1961 and their rapid expansion, which will be dealt with in Volume 2 of this book, was truly remarkable. Yet it was not until five years later that the London dollar Certificates of Deposits made their first appearance – on the initiative of the London branch of one of the big American banks – and it took another two years before sterling Certificates of Deposits also came into existence. The London banking community was definitely slow on the uptake as far as the adoption of the system of CDs was concerned. So in this instance, far from giving the world a lead as it did on so many other occasions, it took a long time to follow the lead given by American banks.

## (2) RIGIDITY OF BRITISH DEPOSIT RATES

Addressing a conference on sterling CDs in July 1968, Mr Paul Bareau attributed this delay in following New York's example to the convention among British clearing banks not to compete directly for deposits. Moreover, he said, the emergence of other parallel markets had blunted the urgency that might otherwise have induced banks to compete for deposits by issuing CDs. British clearing banks felt, and still feel, albeit to a smaller degree, inhibited from borrowing from each other. But that inhibition weakened perceptibly during the late 'sixties, simultaneously with the weakening of their disinclination to be more aggressive in competing for deposits.

The adoption of London dollar CDs, to be discussed in Chapter 13, had naturally gone a long way towards paving the way for the advent of sterling CDs. In any case, British non-clearing banks had already come to borrow from each other in terms of foreign currencies as a matter of course with the advent of the Euro-currency markets. But in order to participate in Euro-dollar dealings without technically breaking with the established tradition, clearing banks adopted the formula of putting wholly owned affiliates in charge of these operations. Such affiliates came to assume considerable importance during the late 'sixties. The mechanism of inter-bank dealing came into being, ready to be applied also to dealings in CDs, first in terms of dollars in 1966 and two years later in terms of sterling also.

As in the United States, the main incentive for banks in Britain to adopt CDs was the realisation of the need for some device to enable large depositors to benefit by the higher interest rates allowed on time deposits without having to immobilise their liquid resources. This motive was particularly strong in Britain because of the clearing banks' rule under their cartel to pay the same deposit rate – 2 per cent below the Bank rate of the day – regardless of the length of the period for which the money was deposited with them and regardless of the size of the deposit. There was no advantage whatsoever in depositing moneys for definite long periods, considering that the interest they received would be the same as for deposits that were subject to seven days' notice. This practice was – and still is, as far as the clearing banks themselves are concerned – quite unreasonably rigid. It deprives clearing banks of the chance to obtain fixed deposits for relatively long periods, to offset credits granted for periods in excess of the customary three months.

(3) WHOLESALE BANKING VERSUS RETAIL BANKING

Another rigidity in the clearing banks' practice under their cartel was, and still is, the lack of any discrimination between large and small depositors. Obviously the cost of handling ten thousand small deposits totalling £1 million is a great many times higher than the cost of handling a single deposit of £1 million.

It is indeed remarkable that the British banks did not stumble much sooner on the formula which is the obvious answer to both the problems arising from the rigidity of their system, and that they did not stumble on it on their own initiative. It is true that the dealing in inter-bank deposits provided a solution to the problem of disriminating between terms applied in wholesale banking and in retail banking, and deposit rates could be made to vary according to the period for which the deposit was fixed. But it still left unsolved the major problem of enabling depositors to regain possession of their money before maturity if and when they should wish to do so.

## (4) NEED FOR MEDIUM-TERM DEPOSITS

The growing demand for medium-term credits resulting from the expansion of capital goods industries provided an additional motive for adopting a device that would facilitate the granting of such credits. Unless banks are able to obtain 'offsetting' medium-term deposits they have to face the risk of losses through an increase in interest rates on short-term deposits. Clearing banks, by paying the same rate on all deposit accounts, could not hope to obtain deposits for fixed periods of twelve months or more.

Non-clearing banks have always been in a position to pay higher rates on medium-term deposits. But before the advent of the CD system not many time deposits exceeded one year, so that when banks granted a medium-term credit they had no means of securing offsetting deposits for the entire duration of a credit for several years. They simply had to live in hopes that the time deposits would be replaced on maturity at interest rates not higher than those of the original time deposit. In the meantime it was a matter of prudence for banks to maintain relatively large liquid reserves, since the average maturity of their claims was longer than the average maturity of their liabilities.

Inter-bank deposits – whether in sterling or in foreign currencies – did go some way, by offering higher interest rates, towards attracting offsetting medium-term deposits. But the number of large depositors who were able and willing to definitely relinquish the use of their money for several years remained relatively small.

There were no doubt many firms and individuals who would have been willing to deposit their money for long periods provided they could retain their freedom to mobilise their funds if the need for them should change their views about the prospect of interest rates.

The great advantage of CDs is that they meet the requirement of depositors who are uncertain whether it suits their interests to tie down their money for a definite period. It is true that time deposit arrangements can contain an escape clause under which the banks are prepared to repay the deposits before maturity while charging the depositor a certain 'penalty'. But that 'penalty' is apt to be relatively expensive because banks do not want to encourage their depositors to make unexpected demands on their liquid resources by prematurely withdrawing their time deposits. CDs provide a solution to the dilemma. Of course they do not offer depositors the same certainty about the cost of recovering their money before maturity as penalty clauses do. If interest rates increase substantially the discounting of a CD might well prove to be costlier than a penalty clause would have been. On the other hand, if interest rates decline it might enable them to recover their money on favourable terms.

### (5) THE CASE FOR CDS

The market in London dollar CDs was the first device by which it became possible in the U.K. to find an answer to this problem. It was very useful for financing medium-term transactions in terms of dollars. But in order to be able to finance medium-term credits in sterling with the aid of dollar CDs it was necessary for U.K. banks to cover the exchange risk, which was often costly. For periods exceeding twelve months this is never a matter of simple routine. So London dollar CDs were not always the answer to the problem of financing domestic medium-term credits, apart altogether from the difficulties created by exchange regulations under which U.K. residents are precluded from buying London dollar CDs without a licence from the Bank of England, which was not easy to obtain until the late 'sixties.

Yet the need for medium-term credits tended to become more insistent as a result of the repeated impositions of credit ceilings and other forms of credit restrictions in the 'sixties. Until then well-established U.K. merchants and manufacturers could feel reasonably safe in assuming that their three months' overdrafts would be renewed again and again as a matter of routine. But the possibility that their branch managers, acting under pressure from the head office, which, in turn, would be acting under pressure from the authorities, might cut their overdraft at an inconvenient moment was a distinct incentive for resorting to medium-term financing.

There was, therefore, a strong case in favour of developing a method by which banks would be in a position to take the initiative to secure for themselves sterling deposits in terms of several years to offset sterling credits granted in terms of years. Indeed, owing to the wider range of fluctuations of interest rates in the late 'sixties, it became advisable for banks to offset even their credit commitments for shorter periods – say for twelve months – if a rise in interest rates was expected, and to offset time deposits obtained by granting credits for corresponding periods if a decline in interest rates was expected.

### (6) DISAPPOINTING INITIAL RESULT

At the end of March 1970 the amount of sterling CDs issued by accepting houses, overseas banks and other banks in the U.K. was £545·3 million compared with £261·3 million a year earlier. Of this £95 million was held by the discount market, compared with £60 million a year earlier when the sterling CD market was a novelty and the dealers had to carry a higher proportion of the certificates until demand developed for them. At the end of January 1970 the total outstanding was £463 million. Of this £64 million was for under one month, £138 million between one and three months, £84 million between three and six months, £163 million between six and twelve months, £11 million between one and two years, £500,000 between two and three years and £1·5 million between three and five years.

As the above figures show, expectations that the new device would attract large amounts of medium-term deposits – deposits of over one year – failed to materialise during the first eighteen months of the market's existence. The Treasury's decision in 1968 to authorise banks to pay gross interest on dollar CDs with maturities up to five years without deduction of income tax at source, which concession also came to be applied later to sterling CDs, failed to produce any noteworthy immediate or early effect. That concession was originally obtained for the sake of attracting medium-term dollar deposits that could be re-lent for periods of years. But at least equally important was the possibility of obtaining dollars which could not be withdrawn for a year or longer. To that end it was essential that issuing banks should be able to pay interest rates without deducting income tax, because non-residents would not want to expose themselves to the delay, uncertainty and loss of interest involved in having to recover from the Inland Revenue the tax deducted at source.

The same was of course true of sterling CDs when they came to be issued. Even though the sterling CDs were meant to circulate primarily in the U.K., the possibility of selling them to non-residents was there. Whenever non-residents do not deem it necessary to cover the exchange risk, or when the cost of forward covering tends to decline below the profit on the interest differential, there is an incentive for non-residents to buy sterling CDs. In actual practice appreciable amounts of sterling CDs for shorter maturities have in fact been sold to foreign residents. But judging by the above figures there has been no great demand for medium-term CDs, either by residents or by non-residents.

### (7) DIFFERENCE BETWEEN STERLING AND DOLLAR CDS

The device of sterling CDs is substantially identical with the London dollar CDs that will be described in Chapter 13. An important technical difference in respect of the practice in the two markets is that sterling CDs are delivered and paid for on the same day, at any rate if the deal is concluded before 2.30 p.m., while dollar CDs are delivered and paid for on the third clear business day after the conclusion of the deal. This is because transactions in dollar CDs, like those in Euro-dollars, are in terms of a foreign currency and are therefore treated as foreign exchange transactions, so that the practice that applies to deliveries of spot foreign currencies applies to them. Payment for CDs is made in bankers' drafts or in London clearing cheques drawn on clearing banks. Dealings up to midday are settled on the same day, while those after midday are settled on the following business day, unless otherwise stipulated.

While U.K. residents are not permitted to acquire dollar CDs without a licence, they are of course free to acquire sterling CDs.

They have to keep sterling CDs, like dollar CDs, with an author-ised depositary, however, because, being bearer securities, such certificates could be used to evade exchange control. Most holders keep their CDs with the issuing bank, or with some other bank.

For reasons of exchange control, only banks which are author-ised dealers are granted a licence to issue sterling CDs. Such licences are granted to U.K. banks and to U.K. branches or subsidiaries of foreign banks. A very large number of licences have in fact been granted. Almost every branch wants to be in a position to issue CDs but the number of banks actively engaged in issuing sterling CDs is relatively small. The licences are issued without limit. During the spring of 1970, two clearing bank affiliates issued between them CDs of the order of £200 million and the market absorbed them easily.

### (8) AMOUNTS, MATURITIES AND RATES

Sterling CDs are issued in units of at least £50,000 up to a maximum amount of £250,000 per unit. Their amounts have to be in multiples of £10,000. They are transferable without endorse-ments. They can be issued for any period from three months to five years. Although they are issued mostly for standard dates, most banks are usually willing to issue them for broken dates to meet specific requirements of depositors. Interest is normally allowed on the basis of the rate for the nearest standard date which is in the bank's favour. Thus if a depositor wants a CD for, say, 135 days and the rate for three months is $8\frac{1}{16}$ while the rate for six months is $8\frac{3}{16}$, the bank allows $8\frac{1}{16}$. It would be difficult to quote a rate that would correspond exactly or even approximately to the period of the broken date in relation to those quoted for standard dates. If the broken date happens to be for a period when money is expected to be particularly tight or particularly easy – such as shortly before or after the turn of year – the rate quoted is apt to depart considerably from those quoted for the nearest standard date.

In certain exceptional circumstances interest is paid on sterling CDs in the form of re-purchase agreements under which depositors buy CDs at a certain price and re-sell them to the same bank at a lower price. Such arrangements are frequent in the United States when banks selling the CDs are not authorised to accept deposits. The device is applied in the U.K. to a much more limited extent.

On both sterling CDs and London dollar CDs interest is paid to the authorised depositary holding the CDs. It is payable on maturity for CDs up to one year, and at the end of each year and at the maturity date of the last year on certificates for periods over one year. Certified receipts given by the depositary are generally used when the CDs are transferred or are employed as securities for loans, in order to minimise the risk of loss or theft or forgery. The issuer of such receipts is expected to confirm their genuineness if called upon to do so. Sterling CDs, like dollar CDs, are printed on maximum security paper and no case of forgery is known to have been discovered so far. It is to the depositary and not to the owner of the certificate that principal and accrued interest are paid on maturity.

### (9) THE PRIMARY MARKET

In the primary market depositors can buy sterling CDs from issuing banks either direct or through dealers who charge no commission for acting as intermediaries. Issuing banks may issue sterling CDs direct to clients who have a deposit or current account with them, or to total strangers, or to dealers or brokers for depositors whose identity they do not know. It is even conceivable that the depositor uses an intermediary precisely because he does not want to disclose his identity to the bank with which he deposits his money. Acceptance of deposits from unknown depositors has a slight disadvantage, because the issuing banks have no means of forming an opinion as to whether the depositor is likely to renew the deposit on maturity. If they are familiar with the depositor's habits they may be able to form some idea whether they may conveniently use the deposits for financing credits for periods exceeding that of the deposit on the assumption that it is likely to be renewed.

Some banks issue sterling CDs on special occasions only and for specific purposes only, while others issue them systematically as a matter of routine and are regular participants in the primary market. Such banks, whether or not they are keen to issue sterling CDs on any particular day, may be anxious not to lose contact with the market even on their 'off' days. They simply fix their rates according to whether or not they happen to be keen to issue sterling CDs on any particular day. They may quote rates which, if some depositors are willing to accept them, are to their advantage even if they are not keen to increase their issue of CDs.

## (10) DIFFERENCE BETWEEN INTER-BANK AND CD RATES

Banks prefer to issue sterling CDs instead of borrowing inter-bank sterling, because the rate allowed on the former is somewhat lower most of the time. Depositors are prepared to accept a slightly lower rate precisely because they retain their freedom to recover their deposit at any time by selling their CDs. But occasions are apt to arise in which, as a result of special circumstances affecting the supply–demand relationship, the rates for sterling CDs rise to par, or even above par, with the rates for the corresponding maturities of inter-bank sterling. Such a situation did actually arise in May 1970 for instance, when selling pressure in both the primary market and the secondary market for sterling CDs pushed their rates above those of inter-bank deposits.

There were two causes responsible for this paradoxical situation. The one was large-scale profit-taking by holders of CDs who benefited by the reduction of the Bank rate. Many of them chose to take their profit by selling out rather than risk a change in the trend of interest rates. The other cause was the issue of CDs by two clearing bank affiliates on a sufficiently large scale to affect the rates perceptibly. In theory it should only have affected the rates of the CDs issued by the two banks directly concerned. But, since they were both of first-class standing, higher rates on their CDs diverted demand from CDs with a lower yield to their CDs, so that the entire market moved upwards and CD rates rose for a short time above rates for inter-bank sterling.

## (11) ADVANTAGES FOR NON-RESIDENTS

The possibility of realising the CDs at any time is of particular importance for non-resident holders of sterling CDs if they are prepared to acquire and hold their sterling assets without covering the exchange risk. Should their views of sterling's prospects change they are in a position to realise their holdings at once and sell the proceeds. If they hold a sterling time deposit the only way to safeguard themselves against a depreciation of sterling before they regain possession of their money on maturity would be through selling sterling forward for the remaining period of their deposit. Amidst a wave of distrust in sterling this might be a very expensive operation. On the other hand if they acquire a sterling CD they can sell spot sterling and their exchange risk is limited to the difference between the exchange rate at which they bought the sterling and the minimum support point for sterling – assuming, of course, that sterling was not devalued in the meantime. The moment sterling appears to become devaluation-prone – devaluations are seldom a bolt out of the blue like the devaluation of the French franc in August 1969 – they may be able to realise their holdings with a smaller loss than they would have to take if they had to cover forward sterling.

It must be borne in mind, however, that if many holders of CDs act likewise the resulting selling pressure would raise the discount rate on sterling CDs in the secondary market, so that late-comers would have to sell their CD holdings at a loss before they could sell their sterling proceeds.

As we shall see later, there is a forward market for CDs in the secondary market and it has promising possibilities. But there are forward operations in CDs also in the primary market. A bank may issue CDs to be delivered and paid for at some future date. The considerations influencing such transactions, and their terms, are similar to those influencing forward transactions in the secondary market.

## (12) HOW RATES FOR NEW ISSUES ARE FIXED

Sterling CDs are on tap at some issuing banks which are very active in the primary market. They quote rates for sterling CDs all day and every day. This is usually because they are anxious to increase their total deposits. Even if they expect an increase in interest rates they issue CDs for long maturities at the prevailing rates, because they can always re-lend the proceeds at the rate prevailing at the time of issue. And even if they should be unable to lend proceeds of CDs to customers they could always re-lend them in the inter-bank sterling market or in the markets for LA or finance house deposits. Notwithstanding this consideration, the outstanding amount is at the time of writing still much smaller than that of inter-bank deposits, and there is ample scope for its further increase. Individual banks may feel from time to time that they have issued enough, in which case they simply lower their rates a shade below the level prevailing in the market. If, however, all or most banks lowered their rates to the level at which they do not compete with LA or finance house deposits – allowing of course for the usual differentials – the outstanding amount of CDs would decline.

Issuing banks communicate to dealers and brokers every morning their range of sterling CD rates. Some banks are in the habit of maintaining the same rates during the whole day – especially for depositors outside the market – unless some change occurs in the general situation or there are substantial movements of rates in accordance with ever-changing supply–demand relationships. But most issuing banks keep changing their rates throughout the day.

Banks may issue CDs to match some large credit they have just granted for over twelve months, or to replace a large deposit just withdrawn. If they issue them for the purpose of offsetting a credit or a withdrawal of a deposit they are only interested in a particular maturity, to match the maturity of the credit or the deposit they are to offset. They then quote relatively higher interest for that particular maturity, to ensure that they get the deposit they want. Otherwise they fix their rates according to their general need for funds, aiming at issuing for maturities whose rates are most advantageous at the moment. The differences between rates for various maturities provide opportunities for playing the yield curve in determining the issuing rates for the various maturities. More will be said about this below.

The issuing banks are willing, at the holder's request, to split their certificates into smaller nominal amounts subsequent to their issue, provided that the amounts of the new certificates are not smaller than £50,000 and are multiples of £10,000. This enables holders to recover part of their deposits while leaving the rest on deposit if this should suit their convenience.

Sterling CDs are often renewed on maturity. But properly speaking such 'renewals' mean the issue of new CDs of the same amount and possibly for an identical period, at interest rates corresponding to those prevailing in the market at the time of each 'renewal'. The rates have to be re-negotiated, and the depositor might find it to his advantage to transfer his deposit to some other bank if he can get a better rate elsewhere, even though the law of inertia does tend to induce relatively unsophisticated depositors to make no change for the sake of diminutive gains. Indeed some depositors of the conservative type, instead of shopping round for the best rate obtainable, leave it to their bank to fix the rate on the original CD as well as on the renewal.

## (13) AMOUNTS OF ISSUES AND LIQUIDITY

All issuing banks make monthly returns to the Bank of England, stating the outstanding amount of this issue, broken down according to maturity. The Bank of England communicates to dealers the total of all outstanding CDs likewise broken down according to maturity, but it treats the amounts issued by individual banks as confidential. Between publications of the issuing banks' balance sheets, the Bank of England alone knows for certain the amounts issued by any individual bank. If it considers the issue of any particular bank excessive it makes its views known to the bank concerned. Even though in theory there is no fixed limit for the amount issued by any individual bank, a hint from the Bank to the effect that a bank has issued too much is sufficient to induce it to stop increasing its issue or even to reduce the amount as and when the CDs mature. But the market itself tends to discourage over-issuing, which is apt to be noticed even in the absence of official information, by quoting less favourable rates for the CDs of the bank in question – unless it is of first-rate standing, in which case its rate tends to influence the standard rate – or by limiting holdings of CDs of the bank concerned.

The self-imposed liquidity ratio of non-clearing banks is much higher than the 28 per cent for clearing banks. The latter hold a multitude of small deposits and are safe in relying on the operation of the law of averages by which withdrawals and new deposits are apt to offset each other by and large. On the other hand, merchant banks hold a small number of large deposits, some of which are very big. Such deposits, representing a high proportion of the bank's total deposits, are liable to be withdrawn unexpectedly and the merchant bank has to be prepared for the resulting sudden demand on its liquid resources. For this reason it has to keep liquid a much higher percentage of its short-term liabilities, which include its CD issues approaching maturity.

But, unless banks issue very large amounts of CDs, their issue need not make any perceptible difference to their self-imposed liquidity ratio. Liquid assets of discount houses are kept mainly in short loans and eligible bills, but they may be kept in the form of sterling CDs issued by big banks, even though the Bank of England discourages the practice by its refusal to accept CDs as collaterals for loans. The market is not in a position to know for certain whether the issuing banks have enough liquid reserves to allow for their CDs adequately except once a year when the balance sheets are published, and even these might be affected by window-dressing.

## (14) ISSUES BY CLEARING BANK AFFILIATES

As stated above, clearing banks do not themselves issue CDs but their affiliates are among the largest issuers. Unlike American bank branches in London, clearing bank affiliates do not lend to their head offices the amounts of deposits borrowed, but employ them to finance the business of their own customers. For if the clearing banks borrowed their affiliates' deposits the rules concerning liquidity ratio, which prevent them from issuing CDs themselves, would apply equally to their liabilities in relation to their affiliates. But indirect availability of credit resources might benefit them through the issue of CDs by their affiliates – or, for that matter, through the acceptance of inter-bank deposits by the affiliates. For the parent institutions might pass on to the affiliates some of the credit transactions proposed to them by their customers or potential customers, thereby indirectly relieving their own tight position with the aid of sterling CDs issued by their affiliates. As a result they are able to lend more to their other customers.

Moreover, affiliates are able to compete effectively with other non-clearing banks by offering high deposit rates to the parent institutions' clients. They can also attract or retain deposits which might otherwise be attracted into LA or finance house deposits. They can attract foreign deposits, including deposits by some smaller Central Banks which have accounts with London banks in addition to their accounts with the Bank of England.

There was only a stamp duty of 2d. on each certificate, payable by the issuing bank, and even that duty was abolished by the Finance Act, 1970. Holders do not pay duties on acquiring, transferring or cashing principal or interest. Each certificate contains the name of the issuing bank, the date of issue, the amount of the deposit, the rate of interest, and the maturity date. The standard size is 8 inches by 5 inches. All certificates are issued at par.

## (15) THE SECONDARY MARKET

The secondary market consists of firms belonging to five categories:

1. Discount houses and other similar dealers who transact business on their own account and play a part similar to that of jobbers on the London Stock Exchange. They keep sterling CDs of various maturities on their books, to be able to match their clients' requirements.
2. Money brokers (also called deposit brokers), who are usually identical with the firms dealing in inter-bank sterling, though some of them specialise in CDs more than others.
3. U.K. banks buying and selling CDs on their own account or on account of their clients.
4. Non-banking U.K. depositors buying CDs through discount houses, brokers or banks.
5. Non-resident banks and non-banking clients of discount houses, banks and brokers.

Discount houses and other dealers perform several distinct functions. They often act as intermediaries between issuing banks and depositors. As observed above, in some cases a depositor may not want his identity to be known to the issuing bank – this may be the case with Communist banks for instance – in which case he buys CDs through a dealer whose discretion he may trust. Much more often the reason why depositors buy CDs from the primary market through dealers is that the latter know the rates quoted by all issuing banks for various maturities and also rates quoted in the secondary market and are therefore in a position to secure for their clients more favourable rates than they would be able to obtain by contacting one issuing bank or even several issuing banks.

Dealers are the sole channel through which it is possible to acquire CDs maturing in less than three months, for as we said above, three months are the minimum maturity for newly issued CDs. With the increase in the amount of CDs, the volume of CDs maturing in less than three months on various dates has increased, so that a fairly good secondary market in short CDs has developed. This market is of particular importance, because only short CDs are eligible for collaterals when discount houses borrow from clearing banks. Banks, too, prefer to confine their holdings of sterling CDs to short maturities.

## (16) FUNCTIONS OF DEALERS

The largest dealers have a variety of maturities on their books so that they are in a position to meet the requirements even of clients interested in sterling CDs maturing on broken dates. Failing this, they can get CDs for the required date from issuing banks. Some dealers specialise in very short maturities, others in maturities of over one year, others again specialise in CDs issued by particular banks or by particular types of banks. They buy CDs from issuers or from other dealers, or from holders wanting to sell before maturity because they need liquid resources; or they buy them because they want to switch out of some other type of short or medium-term investment into CDs; or they buy because they have taken a view on prospects of interest rates in general.

While some dealers aim at a large turnover with their clients, others who take a view on interest rate prospects engage in interest arbitrage on their own account, or hold CDs mainly as investments, as part of their portfolios. It is estimated that on average about 20 per cent of the total CDs issued is held by the market. From time to time when the supply–demand relationship changes considerably holdings of dealers may rise well above that proportion or may decline well below it. At times dealers find themselves overloaded with unsold and unwanted CDs, and they would be unable to unload them without a loss. On such occasions they inform the issuing banks concerned and the latter usually assist them to some extent – without being under any obligation to do so – to enable them to carry the CDs until they are able to sell without a loss. Otherwise the primary market might be liable to be affected by heavy selling detrimental to the interests of the issuing banks.

On the other hand, discount houses do not buy CDs when money is tight in Lombard Street, because on such occasions they may have to borrow from the Bank of England. So they seek to replace their ineligible CDs with eligible securities. In this way tight conditions in the traditional market tend to affect the rates of CDs.

The extent to which sterling CDs are accepted by clearing banks as collaterals for loans is limited, though it tends to increase. Interest rates charged by clearing banks on loans secured by CDs are higher than those charged on loans secured by Treasury bills or commercial bills. Originally the surcharge was $\frac{1}{8}$ per cent, but with the increase of the relative proportion of sterling CDs it increased from time to time to much higher figures, anything up to ½ per cent.

## (17) DEALING IN THE SECONDARY MARKET

While interest on CDs is payable at the end of the period concerned, if a CD is sold in the secondary market it is sold on a yield to maturity basis. The CD is discounted on the basis of the rate accepted by the buyer. Calculations for sterling CDs are based on a 365-day year.

The long-range trend will probably be towards a lengthening of the average maturity of sterling CDs, unless there is a major general setback in financial conditions. But that average is of course bound to have its ups and downs, according to the trend of interest rates and the market expectations of the future trend.

The market in sterling CDs, like the other parallel money markets in London, is a sensitive and sophisticated market and the minor movements of its rates are subject to various cross-currents, apart altogether from the basic trend. For instance demand from abroad may depend on dollar CD rates, Euro-dollar rates, Euro-sterling rates and swap rates. Its extent is apt to affect the market. In given circumstances the advent or withdrawal of a single very large deposit, or the coincidence of the advent or withdrawal of a number of fair-sized deposits, is apt to affect the discrepancy between CD rates and inter-bank rates perceptibly in respect of a wide range of maturities. But if there is a strong or even distinct trend in interest rates in general, such minor influences are liable to be absorbed in the general trend and are quite unnoticed.

## (18) DISCREPANCIES

Discrepancies are liable to arise between rates for various maturities. Operators in the sterling CD market prepare a chart showing the yield curve – a line describing changes in yields for various maturities – as early as possible every morning. The moment the yield on any particular maturity departs from that curve sufficiently for it to become worth while to operate, dealers take advantage of it by unloading CDs giving unduly high yields and acquiring CDs giving unduly low yields. This corrects any deviations from the basic yield curve in a matter of minutes, unless there is some strong reason for the discrepancy, such as special requirements for particular dates, giving rise to strong and persistent buying or selling. The extent to which operators are prepared or even able to deal in a direction opposite to the prevailing trend so as to provide the counterpart required for specific maturities is by no means unlimited, for at a given moment most operators want to increase or reduce their holdings of CDs for certain maturities. Those who are in the lucky position to play the yield curve against the prevailing trend may earn a profit well above the usual margins.

Although the outstanding amounts in dollar CDs are several times larger than those of sterling CDs, the turnover is estimated to be about equal, because sterling CDs change hands much more frequently, largely owing to the demand for them by discount houses that use them as securities against clearing bank credits.

A fairly considerable demand developed for sterling CDs from abroad, especially from Switzerland, after the cost of covering the exchange risk declined towards the end of 1969 and early in 1970, and after the need for covering ceased to be considered imperative in many quarters. Arbitrage between dollar CDs and sterling CDs became more active. The interplay between dollar CD or Euro-dollar rates, forward sterling–dollar rates and sterling CDs tends to affect the rates of the latter. But the volume of sterling CDs is at the time of writing still too small to produce a noteworthy reciprocal effect either on the dollar CD rate or on the forward sterling–dollar rate.

## (19) SHOULD ISSUING BANKS SUPPORT THE MARKET?

Dealers are anxious not to become overloaded with sterling CDs. When they feel that their holdings are becoming excessive they raise their buying rates and price themselves out of the market. Alternatively, as already observed, they approach the banks whose CDs they hold to help them finance their holdings. As we shall see in Chapter 13, this is done systematically with dollar CDs issued by U.S. branches in London. They may even be prepared to give a binding undertaking to assist dealers to a limited extent should it become necessary. Such assistance is practised to a much smaller extent in respect of sterling CDs. Even though some issuing banks are inclined to be helpful, they are reluctant to commit themselves definitely.

The dealers' argument is that, since there is no lender of last resort, in the absence of a good secondary market the issuing banks would find it difficult to issue any substantial amounts of sterling CDs, so that it is to their interest to help the dealer to carry the 'float', or at any rate to be prepared to assist in an emergency.

Against this the issuers argue that the reason why they issue CDs is precisely that they want to divest themselves of the responsibility for providing depositors with an opportunity to regain possession of their money for a definite period. If they felt under obligation to support the market each time there was selling pressure on the CDs it would deprive them of that advantage. Even American branches which are willing to give definite undertakings to assist dealers to carry their holdings of London dollar CDs issued by them are not prepared to give a similar undertaking concerning their issues of sterling CDs. The explanation is that in the United States banks support the secondary market in their dollar CDs – without lending on their own CDs – and, while their London branches may be prepared to apply the same principle to their London dollar CD issues, they feel they are justified in adopting towards their sterling CD issues the same attitude as is adopted by British banks.

### (20) LIMITS FOR NAMES

From the point of view of calculating the total commitments of dealers and holders of CDs in respect of particular names, and also from the point of view of their total commitments for certain maturity dates, sterling CDs and inter-bank sterling are added together or offset against each other as the case may be. Thus an unwanted increase in holdings of sterling CDs can be offset by a reduction in inter-bank sterling deposits and *vice versa*. There may be items of various kinds on the debit and credit side that offset each other from the point of view of reckoning the unused limits for particular names, and any of these items are liable to change as a result of action taken at any moment simultaneously by various departments of the same house. The standing rule is that discount houses have virtually no limit for the names of banks which in practice recognise their moral obligations to help the market to finance their holdings of too large amounts of the CDs issued by them.

Many banks feel inhibited from buying their own CDs or even

accepting them as securities for loans. But if it suits their purpose there is really nothing to prevent them from overcoming that self-imposed inhibition. In fact some clearing banks grant credits on the CDs of their affiliates and charge the same rate as on credits secured by eligible bills. They buy CDs of other banks and lend against them up to a certain percentage of the total of the loans. On the other hand, some banks make it a hard and fast rule never to buy medium-term CDs issued by their rivals, or accept them as securities, because they feel that in so doing they would assist their rivals in granting medium-term credits.

The proportion of sterling CDs which is not held firm by depositors but is floating in the market is estimated at approximately 10 per cent, which is more than twice the estimated proportion of 'float' for London dollar CDs.

### (21) PURPOSES OF ACQUIRING CDS

Sterling CDs of long maturities are held more firmly than short CDs. There is, for that reason, no good market for CDs over twelve months, because the turnover in them is small. In any case, as we saw earlier in this chapter, the total amount issued for over twelve months is not large. The rates on CDs of two years and over are always a matter for negotiation. Of course when interest rates are expected to increase there is no demand for long CDs, unless the rate is made relatively attractive. On the other hand when interest rates are expected to decline it is a simple matter to find buyers of medium-term CDs, prepared to ensure the yield on their deposits on the basis of the prevailing high interest rates.

There is a certain amount of direct dealing between banks in CDs. But there is much dealing by banks, by dealers and by brokers with parties outside the market. Various types of institutional investors and treasurers of big business firms are interested in a wide range of maturities. Very often CDs are sold by holders outside the market in order to invest the proceeds in LA deposits with matching maturities. There is demand for CDs by banks or discount houses which engage in interest arbitrage between CDs and LA deposits of various maturities, taking advantage of the discrepancies between their respective yield curves.

There are banks which systematically play the yield curve of CDs, even though the majority prefer to match maturities. Normally longer maturities command a higher interest rate and the yield curve is shaped accordingly. But towards the end of 1969 and early in 1970 an 'inverted yield curve' developed because a fall in interest rates was widely expected, so that there was a strong demand for CDs with longer maturities and their rates declined below those of shorter maturities.

## (22) FORWARD TRANSACTIONS

There are no dealings in sterling CDs subject to notice, they are all for fixed maturities. But there are dealings for future delivery. There is a certain amount of long–short swap transacted in sterling CDs, but the rates are always a matter for negotiation and there is no active market in such transactions. No swap rates are quoted regularly because operations are few and far between and are usually carried out by combining two separate deals. We saw in Chapter 6 that there are also forward–forward dealings between CDs and inter-bank sterling deposits. There is a good likelihood of an increase in the turnover in the forward–forward market, especially during long inactive periods when dealers have to look around for business to cover their overheads.

The market for broken dates, too, is expected to improve further with the increase in the volume of sterling CDs. On the other hand the outlook for CDs with maturities beyond two years does not seem promising at the time of writing, in spite of the fact that one of the main reasons for creating CDs was precisely to attract offsetting deposits for medium-term credits.

## (23) RELATIONS WITH THE TRADITIONAL MARKET

Thanks to the increasing use of sterling CDs as securities for borrowing in the traditional market, the two markets are becoming more closely related to each other. Tight money conditions in the traditional market can be relieved to some extent by an increased use of CDs as securities by discount houses when borrowing from clearing banks.

The discount market's holdings of CDs has increased year after year. The first time this item appeared in the figures relating to the discount houses in the *Bank of England Quarterly Review* was at the end of 1968. In each subsequent quarter it has increased and in the last quarter of 1969 it increased from £79 million to £97 million. Most of it represented the stock-in-trade of discount houses, but some was held as investment or speculation in interest rates.

The Bank of England has certainly not lost control of the volume of credit in the traditional market as a result of the expansion of the market in CDs, even to the extent to which loans are granted by clearing banks against CDs. For if credit is expanded as a result of such loans to an extent that the authorities consider excessive they can always reverse the process by open market operations or by stiffening the terms of their lendings to discount houses. They can also call up more Special Deposits from clearing banks. They can even impose the equivalent of Special Deposits on non-clearing banks. So the expansion of CDs does not really weaken the control of the banks over the money supply as a whole. This subject is discussed also in Chapter 2.

There is no evidence of any direct dealing in CDs between financial institutions other than banks, discount houses or brokers, or with business firms, even though CDs are held in large amounts outside the market. Nor is there an inter-corporation market in CDs. The difference between the role of brokers and dealers in the CD market is similar to the difference between the role of brokers and jobbers on the London Stock Exchange. Brokers cannot conclude a transaction unless and until they have found a counterpart. Dealers, like jobbers, may themselves provide the counterpart with the intention of reversing the resulting commitments sooner or later, unless they prefer to make a lasting change in their holdings.

## (24) DEALERS' SPECULATIVE RISK

It is not supposed to be part of the dealer's basic function to speculate deliberately on a large scale, but he cannot avoid taking a speculative risk even on his normal stock-in-trade and he assumes additional risk if he does not happen to be able to find fairly soon a counterpart for some large transaction. Unless dealers take a view on the prospects of interest rates they seize the first opportunity to cover any amount which is beyond what they want to keep on their books and they are content with the small return they earn in doing so. In the market for short CDs in particular brokers can usually easily find counterparts for would-be buyers or for would-be sellers. The aim of most dealers is to benefit by an increase in turnover rather than by running even calculated risks for the sake of speculative profit. But they have to keep on their books a selection of maturities in order to perform their functions as dealers efficiently. For this reason unexpected changes in interest rates are liable to inflict losses or confer profits on dealers in CDs as in other types of discount market assets.

Many banks aim at avoiding the speculative risk represented by the possibility of major interest rate changes. They can of course cover the risk that they assumed by granting a medium-term credit, which they would otherwise have to finance with short-term credits. Or they can cover the risk that they assumed when accepting a medium-term time deposit, by lending a corresponding amount in the inter-bank sterling market for the corresponding maturity. It is not always possible to synchronise two deals, but in normal stable conditions the brief time lag between them need not involve the risk of a sufficiently wide adverse movement of the rate to wipe out the profit margin on arbitrage between CD rate and inter-bank deposit rate.

Conservative banks quote rates on the basis of quotations just received on another telephone line and finalise the two deals simultaneously as far as this is physically possible, so that they earn a small return without running any risk beyond the very remote risk of a default by the borrower. Normally the financing of holdings of CDs by dealers presents no problem, because there is ample supply of overnight or short inter-bank sterling deposits available for the purpose of the covering operation. Discount houses also have access to the resources of the traditional market for financing CDs at a lower cost.

There are frequent direct transactions between discount houses. They help with each other's transactions with clients or with banks by meeting the demand for certain maturities in CDs. If one house cannot supply the CD for the required maturity, some other house supplies it.

## (25) PROSPECTS OF THE MEDIUM-TERM MARKET

Although long-term CDs had a very indifferent start, their market is likely to expand. During 1967–68 and the first half of 1969 it was very easy to borrow in the Euro-bond market, so that there was no urgent pressure for medium-term CD facilities. But when the Euro-bond market dries up – as it did during the second half of 1969 and for some time in 1970 – the next best thing for firms in need of capital is to obtain medium-term credits from their banks in the hope that by the time their loans for three to seven years fall due it will be easy to consolidate their liability by bond issues. Thanks largely to the sterling CD market, the banks are now in a better position to meet the requirements of those needing medium-term credits for such purposes.

When a declining trend in interest rates comes to be widely expected, many depositors become keen to ensure a prolonged high yield either by long-term inter-bank sterling deposits or by sterling CDs, according to how likely they are to need their money earlier. Banks should not find it difficult in such circumstances to employ the deposits in medium-term credits, precisely because the prospects of substantial decline in per cents would deter business firms from issuing long-term bonds at the prevailing high rates.

## (26) EFFECT ON CLEARING BANKS

Expansion of the volume of medium-term deposits thanks to a popularisation of long CDs would bring about a basic change in the British banking system. Unless clearing banks swim with the tide and suspend their cartel for the benefit of large depositors their relative importance, which has already declined considerably compared with that of non-clearing banks, will decline further. They will gradually and increasingly confine their activities to retail banking, leaving wholesale banking to non-clearing banks. But the transfer of large accounts to an increasing extent to their subsidiaries, which are not bound by the cartel, may, if practised on a really large scale, solve the problem of differentiating between wholesale and retail banking.

From the point of view of the balance of payments the additional facilities of medium-term credits through the issue of CDs is undoubtedly helpful. Of course the CD market is unable to compete with Export Credits Guarantee Department credits financed at low interest rates. But conceivably cut-throat competition for foreign markets through the granting of artificially cheap medium-term credit facilities might abate, so that the volume of official or officially guaranteed credit facilities might be reduced or their interest charges might be raised. This would increase the demand for medium-term credits by customers of banks, and the need for offsetting medium-term deposits to be raised through issuing more medium-term CDs.

Industrialisation of developing countries could be greatly

assisted by medium-term credit facilities which would enable importers of capital goods to pay cash, or it would solve the problem of exporters financing the transaction. Affiliates in developing countries of business firms in advanced countries need medium credits which could be provided through issuing CDs.

### (27) COMPETITION WITH NON-CLEARING BANKS

Issues of CDs do not reduce the volume of deposits held by clearing banks. For all non-clearing banks have accounts with clearing banks, so that if they issue, buy or sell sterling CDs it only means a transfer of deposits from one account to another, possibly from one clearing bank to another. In all circumstances they would remain in the hands of clearing banks as a whole. If a non-clearing bank uses the proceeds of its sterling CD issues for granting credits to customers the latter too have accounts with clearing banks and the amounts received are paid into those accounts. If they spend them, the recipients act likewise. Even if the proceeds of a bank credit originating from the issue of CDs are paid out in wages to employees who have no bank account, the recipients spend their wages and the money reaches a bank account sooner or later. In this respect the position is the same as with other forms of lendings to customers outside the market, or to non-clearing banks.

It is of course conceivable that non-clearing banks compete with clearing banks for customers who would otherwise borrow from clearing banks. This aspect might become more important after the end of the credit squeeze, because banks will then cease to be prevented from increasing their total lendings. As it is, the demand for credits always exceeds the availably supply, and if a clearing bank loses a customer to a non-clearing bank it merely lends more to its other customers. Possibly, since non-clearing banks are primarily interested in larger firms, a higher proportion of the clearing banks' funds is lent to smaller firms or to private customers as a result of the increase in the CD issue. We propose to return to this aspect of the subject in Chapter 16. But clearing banks are by no means indifferent to the loss of some good customers to non-clearing banks.

Owing to the high minimum limit for CDs, as for LA and finance house deposits, clearing banks necessarily retain deposits of smaller amounts, and these, together with current account balances, constitute, after all, the bulk of the funds they hold for customers. Any deposits in excess of £50,000 can be retained 'within the family', if clearing banks can persuade depositors to deal with their affiliates. So in practice the cartel only applies to deposits under £50,000, or to larger deposits held by a diminishing number of unsophisticated depositors. But even large customers of clearing banks are reluctant to burn their boats, and they want to retain their goodwill with their clearing bank, possibly by transferring the bulk of their deposits to its affiliates. Whether this is in the form of inter-bank sterling or CDs depends partly on the difference between penalty clauses applied to time deposits and the differential between inter-bank sterling and sterling CD rates.

## (28) INFLUENCE ON INTEREST RATES

The volume of sterling CDs is at present not high enough to represent a major influence on the trend of interest rates, though occasionally the appearance of a large amount of excess supply or demand might conceivably tip the balance slightly. Should the volume increase to several times its present size – which is well within the realm of possibility – it might well become a major factor as it did in the United States during the early 'sixties. Although a separate market, it is not a watertight compartment, and its tendencies are liable to affect the general tendency of interest rates. At present sterling CD rates are determined by the trend in the money market in general and in two of its sections in particular – the inter-bank sterling market and the LA deposit market. To a very large degree sterling CDs are interchangeable with inter-bank sterling deposits of corresponding maturity; there can be no lasting discrepancy between them beyond the $\frac{1}{8}$ per cent or so which depositors consider it worth their while to concede for the sake of marketability. As for LA deposits, since issues of CD are used to a large degree for reinvestment in them for the sake of their higher yield, any change in LA deposit rates is liable to react on sterling CD rates.

Abolition of the cartel among clearing banks would mean that they competed directly for deposits instead of competing through affiliates by issuing sterling CDs. They would be siphoning off each other's deposits through the sterling CD market or the inter-bank deposit market, as the American banks do in the dollar CD market and in the Euro-dollar market.

# CHAPTER NINE

# Local Authority Deposits

## (1) ONE OF THE MAJOR FACTORS

DURING the late 'fifties and early 'sixties a new short-term and medium-term money market developed in London as a result of systematic short-term borrowing by Local Authorities on a large scale. Local Authorities developed the practice of borrowing by means of offering relatively attractive interest rates for deposits. There had been a fair amount of short-term borrowing by Local Authorities in earlier periods, but not in a form that would constitute a money market. Twenty years ago little interest was taken in the City in Local Authorities short-term borrowing – apart from their accounts and their overdraft arrangements with clearing banks – and none in foreign financial centres. Today the market in Local Authorities deposits has become one of the major factors in the London financial mechanism. It has become an influence that affects international movements of funds to and from London, at times to a considerable degree, in addition to influencing the trend in the domestic money market to an appreciable extent.

The market in LA short-term deposits comes within our scope because it has created a parallel money market which in a sense bears comparison with the all-important inter-bank sterling market. All kinds of British Public Authorities (with the exception of Parish Councils) – Municipalities, boroughs, towns, cities and counties numbering over 1,500 – are in a position to borrow against deposit receipts. A number of Public Boards other than Municipalities also accept deposits. They include Water Boards, Port Authorities, etc. But Local Authorities are by far the most important public sector borrowers in the deposit market. Between them they have come to attract large short-term funds from banks inside and outside the U.K., from other financial institutions, and also from large private firms and individual investors. Their medium-term borrowing, too, has assumed considerable importance, and their bill issues have created a new type of bills eligible for rediscount by the Bank of England.

## (2) VARIOUS FORMS OF BORROWING

The change that led to the development of the market in LA deposits dates from 1955. Until 1952 Local Authorities covered their capital requirements by borrowing from a Government institution, the Public Works Loan Board. From 1953 till 1955 it was left to Local Authorities to decide whether to borrow from the Board or from the market. But in 1955 the Government decided that the Local Authorities should no longer be allowed a free option to borrow at will from the Board. The rule was laid down that henceforth the Board would only consent to grant loans in instances in which it was satisfied that the Local Authority applying for a loan was not in a position to raise the money on its own credit in the market or through private channels.

As a result of this change a substantial market providing short-term credit facilities for Local Authorities developed during the course of the next two years. Their borrowing assumed various forms – long-term stocks in large amounts, mortgages with an active secondary market, bonds and bills, bank overdrafts and deposits. It is with the latter that we are primarily concerned.

It goes without saying that none of the well-known Local Authorities has found any difficulty in raising the necessary money either privately or through public issues since 1955. Only some small and little-known Local Authorities were ever in a position to satisfy the PWLB that they had been unable to cover their requirements through such channels. About 90 per cent of borrowing by Local Authorities was from private lenders.

## (3) INCREASED SHORT-TERM BORROWING

Treasurers of Local Authorities found during the early 'sixties that it cost them much less to cover a very large part of their requirements by short-term borrowing than by long-term borrowing, because short-term interest rates were most of the time much lower than long-term interest rates. As a result, the increase in the amount of the floating debts of Local Authorities reached proportions that gave rise to growing concern in Whitehall. Consequently in 1964 the Treasury laid down the rule that no Local

Authority was permitted to borrow for the short term in excess of
20 per cent of its total debt. The Authorities were required to
adapt their ratio to the prescribed limit by 1968, but later the
time limit came to be extended to March 1969. The PWLB was
authorised to assist in certain circumstances in the funding of
excessive short-term debts.

The bulk of short-term money is raised in the form of deposits
against the issue of Deposit Receipts. The shortest deposits are
deposits overnight or money at call. There are deposits subject to
two days' notice or to seven days' notice by either side. But there
are also deposits for fixed maturities in terms of months, up to
364 days. Or after a fixed period of one to nine months they may
become subject to seven days' notice by either side. There are also
short-term bonds for twelve months that soon became popular
under the name of 'yearlings' even though their maximum
maturity was later extended to two years. There are longer loans
for fixed periods of up to five years or subject to notice. There is a
market with fluctuating rates for medium-term mortgage.

The reason why most Municipal treasurers preferred to borrow
as much as possible in the form of short-term deposits in addition
to the lower level of short-term interest rates was that they
expected a decline in long-term interest rates. In consequence of
this preference by the end of 1965 the outstanding amount of
temporary borrowing was £1,789 million, an increase of £682
million in four years. By the beginning of 1970 it rose to about
£2,650 million. Of these amounts between 75 and 80 per cent was
repayable within seven days, and a large proportion was borrowed
overnight. But only the Greater London Council and a few of the
largest Municipalities are in the habit of borrowing overnight
systematically. Other Local Authorities rarely borrow for less
than seven days.

### (4) HOW THE MARKET WORKS

The mechanism of the LA deposit market is similar to that of
other parallel money markets. Business is transacted mostly
through private telephone lines between brokers, potential lenders
and potential borrowers.

The market begins its activity very early in the morning. Some
treasurers are at their desks at 8.30 a.m. and inform the deposit
brokers about their borrowing requirements or about the surpluses

they may have at their disposal. Often they have to wait till their banks open in order to ascertain how they stand – whether they have a surplus or a deficiency. As soon as inter-bank sterling deposit rates, on which initial quotations of LA deposit rates are largely based, are available the brokers quote them rates 'for information' to give them an idea, solely for their guidance, of the prevailing trend.

Later the brokers may receive firm quotations of rates either from treasurers or from the potential depositors. They then contact the other party. Some treasurers are very hard bargainers and when they receive a firm offer they try to improve on the rate quoted to them by inquiring in other quarters. But they run the risk of thereby missing the opportunity to obtain the deposit at the rate quoted to them if the rate should move against them or if the depositor should find a taker in the meantime at the rate he quoted.

A high proportion of inter-bank sterling deposits is invested in the market in LA deposits. For this reason the two markets influence each other reciprocally, but the rates for LA deposits are influenced to a much higher degree by the rates for inter-bank sterling. This is because the turnover in the inter-bank sterling market is much larger than that in LA deposits, even though the outstanding amount of LA deposits is probably larger. But since there is no secondary market in them the turnover in the market for inter-bank sterling deposits, where the same deposits may be re-lent again and again, is incomparably larger.

## (5) OVERNIGHT DEPOSIT RATES

Overnight inter-bank deposit rates do not influence overnight LA deposit rates to nearly the same extent as longer maturities of LA deposits are influenced by corresponding maturities of inter-bank deposits. For instance when the overnight inter-bank deposit rate rose to 32 per cent at the end of March 1970 the overnight LA deposit rate only rose to 18 per cent. At the same time twelve months' LA deposits rose by $\frac{1}{2}$ per cent, in sympathy with a similar rise in twelve months' inter-bank deposits.

Overnight rates in both markets are liable to be affected by separate sets of fortuitous influences that are largely independent of each other, in addition to the influence of the general trend. Nevertheless, they react to each other to some extent. Municipal treasurers may find themselves short of funds, or they may find themselves in possession of large cash surpluses, for reasons that are quite unrelated to the general market conditions affecting inter-bank rates. The sudden demand for funds, or the unloading of surplus funds on the market by treasurers is, however, liable to influence the inter-bank market to some extent. Conversely, even though banks are not in a position to withdraw funds from the market in LA deposits – except by giving notice for deposits that are subject to notice – their willingness to lend new deposits to Local Authorities overnight or for short maturities, and therefore the rates they are prepared to accept, is naturally affected by their own cash position. There is also a certain amount of reciprocal influence between the LA deposit market and the rival parallel markets – the market in sterling CDs and the market in finance house deposits.

## (6) SOME TECHNICAL DETAILS

In the LA deposit market the minimum deposit is £50,000, but it is possible to negotiate smaller amounts. On the other hand, £500,000 and £1,000,000 are standard amounts, and deposits of £5,000,000, £10,000,000 and even £25,000,000 are occasionally transacted. On some days the turnover runs into tens of millions of pounds and the average turnover is very high.

A specially printed form of receipt is used for these deposits. The depositor pays the deposit into the Local Authority's bank, which may be authorised to issue receipts on behalf of the Local Authority for overnight deposits in order to save time. The Authority itself issues receipts for deposits for all other maturities. The Deposit Receipts are not transferable, so that no secondary market can exist in them. Owners of LA deposits with fixed dates have to hold them till maturity, and owners of deposits subject to notice are bound by the terms of the notice as stated on the receipt. For deposits up to eleven months either party is entitled to give notice, but in the case of deposits for one year or longer the borrower may agree that the depositor alone should have the option to give notice.

For money at call notice must be given by telephone before noon on the day on which repayment is wanted. For deposits subject to two days' notice, notice is to be given by telephone before noon (to be confirmed by mail on the same day) for repayment on the third clear day. Seven days' notice may be given any time during the customary office hours, and it takes effect a week from that day – that is, on the same day of the following week. If notice is given by mail without previous notice by telephone it becomes effective on the first clear day after the posting as indicated by the postmark, or on any subsequent day, as stated in the notice.

## (7) CALCULATION OF INTEREST

Interest on loans maturing before an interest date is payable at the time the loan is repaid. For longer deposits interim payments of interest are made half-yearly or quarterly, according to the terms of the arrangement. Interest from the last interest date to the date of repayment is paid on repayment. The interest is reckoned on the basis of 365 days a year, by multiplying $\frac{1}{365}$ of a full year's interest by the number of days for which interest is to be paid, counting the first day but not the last day. Repayment is normally made in the same form and in the same manner in which the deposit was received.

Interest on LA deposits up to 364 days can now be paid without deduction of income tax. This fiscal concession has greatly increased the popularity of such deposits abroad.

## (8) HOW SECURE ARE LOANS TO LOCAL AUTHORITIES?

Deposit Receipts and all other securities issued by Local Authorities are Trustee securities. They are a charge on the rate revenue of the Authority. They are not guaranteed by the Government in the legal sense, but it is a widely – though not generally – accepted assumption that the Government has a high degree of moral obligation that impels the Treasury to ensure repayment. For this reason it would not allow any Local Authority to default on its liability. There has indeed been no actual default on Municipal debts in Britain in modern times. When difficulties due to political reasons arose in Poplar soon after the First World War the Treasury took over the control of the finances of the local Council by putting its own auditors in charge to tidy up the situation. Moreover, *pour décourager les autres*, members of the Council responsible for the default were sentenced to short-term imprisonment.

Even so, while most people consider it inconceivable that the Government should ever change its attitude as far as the debts of the well-known authorities are concerned, many banks and other depositors have limits for the names of all Local Authorities. When it comes to less well-known or entirely unknown Local Authorities opinion among potential depositors is sharply divided as to whether it is safe to take Government intervention to prevent default for granted. While treasurers of some banks and of other depositors unhesitatingly invest in any of the 1,500-odd Local Authorities in the United Kingdom, others are more selective. For this reason unknown or little-known authorities usually have to pay somewhat higher rates, but the differential is seldom more than $\frac{1}{4}$ per cent. Since the Mersey default it became wider.

Some banks treat Local Authorities in the same way as they treat private borrowers from the point of view of fixing limits for their names. They take into consideration the size of their outstanding indebtedness in general and of their short-term debts in particular, and relate these to the size of their populations or of their rate revenues. At the other extreme, some depositors, when giving orders to brokers, merely state the amounts they want to deposit and the maturities for which they want to deposit the amounts and do not even specify names. In between the two extremes there are many depositors whose brokers usually deem it advisable to ask their client whether he is prepared to accept Local Authorities whose names are not household words. Some depositors give brokers a list of Local Authorities whose names are acceptable, or they give them the names or categories of those which are unacceptable.

I have heard of instances in which treasurers of banks or business firms, having deposited their firms' money with some unknown Local Authority, were taken severely to task by their General Managers. 'How do you know that this —— place exists at all?' one treasurer was asked by his irate chief, and he had to produce a map of the U.K. to prove that it did in fact exist. Having regard to the fact that the deposit was made through a well-known broker specialising in LA deposits, this distrust was surely unwarranted.

As things are now the assumption that the Government would intervene may be depended upon with an even higher degree of certainty than the assumption that the Bank of England would rescue any British bank of importance. While the Bank of England might feel it could afford to allow small banks which got into trouble through faults of their own to fail, the Government could ill afford to allow the reputation of Local Authorities as a whole to be damaged through default by any one of them. In particular since the Government discovered the possibility of raising foreign exchange by Municipal borrowing abroad, it has become particularly important to maintain that reputation unblemished.

In spite of these considerations, London branches of American banks have not always found it easy to persuade their head offices that British Municipal securities are virtually gilt-edged and well worth holding for the sake of the higher yield they offer compared with the yield on corresponding Government securities. Their head offices have found it even more difficult to make their clients realise this fact. Even now many American and other foreign banks and investors are only interested in well-known Municipalities.

In reality there is very little to choose between the Deposit Receipts of various Municipalities from the point of view of their security. Nevertheless, as already pointed out, many banks have limits for names and refuse certain names altogether. Yet there are sometimes interesting discrepancies between interest rates paid on them. Discrepancies are also liable to arise because the extent and urgency of requirements of various Municipal treasurers is apt to vary widely. If a treasurer finds himself suddenly short of cash he may be prepared to pay rates above those prevailing in the market, especially on overnight deposits or on very short deposits, pending the advent of the expected rate payments or Government grants, or in anticipation of the issue of long-term loans, or of short-term borrowing on more favourable terms.

If Local Authorities get into difficulties they may be able to fall back upon the PWLB as lender of last resort, though the extent to which this has been done in recent years is moderate. They also have overdraft facilities with banks. Nevertheless many treasurers prefer to square their positions in the market.

## (9) INTER-AUTHORITY DEPOSIT MARKET

Local Authorities have a deposit market of their own through which they can circumvent the City – an equivalent of the market for inter-corporation deposits dealt with in Chapter 7. It is a kind of official clearing house through which deficiencies of some Local

Authorities are met out of surpluses of other Local Authorities. This function is performed by the Local Authority Loans Bureaux. There are about a dozen such institutions. Their managers are known as Area Liaison Officers, because each Bureau covers a certain area and keeps in touch with Municipal treasurers within its area. They also keep in touch with each other.

The reason why many Local Authorities prefer to deal through these Bureaux rather than dealing through deposit brokers is that they save the ⅛ per cent commission they pay to brokers. (In the LA deposit market only the borrowing Local Authorities pay commission to brokers, not the depositors.) But many of the more sophisticated treasurers are aware that they stand a better chance of obtaining deposits at lower rates if they deal through brokers who are in close contact with a wide range of potential depositors, including Local Authorities with surpluses. Brokers often act as intermediaries between two Local Authorities, and are often able to secure for them better terms than they could get through Loan Bureaux, even allowing for the commission. Nevertheless, the Loan Bureaux too have their *raison d'être*, judging by the fact that their annual turnover is estimated at £200 million, which is not negligible, even though it is a bare fraction of the estimated turnover in the deposit market.

Some treasurers aim at establishing a direct relationship with some regular depositors. Having been introduced to them by a broker, they seek to 'chisel' him out of his commission – to use this apposite Americanism – on subsequent transactions by dealing with his client direct behind his back. The Institute of Municipal Treasurers and Accountants does not encourage this practice, which, apart altogether from ethical considerations, is often detrimental to the interests of the Municipalities concerned. As is the case with treasurers who deal through Loan Bureaux, those dealing direct with depositors might fail to secure the most favourable terms that are obtainable in the market.

Brokers are better placed to secure favourable terms for their clients because they have frequent contact through their private telephone lines with big depositors and with the treasurers of all the important Municipalities. One of the brokers told me that his dealers are in communication with the G.L.C. treasurer's department alone between twenty and thirty times a day on average.

The inter-bank market is by far the best source of LA deposits and brokers are in a position to follow its ups and downs much better than either Municipal treasurers or Loans Bureaux. A sudden dip in inter-bank deposit rates would provide them with ample opportunities to secure for Municipal treasurers better rates than they could possibly obtain if they circumvented the market. On the other hand, if the inter-bank deposit rate rises suddenly Municipal treasurers can always try to secure their deposits from less sophisticated quarters which, not being in close touch with the market, have not yet realised the change.

Owing to the high proportion of inter-bank deposits invested in LA deposits, rates in the two parallel markets tend to fluctuate in sympathy with each other. While we saw earlier that fortuitous circumstances are liable to widen the differential for a short time for overnight deposits, for longer maturities discrepancies seldom exceed $\frac{1}{4}$ to $\frac{1}{2}$ per cent for any length of time, because wider differentials lead to arbitrage between the two markets.

## (10) SEASONAL CHANGES IN REQUIREMENTS

Requirements of Local Authorities for deposits are subject to regularly recurrent seasonal variations. They decline when rate payments are received twice a year, in the early spring and in the early autumn, though this seasonal factor has become somewhat less pronounced since it has become possible to pay rates in monthly instalments. The receipt of Government grants at regular intervals also reduces the current requirements of Local Authorities from time to time. Otherwise the demand is fairly even. Although expenditure by various Local Authorities has its ebbs and flows, it rises and falls in different places at different times of the year, so that by the law of averages these fluctuations tend to offset each other. For this reason, in spite of the seasonal influences referred to above, the fluctuations of LA deposit rates depend not so much on the demand for such deposits as on the ups and downs of interest rates in other parallel markets, especially in the inter-bank sterling market.

Local Authorities have overdraft facilities with clearing banks on the informal understanding that they do not make use of them as a matter of routine but solely temporarily amidst tight conditions. It is extremely useful for treasurers to know that they are in a position to fall back upon these facilities in case of real need. It enables them to avoid having to pay abnormally high rates which might prevail for a short time. For instance when in March 1970 the overnight deposit rate rose to 18 per cent, Local Authorities who needed the money urgently were able to borrow it from their banks instead of having to borrow in the market regardless of cost.

Treasurers were worried about the wide fluctuations of interest rates during the late 'sixties and in 1970. Those fluctuations upset their Budget calculations by changing the cost of their debts, and they increased the difficulties of their debt management. While usually the inter-bank deposit rate dominates, Euro-dollar rates also have a considerable influence on LA deposit rates, especially since the closing months of 1969 when many non-resident investors ceased to consider it essential, for the time being at any rate, to cover their LA deposits against exchange risk. When it is necessary to cover that risk the cost of forward covering reduces the differential between the yield obtained on these deposits and on comparable investments abroad.

## (11) EFFECT OF GOVERNMENT POLICIES

The demand for LA deposits by Municipal treasurers is supposed to depend to a very large degree on the policy pursued by Governments of the day regarding meeting those requirements through the PWLB. Substantial reductions in the demand for LA deposits are liable to be caused by Government decisions to increase the limits of PWLB loans. For instance in April 1970 an additional £200 million was conceded. But under a Conservative Government the limits are more likely to be reduced than increased.

The Conservative Government is likely to be inclined to divert much Municipal borrowing from the PWLB and to make the Local Authorities more dependent on the market. Apart from that there does not seem to be much difference between the amount of capital requirements, for Tory-controlled Councils are also inclined to overspend, just like Socialist-controlled Councils, though there may be a difference of degree. A high proportion of capital and current requirements of Local Authorities depends on Government policies on housing, education, public health, etc., and Local Authorities merely carry out Government policy. The size of Government grants may tend to be lower under a Conservative Government.

Although the basic principle that inspired the establishment of the PWLB was that Local Authorities should finance current expenditure out of rates and the Government should only provide money for capital expenditure, in practice in most Municipal budgets the two types of expenditure are hopelessly intermingled. The capital raised in the market, too, is just as likely to finance current expenditure as capital expenditure. And deposit and other short-term borrowing often finances long-term capital spending.

Thanks to the existence of a good market for Local Authority borrowing, the Exchequer is relieved of a substantial portion of the burden of financing the capital expenditure of Local Authorities. From the investors' point of view it provides them with a wider choice of safe investment facilities with yields distinctly above those of Government issues. It increases the activities of the London money market. Last but by no means least, it attracts funds from abroad.

### (12) MARKETABLE BILLS

Although the market in LA deposits receives most attention in the Press, it is by no means the only Local Authority market. There is a market for bills issued by Local Authorities. These bills are very much sought after at a time when the volume of Treasury bills is low or when allotments to discount houses are reduced by heavy outside tendering. LA bills are eligible for rediscount by the Bank of England and as collaterals for loans from the Bank or from clearing banks. For this reason, although their yield is higher than that of Treasury bills, it is lower than that of sterling CDs. The rates for CDs largely determine the rates for LA bills for corresponding maturities. The differential is usually around $\frac{1}{16}$ per cent. Clearing bank affiliates and other banks often issue CDs for the purpose of investing the proceeds in LA bills.

Before 1935 various Local Authorities obtained parliamentary authorisation to issue bills. This practice has been resumed since 1965 when the Manchester Corporation was authorised to issue such bills. The Greater London Council has obtained authorisation to issue up to £25 million, and the Greater London Boroughs up to a total of £50 million. The rule is that a Local Authority which can apply for permission has to have a rate income of at least £3 million. Applications must be limited to sums of up to 20 per cent of the total debt. Altogether over eighty Local Authorities obtained such authorisation by the beginning of 1970 to a total of £138 million, of which £76 million was actually issued. The official policy is to keep these issues limited, and each issue has to be sanctioned by the Discount Office of the Bank of England, precisely because the bills are eligible for rediscount and as security for loans.

## (13) BOND ISSUES

There is a special market for funds for mortgages. Units vary from £50,000 to £1,000,000 and even larger. These mortgages are for periods of one year or more, so that a large proportion of them are medium-term loans. Since 1963 Local Authorities have been authorised to issue bonds, most of them for one year or two years. 'Yearlings' are particularly popular. Maturing bonds are often re-financed through the issue of new bonds. They are issued by merchant banks and many of them find their way into the discount market. Although the Bank of England does not accept such bonds as security, the clearing banks accept them to a limited extent. Anyhow, it is a fairly active market for medium-term loans, and bonds which are approaching maturity provide a market for short-term investments.

Although many of the Municipal bonds are issued on the Stock Exchange and obtain quotations there, others are taken up by discount houses. But these can only hold a relatively small proportion of their assets in that form, because the bonds are not accepted by the Bank of England as securities for loans, and clearing banks accept only limited amounts as securities for loans.

Originally the object of short-term borrowing by Local Authorities was the anticipation of revenue or of the proceeds of impending long-term borrowing. But during the 'fifties and since, many treasurers have become inclined to take a view on interest rate prospects, and whenever they expect a decline they prefer to finance their requirements by short-term borrowing, renewing their deposits or other forms of short term loans again and again. They may even engage in interest arbitrage by raising amounts in excess of their immediate requirements and re-lending the surplus either to other Local Authorities or even in one of the parallel markets.

While most types of Local Authority issues follow the traditional types there is at least one type actually devised by that market. It differentiates between loans which are subject to notice by either side and those which are subject to notice by lenders only. The interest differential between the two types is normally of the order of $\frac{1}{8}$ per cent to $\frac{1}{4}$ per cent, but it is liable to widen when future prospects become more uncertain, so that the advantage of a unilateral option for the benefit of lenders becomes potentially more valuable.

## (14) WHY DEPOSIT RECEIPTS ARE NOT TRANSFERABLE

It may appear somewhat perplexing that the legislation empowering Local Authorities to accept deposits did not empower them to issue transferable Deposit Receipts. As it is, there can be no secondary market in them. The depositor must part with his money until maturity and cannot use the receipts as collaterals for loans. If LA Deposit Receipts were marketable the Authorities issuing them would be able to borrow at a lower rate. LA deposits would be more popular short-term investments and they would attract more money from abroad.

It has been suggested that the Government's decision to make the Deposit Receipts non-transferable was inspired by its intention to prevent an undue expansion of this type of Municipal short-term borrowing. But the same end can be attained by maintaining the 20 per cent limit for short-term borrowing, or by fixing a separate limit for borrowing in this particular form.

What is more likely is that the Government has no wish to create a short-term security which would compete with Treasury bills by enabling Municipalities to increase unduly their issues of transferable Deposit Receipts. Also if those receipts were transferable they would be eligible for rediscount by the Bank of England or at any rate as collaterals for loans from the Bank of England and from clearing banks. Even though the volume of credit is determined by Government policy, its enforcement would become more difficult if the Bank of England had to cope with an additional volume of credit.

As it is, LA deposits are an influence making for consolidation, by preventing the money invested in them from producing a dual inflationary effect. If the receipts were marketable this would make for expansion in addition to the inflationary use of the proceeds by the Local Authorities in spending the money. Since the depositors themselves renounce the inflationary use of their money for the duration of the deposits this may go some way towards offsetting the inflationary effect of its use by the Municipalities.

## (15) COMPETITION WITH OTHER PARALLEL MARKETS

It is true that the higher interest rate the Local Authorities have to pay to compensate depositors for the non-transferability of the Deposit Receipts might divert some demand from the market for Treasury bills by holders of funds who are reasonably certain that they will not need their money until maturity.

But marketable Deposit Receipts would also compete with CDs or, in the case of non-residents, with dollar CDs. They might reduce demand for these, which would narrow the discrepancy between their rates and those of inter-bank sterling or Euro-dollars respectively. Or they might divert demand from commercial bills. So the whole weight of their change into marketable paper would not fall on the Treasury bills.

Since Deposit Receipts are non-transferable the amount of Local Authorities short-term issues which can be re-sold and which can be used as security is comparatively limited. The bulk of Local Authorities borrowing has to be in long-term loans, marketable or otherwise, or non-marketable short-term loans.

Before concluding this chapter it is necessary to refer briefly to the partial default on the Mersey Docks Authority towards the close of 1970. Its immediate effect was heavy withdrawals of LA deposits. The PWLB had to support some of the Municipalities to enable them to meet their liabilities. But the sum total of this Government support was merely £42 million – a bare fraction of the outstanding amount, and the withdrawals caused *after* two days. The market came to realise that the Government does not have the same moral responsibility for debts of autonomous institutions such as harbour boards as for those of Municipalities. After the first panic, the LA deposit market settled down and conditions became normal.

# CHAPTER TEN

# Finance House Deposits

## (1) EXPANSION OF HIRE-PURCHASE BUSINESS

BRITAIN and most other advanced countries of the free world have witnessed since the war a most remarkable expansion in the use of hire-purchase credit. Of course the system existed before the war – indeed it can be traced back to Ancient Roman times when during the 1st century B.C. Crassus sold houses on the instalment system – but its spectacular expansion after the Second World War must be regarded as an institutional change.

This expansion may be attributed to the coinciding of several basic economic, social and technological changes. While amidst the mass unemployment existing before the war uncertainty of future earnings tended to discourage many consumers from mortgaging their future incomes, after the war the existence of a virtually uninterrupted high level of employment made it appear perfectly safe to buy now and pay gradually out of future earnings. All the more so since wages and other earnings were rising, so that a great many people felt they could depend on being able to spare the money needed for the redemption of their hire-purchase debts out of their increased incomes. Even to the extent to which the increase in earnings was only in terms of money and not in real terms, most debtors were able to meet instalment payments without unduly reducing their increased money incomes available for current spending.

Indeed the gradual realisation that the real value of money in terms of goods tended to decline through creeping inflation induced consumers to anticipate the rise in prices by buying goods before they could afford to pay cash, on the assumption that if they waited prices would rise even higher. Those who could not afford to finance their purchases out of their current incomes deemed it to be in their interests to buy nevertheless, by incurring hire-purchase debts that would be repayable with depreciated money out of increased money incomes. In any case a great many people expected their real incomes, too, to increase.

## (2) 'KEEPING UP WITH THE JONESES'

The increase in real incomes – in other words the rise in the standard of living – stimulated buying on the instalment system, especially buying of consumer durable goods, whose use ceased to be confined to the upper income groups, largely as a result of the ease with which they could be bought on hire-purchase terms. Refrigerators, washing machines, costly TV sets and, above all, motor cars ceased to be considered luxuries reserved for the privileged few. They came to be regarded as necessities by a large and growing number of people who could not afford to pay cash for them. Technological progress produced new goods and new temptations for consumers. Such goods are particularly suitable for hire-purchase transactions, because they are supposed to be sufficiently durable to last at least until the instalment payments have been completed.

The urge to 'keep up with the Joneses' has become increasingly strong with the increase in earnings. The possession of certain consumer durables – especially motor cars and TV sets – which most people could only acquire on the instalment system, has become increasingly a status symbol, and this new kind of snobbery has provided a strong motive for buying goods obtainable through hire purchase. Demand for hire-purchase facilities for furniture and fittings – which was the original basis for the hire-purchase system between the wars – has also increased, thanks to the rising standard of living. Holidays can now be financed on the hire-purchase system.

Apart altogether from financing increased consumer demand, hire purchase has also developed and expanded since the war in the sphere of industries supplying equipment for industrial producers of every kind – for distributive trades, for transport, for agriculture. In many instances small producers have only been able to benefit from technological progress thanks to the purchase of more up-to-date equipment on the instalment system. Transport vehicles, shop equipment, increasingly modern office equipment ranging from filing cabinets to computers, have also become available under a system of deferred payments. The operation of the hire-purchase system has tended to increase not only consumption but also production – albeit to an incomparably smaller degree.

## (3) FINANCING OF HIRE PURCHASE

The expansion of instalment selling gave rise to growing problems of financing. In the old days many manufacturers and merchants were able to finance the relatively small volume of their hire-purchase business out of their own capital resources, or with the aid of funds borrowed from their banks in the ordinary way. With the increase in the volume of goods sold on the instalment system the financing of that activity necessarily became increasingly separated from the production and sale of the goods concerned. Some large firms formed subsidiaries for that purpose, but most firms came to rely on independent institutions which became known as 'finance houses' – an abridgement of the original term 'hire-purchase finance houses' – specialising in providing capital for financing the sale of goods on hire-purchase terms.

The terms on which goods are sold on the instalment system must necessarily allow for losses through bad debts. Although such losses were surprisingly moderate even during the long depression of the 'thirties, the risk is undoubtedly there and sellers want to err on the cautious side when fixing their terms for goods sold on deferred payments. They were in a position to benefit from the psychological effect of doing away with the necessity for buyers to part with cash immediately. If one need not pay cash at once one is inclined to overspend, and consumer resistance to higher prices for goods on HP terms is liable to weaken.

This meant that firms selling on the instalment system could afford to pay high interest rates to finance houses, rates well above those charged by banks on overdrafts. Many of the minor finance houses, being unable to borrow from banks or in the capital market, were prepared to pay abnormally high rates to depositors. The system of financing hire purchase with the aid of deposits developed after 1947 when Government restrictions imposed on bank credits to finance houses compelled the latter to secure alternative resources. During the early period there was no market and many finance houses had to try to obtain deposits from the public by offering tempting interest rates.

## (4) DEMAND FOR DEPOSITS

It was not until much later that a proper market developed in finance house deposits, in which interest rates came to be determined by ever-changing supply–demand relationships, subject of course to the influence of rates prevailing in other parallel money markets. Meanwhile, many finance houses went out of their way to attract deposits direct from the public. There were frequent advertisements in the late 'forties and in the 'fifties, offering deposit rates of the order of 12 per cent, at a time when this was several times higher than the prevailing rate on bank deposits.

Many such finance houses had inadequate resources of their own and some of them got into difficulties. Many depositors lost their money. The outcome was the adoption of the Protection of Deposits Act of 1963, making it compulsory for finance houses which advertise for deposits to publish fuller details on their deposits and also on the nature of their lending transactions.

On many occasions after the war more or less drastic restrictions were adopted by the Government of the day in order to keep down or reduce the volume of demand stimulated by hire-purchase facilities. Such restrictions were apt to be maintained for prolonged periods. A minimum initial deposit on goods bought on deferred payments was made compulsory, though its size varied according to the prevailing economic climate. The maximum limit for the period of repayment was reduced from time to time. These measures were modified some two dozen times in twenty years. They were often relaxed, and on two occasions actually repealed when conditions appeared to have improved, but they were reinforced again and again on the occasion of the next crisis. But for this, the volume of hire-purchase debts and that of the credits financing them would have risen much more steeply.

Even as things were, in face of the growing pressure of demand for hire-purchase facilities by the public, there was a correspondingly insistent demand for credits to finance such facilities. Although there have been for many years a number of highly reputable houses engaged in this type of financing and they had access to bank credit, their total capital resources and bank credit facilities were far from sufficient to cope with growing requirements.

### (5) BANKS TAKE AN ACTIVE INTEREST

At this stage, in the middle of the 'fifties, a number of banks decided to take an active part in hire-purchase finance by acquiring an interest in finance houses. The National Commercial Bank of Scotland was first in the field. In 1954 it acquired the share capital of the Scottish Midland Guarantee Trust. Other banks followed its example, but the movement did not gather momentum until 1958 when the Government removed the restrictions on hire purchase in order to reflate the economy. Banks were anxious to take their share in meeting the increased demand. The financial requirements of finance houses increased and banks came to assist more actively in meeting them, by lending the prestige of their names to the houses they acquired.

The National Provincial Bank bought the Forward Trust Co. The National Commercial Bank of Scotland, in partnership with Lloyds Bank, gained the control of Olds Discount Co., and amalgamated it with the Scottish Midland Guarantee, forming the Lloyds and Scottish Co. Substantial minority shareholdings were acquired by Barclays Bank in the United Dominions Trust, by the Westminster Bank and Martins Bank in the Mercantile Credit Co., by the District Bank in Astley Imperial Trust, and by Lloyds Bank, in addition to its holding referred to above, in Bow-makers. The National Bank secured an interest in St Margaret's Trust, the Three Banks Group (William Deacons & Co., Glyn Mills & Co., and the Royal Bank of Scotland) linked up with British Wagon Co., but later that house was taken over by the United Dominions Trust. The Bank of Scotland formed an association with North West Securities.

The above list of participators does not represent the present position, as in recent years there have been several amalgamations among the parent institutions as well as among the finance houses, and the picture has changed in many respects. There are many inter-locking shareholding arrangements between finance houses and non-clearing banks, too, while insurance companies have acquired minority shareholdings in several finance houses.

British banks have taken an active interest in hire-purchase finance in a totally different way from American banks, which themselves have been actively engaged in granting hire-purchase credits to their own customers. Some American banks have special counters where hire-purchase debtors pay their monthly instalments. They actively advertise their instalment credit facilities. British banks prefer to leave it to specialist finance houses to finance hire-purchase credits, either direct to buyers or through manufacturers, wholesalers or retail distributors.

## (6) LARGE VERSUS SMALL DEPOSITS

What concerns us here is that, as a result of the acquisition of control, or even of a substantial minority interest in the capital of finance houses by banks of high standing, finance houses are now placed in a position to borrow more extensively and at lower cost. Their bills are accepted by banks and such finance paper is well received by the discount market. What is more important, finance houses are in a better position to obtain time deposits from depositors of all types. Most of the deposits are for three months or six months, and the rates they have to pay, though higher than those paid on inter-bank, CD or LA deposits, are relatively reasonable. The discrepancy between three and six months' deposits is usually ¼ per cent. A regular market in such deposits has developed.

Many of the deposits still come from outside the market. Some of the finance houses – even some of the biggest of them – advertise for such deposits. The policy they pursue in respect of accepting small deposits varies from finance house to finance house. The Mercantile Credit Co., for instance, does not accept deposits smaller than £5,000, but the United Dominions Trust introduced in 1968 a savings scheme under which deposits from £1 upwards are accepted. Such private depositors are paid a uniform interest rate that may vary from finance house to finance house and may or may not be adjusted in relation to changes in the Bank rate. There is no cartel among finance houses in respect of fixed deposit rates paid to the public, which are usually relatively high. In addition to this form of borrowing, finance houses have also become takers of large outside deposits whose rates are a matter for negotiation.

Above all, finance houses seek to attract deposits from the market for finance house deposits that has come into being and has become one of the important parallel markets. The average level of interest rates paid on deposits is a matter of considerable importance to finance houses. They usually grant credits up to three years to firms financing hire purchase and the average extent of outstanding credits is usually of the order of eighteen months, which means that during a period of rising interest rates such as was experienced during the late 'sixties they are liable to have to renew maturing deposits, or re-borrow the amounts withdrawn, at the higher rates current at the time of renewal.

The reason why some finance houses prefer to borrow a large number of small deposits rather than a smaller number of big deposits – or in addition to the big deposits – is that they can depend on the operation of the law of averages as far as the multitude of small deposits are concerned. Withdrawals are liable to be offset by new deposits. On the other hand if individual deposits are very large finance houses are exposed to the possible coinciding of unexpected withdrawals of several of them. That contingency is liable to arise at any time, so that finance houses have to keep a high ratio of liquid assets to meet the demand for repayments of large deposits if and when it should arise. The alternative is to depend on being able to re-borrow – at a price – at short notice the large amounts required.

Nevertheless, finance houses have to depend to a high degree on large deposits borrowed in the market. The minimum amount of market transactions is £25,000; the maximum is in terms of millions of pounds, but individual items are on average smaller than in the market for LA deposits. In spite of the relatively high costs of such deposits, finance houses have to resort to them to satisfy their requirements. At the end of 1969 the total deposits of finance houses amounted to £636 million, out of which £519 million was from U.K. banks and other financial institutions and from U.K. non-financial companies. This means that they are certain to have been obtained in the market at rates prevailing in the market, and not at the lower rates paid on smaller deposits. Even part of the £101 million deposited by 'other U.K. residents' and the £24 million from 'overseas residents' must have represented market deposits.

## (7) RATES AND MATURITIES

This accounts for the high average deposit rates paid by finance houses. According to the chairman's report of one of the leading finance houses for 1968, although traditionally borrowing costs had ranged between Bank rate and $\frac{3}{4}$ per cent above it, more recently average borrowing rates were running at up to 2 per cent above that level. As many of the credits were granted by the finance houses at a lower interest rate for periods of up to three years – and in the case of capital goods up to seven years – renewals of short-term deposits at increased rates reduced their profit margins and in many instances resulted in losses.

Most finance houses make it a rule never to refuse any deposits offered to them, whether direct by depositors or through brokers. If they do not want any more deposits, or if they are not interested in receiving any for the maturities offered to them, they quote unattractive rates.

The extent to which finance houses could depend on acceptance credits was limited by the credit squeeze. Although banks and discount houses are favourably disposed towards finance house bills, which are essentially self-liquidating – albeit at a slower pace than the sale of consumer goods against short-term credits – and are obviously based on genuine commercial transactions, official limitations made finance houses depend increasingly on the market for deposits. Even the amounts raised by such means remained more or less static during recent years. This was due to the levelling out of the demand for facilities resulting from restrictions imposed on hire-purchase terms.

The number of finance houses in the U.K. is about 1,500, but as a rule only members of the Finance Houses Association borrow in the market. Some finance houses keep in close contact with the market, and have a number of private telephone lines to brokers. The number of transactions in the market is, in the case of one of the biggest houses, between twenty and forty a day, the individual amounts varying between £20,000 and £2 million. Some brokers have reduced their commission to $\frac{1}{16}$ per cent, but others still charge the finance houses $\frac{1}{8}$ per cent. Although most deposits are for three months and six months finance houses often borrow for much shorter periods if they are in urgent need of resources or if they expect a fall in interest rates. They accept deposits for seven days and even overnight. The main factor determining finance house deposit rates is the inter-bank sterling rate. Like inter-bank deposits, Euro-dollar deposits and CDs, finance house deposits are unsecured. Their security lies in the continuous flow of repayments of hire-purchase debts by the ultimate debtors and by the latter's immediate creditors, and of course in the association of leading finance houses with banks of high standing.

Many finance houses have several subsidiaries, some of which are also in the habit of borrowing deposits in the market. Channel Island subsidiaries too borrow both private deposits and market deposits.

## (8) RELATIONSHIPS WITH BANKS

Although many finance houses are now associated in some degree with banks, the credit squeeze prevents the latter from assisting the finance houses to a sufficient degree. So they have to depend largely on the market. They are not permitted to issue CDs, but this obstacle may be overcome indirectly if the associated non-clearing banks issue CDs for the benefit of finance houses.

Some of the deposits of finance houses are subject to notice – usually three months – but most of them are for a fixed period. Some houses transact a certain amount of forward-forward business, which means they obtain deposits in advance for future dates. This is necessary to provide for withdrawals on the eve of window-dressing dates. Such business is usually for short periods, up to a maximum of two months.

Needless to say, the banks associated with finance houses have no legal liability for the latter's deposits, not even if they own the full share capital of the finance houses. But since the main reason why many depositors trust the latter to a sufficient extent to deposit their moneys with finance houses at a relatively low rate is their publicly acknowledged association with banks of high standing, the banks have a strong moral responsibility which they would be most unlikely to repudiate. This consideration enables the finance houses concerned to raise large amounts, but they nevertheless have to pay rates above those paid on CDs or even on LA deposits.

## (9) THE FINANCE HOUSES ASSOCIATION

The finance houses which are members of the Finance Houses Association naturally have a higher standing than the rest, in the same way as merchant banks which belong to the Accepting House Committee have a higher standing than those which do not belong to it. A condition of membership is the possession of at least £500,000 capital and free reserves. The deposits of members represent 95 per cent of the total deposits of all finance houses. Their deposits amounted to £609 million at the end of 1969, out of a total of £636 million held by all finance houses.

As the deposits are unsecured, differentials between the rates on them are influenced by the standing of the finance house and also by its relationship with some important bank. Although large deposits are often negotiated by depositors direct with finance houses, many more are transacted through the intermediary of brokers. Finance houses may obtain deposits from the banks with which they have a special relationship if those banks happen to have liquid funds to spare and if their credit ceiling has not been reached.

Credit restrictions on banks limited the extent to which they could lend to finance houses – even to those closely associated with them – whether in the form of acceptance credits or over-drafts or deposits. At the end of 1969 the total deposits obtained by finance houses from U.K. banks amounted to £104 million, while finance house bills discounted with them amounted to £97 million. Against this, deposits from U.K. non-financial companies and individuals totalled £423 million, more than twice the total amount of credits obtained from banks. Industrial and commercial firms were by far the largest depositors. Treasurers of large firms came to appreciate the high yield obtained on finance house deposits compared with alternative forms of short-term employment of their resources.

Overseas residents, too, came to appreciate the advantages offered by the new market. Foreign brokers often acted as inter-mediaries for placing Euro-sterling deposits with finance houses when finance house deposit rates were more attractive. At the end of 1966 finance houses held £130 million in foreign HP deposits. But this figure declined year by year, and by the end of 1969 it was down to £26 million. The possibility of a revival of non-resident interest in HP deposits exists, however, even though LA deposits, offering slightly lower rates, came to be widely regarded abroad as a more attractive form of employing sterling balances.

U.K. institutional investors other than banks are among the regular depositors, their total holdings fluctuating between £80 million and £100 million during 1969. All classes of depositors confined their deposits almost entirely to members of the Finance Houses Association.

## (10) OPERATION OF THE MARKET

There are apt to be discrepancies between the deposit rates obtainable from different finance houses, not only because of differences between their relative standing or between the stand-ing of the banks with which they are associated or between the degrees of closeness of these associations, but also because at any given moment finance houses are not equally keen to increase their deposits in general or their deposits for particular maturities. The rates that even first-class houses have to pay to attract the deposits they need are apt to rise distinctly above the prevailing standard rates if they are in urgent need of large amounts. The spread between deposit rates for various finance houses is apt to be wider than the spread between CDs issued by various banks, and even wider than the spread between LA deposits for various Municipalities.

Practice in the finance house deposit market is the same as in other parallel markets. In the morning brokers contact the finance houses to ascertain their requirements and to inform them about the likely rates at which it will be possible to obtain deposits. The finance houses for their part inform the brokers about their requirements regarding amounts and maturities, and also about the maximum rates they are prepared to pay. The brokers then contact their clients inside and outside the market. The rates are subject to fluctuation during the course of the day in accordance with the general trend, but also under the influence of the changing requirements of finance houses or the changing demand for this type of deposit.

## (11) RESTRICTIONS AND TRENDS

The turnover in finance house deposits is seldom sufficiently large to influence the general trend to any noteworthy extent. Like the market in LA deposits, this is a one-way market, for deposits, once lent, cannot be recovered through the sale of the Deposit Receipts, which are non-transferable. There is therefore no secondary market. An important factor in determining interest rates is the degree of willingness of depositors to renew maturing deposits.

There are seasonal factors affecting deposit rates, such as the pre-Christmas trade, and even more the spring demand for motor cars, which always account for a high proportion of all hire-purchase business. But the operation of the credit ceiling reduces the importance of the fluctuations, for potential demand for credits from finance houses exceeds their permitted limits almost all the time. In 1965 the Bank of England requested the finance houses to restrict the volume of their lendings to a maximum of 105 per cent of their figures of 31 March 1965. Later the limit was fixed at the amount actually outstanding on 31 October 1967. In 1968 this limit was reduced to 98 per cent, but in April 1970 it was raised to 103 per cent.

The market is sensitive to recessions and recoveries, and also to changes in Government restrictions of hire-purchase terms. The appearance of new types of goods or services that come to be financed on hire-purchase terms – such as holidays, for instance – tends to affect demand for deposits. Above all, the ups and downs of the motor car trade are a major factor. But the decline in domestic sales of cars in 1969–70 did not mean any overall slackening of the demand for HP financing, for there were other outlets for the facilities that became available as a result of the decline in the demand for financing car purchases.

Deposit rates depend to some extent on the limits to which finance houses can meet their requirements through bank credits, for which banks usually charge 1 per cent above the Bank rate. To the extent to which they can meet some suddenly increased requirement by this means there is no need for them to pay higher deposit rates, unless these are below the rate charged for bank credits. Usually the cost of acceptance credits is more or less the same as that of deposits, but finance houses usually prefer deposits because the procedure is simpler.

Unlike Local Authorities or banks, finance houses never employ their surplus funds in deposits with their rival borrowers. If they have liquid funds they employ them in one of the other parallel markets.

## (12) DIVERSIFICATION

Diversification has broadened the sphere of activities of the larger finance houses. Some of them are now also active in investment banking, export financing, financing of building and construction, financing of equipment leasing, portfolio management, etc. The United Dominions Trust owns the London Produce Clearing House. The Mercantile Credit Co. has associated itself with the Post Office Giro's lending activities, etc. Some of them have extended their activities in overseas countries with the aid of affiliates.

All this is worth mentioning to show that the deposits obtained by finance houses are not earmarked specifically for financing hire purchase but are added to the general pool of funds of the finance houses, so that depositors are not putting all their eggs into one basket. Moreover, since restrictions on hire-purchase business and on its financing have prevented the finance houses from expanding in their original sphere of activity, diversification has opened up new fields for them. As a result of progress in these directions, the security of their deposits will cease to depend too unilaterally on hire-purchase business, which is an advantage.

# CHAPTER ELEVEN

# Euro-Dollar Deposits

## (1) A RIVAL TO LOMBARD STREET

HITHERTO we have been dealing with the London parallel money markets operating in terms of sterling. But parallel money markets in a financial centre need not all be for transactions in terms of the centre's local currency. Indeed, as we shall see in Volume 2 of this book, dealing with continental money markets, in several European financial centres the markets in Euro-currencies other than the currencies of the centres concerned are the only effective money markets in the real sense of the term.

Until the late 'fifties the development of a money market in London in terms of any currency other than sterling would have been considered inconceivable. In spite of sterling's frequently recurrent troubles between the two World Wars, culminating in the suspension of the gold standard, and again after the Second World War, the London money market where all transactions were of course in sterling remained without equal, owing to its unique technique. The New York money market was, however, gradually gaining ground in their rivalry for supremacy, owing to the increase of the relative prestige of the dollar as a much more dependable currency.

Even after the emergence of the Euro-dollar market in the late 'fifties the money markets in sterling continued to dominate the London financial scene for some time. During the early years of its existence the Euro-dollar market merely supplemented the facilities of the traditional money market in the international sphere, and its activities were considered to belong to the sphere of the foreign exchange market rather than to that of the money market.

It is true that at the beginning of the 'sixties the Euro-dollar market was often referred to as the merchant banks' money market, because it provided merchant banks with facilities to offset each other's surplus funds and deficiencies – a function which had been until then the monopoly of Lombard Street. Thus already at that stage the Euro-dollar market was beginning to be regarded as a parallel money market. But for years the outstanding amount of Euro-dollar deposits and the turnover in them was too small to constitute a serious challenge to the quasi-monopoly of Lombard Street. In any case the dollar denomination of the deposits introduced an element of complication that limited their use in the domestic sphere.

## (2) LONDON'S MOST IMPORTANT MONEY MARKET

Today the total amount of Euro-dollar deposits and the turnover in them in London is a multiple of the corresponding figures for the traditional market. Indeed the outstanding amount – though not necessarily the turnover – exceeded in 1969 the grand total of all the parallel money markets in London in which business is transacted in sterling. The expansion of the Euro-dollar market assumed a truly remarkable extent at the end of the 'sixties, even if the revaluation of the D. mark was followed by a setback at the close of 1969 and continued during 1970.

The London Euro-dollar market is beyond doubt the most important money market in London at the time of writing, and is likely to retain its supremacy in the long run, apart from any temporary setbacks. On the face of it, this is detrimental to London's prestige as a world financial centre, because the growth of the Euro-dollar market has been one of the major causes of the decline of sterling's importance as the leading international currency. But according to the new way of thinking, it is more important for Britain that financial business should be transacted in London than that it should be transacted in sterling. From this point of view there can be little doubt that the turnover in the London banking centre has increased to a much larger extent as a result of the expansion of the Euro-dollar market than it would have done if all the business had continued to be transacted in sterling, having regard to the decline in the international use of sterling which would have occurred even if no Euro-dollar market had come into existence.

## (3) HOW THE MARKET DEVELOPED

For a detailed history of the advent and expansion of the London market in Euro-dollars, its practices and techniques, its significance in various national and international spheres, and its theoretical implications, the reader must be referred to my *Euro-Dollar System – Practice and Theory of International Interest Rates* (4th edition), which brings the material up to date until the beginning of 1970. Euro-dollars have a very extensive literature. In this book we are only concerned with the role that the London Euro-dollar market plays as one of the parallel money markets of London.

Owing to the continued existence of exchange control which prevents U.K. residents from making free use of the facilities of the Euro-dollar market, it is primarily an international money market geographically situated in London, in the same way as the Euro-bond market is primarily an international capital market geographically situated in London. The difference is that British banks, or at any rate banks resident in the U.K., play a much more important part in operating the Euro-dollar market than they do in operating the Euro-bond market.

Before describing the relatively limited role the Euro-dollar market plays in the British money market and its incomparably more important role in the international money market, it is necessary to summarise briefly its evolution, its organisation, its essential characteristics, and the nature and technique of its operations. Although there had been many earlier instances of inter-bank dollar deposits, the beginning of systematic operations in inter-bank dollar deposits on any appreciable scale dates from 1957 when, for the sake of the reinforcement of British exchange control in defence of sterling, the granting of sterling acceptance credits for financing trade between non-sterling countries was banned. Much of the facilities essential for international trade continued to be provided by London accepting houses and by other London banks with the aid of dollar deposits borrowed for that purpose. The volume of such deposits increased considerably as a result of the restrictions placed by Regulation Q on the deposit rates American banks were permitted to pay. Central Banks and other foreign holders of dollars found it more advantageous to lend their dollars in the new market in London, which gradually came to attract American corporation deposits also.

## (4) THE MECHANISM OF THE MARKET

The organisation, operation and techniques of the Euro-dollar market are virtually identical with those of the inter-bank sterling market described in Chapter 6. (To be correct I should have said that the inter-bank sterling market is organised and operated on the same lines and applies the same techniques as the Euro-dollar market, since the latter preceded the former in chronological order and evolved the system later adopted by the inter-bank sterling market.) Business is transacted in large round amounts. The usual unit for Euro-dollar transactions is $1 million, but items of $500,000 and $250,000 are frequently encountered, and occasionally there are market transactions of the order of $100,000. On the other hand, transactions of $5 million and $10 million are not infrequent, and American branches have dealt at times in much larger single items – anything up to $100 million and even $150 million.

The average amounts of individual transactions between banks and their customers are of course smaller, but seldom less than $50,000, and they are usually in round amounts. Interest paid on deposits from outside the market – unless they are from one of the big international firms such as the oil companies which are in a position to obtain good rates – is distinctly lower than the rates quoted in the market for corresponding maturities. Lending rates to borrowers outside the market are correspondingly higher.

As in the inter-bank sterling market, some banks run books of graded maturities without having overall commitments in the form of an excess of total deposits lent over total deposits borrowed or *vice versa*. Others are not afraid of having net excesses of claims or liabilities in dollar deposits. Some banks never swap their borrowed deposits into any other currency, but others do so systematically.

Forward dealing in Euro-dollars, as in inter-bank sterling or in CDs or LA or finance house deposits, is confined to a small number of banks, but it is tending to increase in volume and complexity. It is likely to increase in importance during prolonged inactive periods when dealers have to find or invent new forms of activity.

Temporary setbacks apart, this market increased its turnover and the outstanding amount of deposits until 1969. Although the Euro-dollar market is not confined to London, the overwhelming majority of Euro-dollar business is transacted in the London market. This is partly because of the initiative taken by London banks in developing the market and the technical skill with which they operate money markets, but also because London is, and has always been, easily the most important market in dollars. Since a high proportion of Euro-dollar transactions is linked up with foreign exchange transactions this advantage has been of decisive importance in the achievement and maintenance of London's supremacy as the principal Euro-dollar market. The high reputation of the London banking community for soundness – there was not a single bank failure between 1919 and 1965 – continued to inspire confidence throughout the world even during the years when international confidence in sterling was declining fast.

### (5) MONEY MARKET OR FOREIGN EXCHANGE MARKET?

It is always difficult to adjudicate between the conflicting claims of various banks to have been first in the field. For a long time banks active in the market were reluctant to talk about it to the financial Press, for fear that publicity might induce the authorities to adopt measures to restrain its growth. But once the market emerged and its existence came to be increasingly recognised, practically all non-clearing banks came to take a hand in it. Some of the clearing banks began to operate at a relatively early stage through their affiliates, but one or two of them were slower off the mark than the rest. It was soon discovered that the new market had promising possibilities. It brought new accounts from abroad and attracted additional foreign exchange business and other banking business.

For a long time the Euro-dollar market was regarded as a branch of the London foreign exchange market, because its transactions were in terms of a foreign currency. Most London banks transacted their Euro-dollar and other Euro-currency business in their foreign exchange dealing rooms, with an increasing number of their dealers specialising in Euro-currency transactions. Foreign exchange brokers and not money brokers acted as intermediaries. It is true that some banks handled Euro-dollar transactions through their money market departments, especially American bank branches, for which Euro-dollar transactions were not foreign exchange transactions. But until the late 'sixties the foreign exchange aspects of the market overshadowed its money market aspects.

## (6) HOW BUSINESS IS TRANSACTED

Business is transacted in the same way as foreign exchange business or inter-bank sterling business – by telephone and teleprinter – but, while there is hardly any direct foreign exchange dealing between London banks, part of the Euro-dollar business is transacted direct between banks without the intermediary of brokers. This is probably largely because the lender of deposits always wants to know the borrower's name, so that brokers are not in a position to conceal the identity of the latter until the deal has been concluded, as they do in respect of foreign exchange transactions. Nevertheless, as in the case of inter-bank sterling and of the other parallel markets, most banks find the services of brokers useful, so that a high proportion of the Euro-dollar business is done through them.

As in other parallel markets, many banks specialise in certain types of transactions. Some of them aim at earning a narrow profit margin by operating in deposits with matched maturities without taking any risk. Others use the proceeds of borrowed deposits for financing international trade. It was largely for the sake of avoiding the loss of clients as a result of the ban on acceptance credits in 1957 that London accepting houses came to operate in Euro-dollars. Overseas banks use Euro-dollars mainly for financing trade with the countries or areas in which they specialise. Some banks prefer to deal in overnight deposits and in other short maturities, others specialise in long maturities – anything up to five years and even seven years. Transactions for such long maturities can seldom be covered immediately for the full period, so that there is a certain amount of risk involved in case of major changes in interest rates. There is ample scope for time arbitrage also in shorter deposits. All this is similar to corresponding operations in the inter-bank sterling market. Euro-dollars also provide an opportunity for speculative operations if the borrower sells the spot dollars without covering the forward dollars.

## (7) TIME ARBITRAGE

Time arbitrage often involves a speculative element, because banks borrowing short Euro-dollars against lending long Euro-dollars have no means of knowing for certain whether they will not have to renew their borrowing at higher rates. On the other hand, they have a chance of making a profit by being able to renew the deposits at lower rates. Since most of the time short deposit rates are lower than long deposit rates arbitrageurs may be able to make a profit even if the rate does not move in their favour by the time they have to renew the deposits they have borrowed. On the other hand, the dice are loaded against them if they lend short and borrow long. Such operations are undertaken either by dealers who have strong views about the prospects of an increase in Euro-dollar rates or by borrowers who want to ensure possession of large amounts for long periods – just in case it should be difficult or more costly to borrow later – but have no immediate use for the entire sum borrowed.

Such transactions of borrowing or lending long deposits against short deposits are liable to provide one of the connecting links between the foreign exchange aspects of Euro-dollars and their credit aspects. Facilities for such operations create a money market in which possessors of funds and would-be borrowers can offset each other's requirements. One of the two parties in the transactions may be an arbitrageur or a speculator while the other is a genuine lender or a borrower.

### (8) HOW THE BRITISH MONETARY SITUATION IS AFFECTED

Gradually the money market aspects of the Euro-dollar market – its role as a source of credit rather than as a sphere of foreign exchange arbitrage – gained prominence. To an increasing extent it came to be regarded as a channel through which banks – especially in the United States – could adjust their cash positions and liquidity positions, rather than a channel through which foreign exchange dealers could practise increasingly sophisticated types of arbitrage or speculation. From the very outset the new market had some implications that concerned not only the international money markets but indirectly even the domestic money market. Since Euro-dollar credits came to replace acceptance credits to a large degree, this induced accepting houses to increase their domestic acceptance credits to U.K. firms. The emergence of the Euro-dollar market contributed considerably, albeit indirectly, towards the expansion of the market for domestic trade bills in London during the late 'fifties and the early 'sixties. Such bills are well received in Lombard Street and are increasingly popular as a result of the decline of sterling bank acceptances originating from international trade and of the decline in Treasury bill allocations.

Another way in which the Euro-dollar system reacted on the British domestic monetary scene was through providing the means by which London branches of American banks financed the large and increasing number of branches and subsidiaries of American firms in the U.K. The use of Euro-dollars for that purpose increased considerably after President Johnson's guidelines directed American banks to finance foreign branches and affiliates of American firms by means of money raised abroad. At the same time the Bank of England discouraged the use of sterling credits for the financing of foreign branches or affiliates. Having regard to the almost continuous existence of some degree of credit squeeze in the 'sixties, this enabled London banks to increase facilities available for their British customers – or at any rate to avoid reducing those facilities – with the aid of sterling amounts formerly used for financing American firms in this country, which now came to be financed with the aid of Euro-dollars.

Merchant banks and other non-clearing banks came to make more use of the Euro-dollar market for increasing their liquidity on the eve of awkward dates and during tight periods in general. Borrowed Euro-dollars are outside the limits fixed by the Bank of England for the foreign exchange commitments of every authorised dealer in the U.K., and it was feasible to increase the resources of London banks by borrowing Euro-dollars and switching the deposits into sterling. It was also possible to invest the proceeds of such swaps into other parallel markets, such as the LA deposit market or the finance house deposit market. This was done on a very large scale at a time when the cost of the swap transaction was kept artificially low by systematic official support of forward sterling and when Local Authorities and finance houses were prepared to pay very high interest rates compared with those obtainable in other money markets in London or abroad.

It is true that Euro-dollars were not available for the financing of British domestic production and trade, because until the late 'sixties very few licences were issued for borrowing for purely domestic purposes. Even for financing British imports or exports it was necessary to obtain a licence from the Bank and until 1969 such licences were not very freely forthcoming. On the other hand, licences for insurance companies and other institutional investors came to be granted during the late 'sixties for the purpose of financing investments in foreign securities.

Taking this into consideration it is justifiable to regard the Euro-dollar market as a minor parallel market even from a domestic point of view. The Bank for International Settlements grossly understated the importance of the Euro-dollar market as a British money market when it said in one of its reports that it had barely had any impact on the British economy. To give only one instance, during the 'sixties a considerable part of British exports to Latin America was financed with the aid of borrowed Euro-dollars.

## (9) AN INTERNATIONAL MONEY MARKET

But the Euro-dollar market became from the very outset an overwhelmingly international money market. It came to be used increasingly for financing international transactions which did not concern the U.K. in any way, except that a high proportion of the Euro-dollar transactions was carried out by British banks. Even in that respect the balance of power was changing gradually during the late 'sixties as a result of the increase in the number of American and other foreign bank branches and of internationally owned banks in London. Although the volume of Euro-dollar business transacted by British banks and by British overseas banks continued to increase with the expansion of the market, their relative share in the turnover declined, especially after the 'invasion' of the City by American banks. The biggest of the American branches operated on a scale that overshadowed the activities of any British bank. In 1968–69 the grand total of their Euro-dollar transactions came to assume gigantic dimensions.

Even in earlier years American lending in the London Euro-dollar market gradually assumed considerable importance as and when U.S. corporations discovered the advantages of employing their liquid reserves in the Euro-dollar market, where they were able to earn much higher interest rates than they were allowed to earn under Regulation Q. This practice came to be discouraged under President Johnson's guidelines though it was not stopped altogether. But by 1968 American borrowing of Euro-dollars outweighed all other influences affecting the market. The credit squeeze in the United States and the prevention of American banks from attracting domestic deposits by paying high interest rates made it appear expedient for American banks, especially those with branches in London, to make increasing use of the Euro-dollar market for covering their requirements.

### (10) A BRANCH OF THE NEW YORK MONEY MARKET?

It may be said with very little exaggeration that by 1968–69 the London Euro-dollar market had become virtually a branch of the New York money market. At the earlier stages of its development it was a truly international market which served as a clearing house for dollar surpluses and requirements of banks and others all over the world. The interest rate that emerged from the conflicting currents of supply and demand in Euro-dollars was a truly international interest rate that differed considerably both from the local London interest rate and from the local New York interest rate.

But owing to the large size of American borrowing, and to the extent to which its size was influenced by the monetary policy measures of the United States authorities and by changing trends in the New York market, the Euro-dollar market became an overwhelmingly American money market. The relative extent to which non-American influences affected its trends became greatly reduced. Although geographically the market remained in London in reality it might as well have been in Wall Street, but for the discrepancy between business hours on the two sides of the Atlantic. Even that discrepancy is now tending to disappear. American branches keep in touch with their head offices until the New York market closes at 10 p.m. London time. Several British banks, too, keep a senior dealer on duty while New York is open, and there is a small but increasing volume of dealing in Euro-dollars between 4 p.m. and 10 p.m. London time. This practice is liable to spread, and a stage might be reached some time at which London and New York would become virtually the same market.

### (11) IMPACT OF AMERICAN BORROWING

The main reason why so many American banks opened branches in London in the late 'sixties is that they felt the need to gain direct access to the London Euro-dollar market. Of course American banks can place orders with their London correspondents for borrowing or lending Euro-dollar deposits. But during hectic periods, and even during calm periods when the spreads are narrow, direct access has distinct advantages. On the other hand, the idea that large-scale borrowing of Euro-dollars in London tends to mitigate the credit squeeze is fallacious. It is based on the widespread belief that Euro-dollars are dollars that are somehow physically held in Europe, so that by borrowing them American banks are in a position to increase not only their own liquid assets but also the total liquid assets of the entire American banking system.

The truth is that Euro-dollars are in no way different from ordinary dollars. They must be dollars held on deposit in the United States, with a bank resident in the United States. It is true that they are owned or held by depositors resident outside the United States. But if such a depositor lends his deposit, whether to a resident in the United States or to someone resident outside the United States, or if he spends it on goods or uses it to repay a debt, the dollars remain in the United States and are merely transferred from the lender's account to the borrower's account – or, in the case of purchases or debt repayments, from the debtor's account to the creditor's account – whether with the same American bank or with some other American bank. The total of American deposits held by the American banking system as a whole remains unaffected.

This means that when an American bank borrows Euro-dollars in London all that happens is that it increases its own deposits at the expense of some other American bank. Those with direct access to the Euro-dollar market are in a better position to siphon off the deposits of other American banks than those without direct access to the London market. The main object of the presence of at least some of the new American branches in London is not so much to increase their deposits at the expense of other American banks as to prevent other American banks from siphoning off their deposits. When Regulation Q prevented them from competing for big deposits in the domestic field, they competed for them in the Euro-dollar market. Those who are successful in attracting large amounts of Euro-dollars because they have a branch in London and because their names are taken for large amounts are able to increase their resources and their capacity to lend to their clients. But the volume of deposits and credits in the United States as a whole remains substantially unaffected, even though banks which lose deposits as a result of Euro-dollar borrowing by their rivals may be able to avoid having to cut credits to the full extent of their losses through a fuller use of their resources.

The extent to which the Euro-dollar market has become a parallel market of the New York money market as well as of the London money market is indicated by the size of the transactions in Euro-dollars carried out by American branches. As observed above, before their advent transactions over $10 million were exceptional and the rates for such amounts were a matter of negotiation. In 1969 items of $100 million are known to have changed hands on a number of occasions, and I have even heard of higher amounts.

## (12) FINANCING SPECULATION AND INVESTMENT

Another way in which the Euro-dollar market fulfils its functions as a parallel money market in the international sphere has been by providing credit facilities for speculative purposes. Speculation in gold was financed almost entirely with the aid of Euro-dollars. The greater part of the flight into D. marks in 1968–69 in anticipation of the German revaluation was financed with the aid of borrowed Euro-dollars which were sold against D. marks. Oddly enough even a reversal of this flight from Euro-dollars into D. marks caused a demand for Euro-dollars – this time by German banks which, having lost large amounts of foreign deposits, were seeking to improve their liquidity by borrowing Euro-dollars after the D. mark revaluation had turned out to be not nearly as large as the rise prior to revaluation.

Although there has been no major dollar scare since the spectacular growth of the Euro-dollar market during the second half of 1968 and in 1969 it seems certain that its expansion would greatly increase the difficulties of the United States authorities in defending the dollar, should a major dollar scare occur. Many billions of Euro-dollars would be borrowed for the purpose of going short in dollars by selling the proceeds of the deposits.

International investment, too, was financed largely with the aid of borrowed Euro-dollars. The Euro-bond market benefited by it in more than one way. Issuing syndicates which had to take up the bonds they were unable to place with investors immediately financed them by borrowing Euro-dollars. Many investors subscribed or bought Euro-bonds by similar means. This explains why the sharp rise in Euro-dollar rates in 1969 brought about a sharp setback in new Euro-bond issues and caused a decline in the secondary market.

Long Euro-dollar deposits compete with short Euro-bonds. Euro-dollar rates influence Euro-bond issue terms and yields in the secondary market, and they actually determine the interest rate of bonds with flexible interest rates which are adapted to Euro-dollar rates every six months.

A high proportion of the Euro-dollars attracted to the market by the high rates continued to be borrowed by American banks after the revaluation of the D. mark, even though the total declined after the revaluation and especially after the mitigation of the credit squeeze in the United States. A fact which is not generally realised is that Euro-dollars which are borrowed by American banks are owed by the United States twice over. Even if the banks repaid these deposits most of them would still remain deposits owned by residents outside the United States. This is what happened in 1969–71 when a large proportion of the Euro-dollars borrowed earlier by American banks came to be repaid. The extent of such repayments became a major factor in the London market.

## (13) HIGH INTEREST RATES

Meanwhile London – and to a much less extent other financial centres dealing actively in Euro-dollars – has a gigantic parallel market in dollars which overshadows the markets in local currencies. Until 1970 Euro-dollar rates were high in spite of the function of forward margins in bridging the gap between interest rates. At the time of writing the Euro-dollar market is even larger than the market in forward dollars, so that the latter is liable to adapt itself to the former to a larger extent than the former is liable to be influenced by the latter.

The mechanism of the Euro-dollar market is the same as that of the other parallel markets. There is no meeting place for dealers and brokers. All business is transacted by telephone, or with overseas centres by long-distance calls or by teleprinter. Even in continental financial centres which have a meeting place for foreign exchange transactions for certain limited purposes no Euro-dollar or other Euro-currency business is transacted there.

The Euro-dollar market is confined to inter-bank dealing. We saw in Chapter 7 that there is a certain amount of inter-corporation dealing in inter-bank sterling, but there is no such dealing in Euro-dollars in London, except perhaps between affiliates and branches belonging to the same combine. But non-banking depositors of Euro-dollars may deal with market operators either directly or through brokers.

## (14) MANIFOLD ACTIVITIES

As pointed out earlier, many banks specialise in particular types of Euro-dollar transactions. They may aim at matching the maturities of deposits borrowed and lent and they never conclude a deal unless they can undo the resulting commitment simultaneously. Others are not quite so conservative and job in and out of the market for the sake of a quick return, but take care not to have open commitments for any length of time. Others again speculate on prospective changes in Euro-dollar rates and borrow long deposits against short deposits or *vice versa*. Some banks swap the proceeds of Euro-dollar deposits into sterling or into some other currency. Others again employ most of the deposits for financing their clients. The growing number of American branches and affiliates in the U.K. largely finance affiliates of American corporations. They might even poach on the preserves of U.K. banks by granting credits to U.K. firms. This is all the easier when the credit squeeze prevents U.K. banks from satisfying the full requirements of their clients. The credit ceilings fixed by the Bank of England for new American branches are very low, but they only affect sterling credits. American banks are always in a position to borrow Euro-dollars and switch them into sterling to lend the proceeds to U.K. clients. The British authorities welcomed such transactions during the period of adverse balance of payments because they tended to increase the official dollar reserves or assisted the authorities in the repayment of foreign credits contracted between 1964 and 1969. Even U.K. firms were permitted to borrow in foreign currencies. But in 1971 the improvement of the balance of payments induced the authorities to check such borrowing except for periods of at least five years.

Owing to its large turnover, the London Euro-dollar market is able to quote fine rates and is usually able to absorb very large transactions without their producing an unduly marked effect on rates. For this reason among others, London often acts as intermediary between other Euro-dollar markets, absorbing their surpluses and covering their deficiencies. Heavy commitments assumed by dealers in other Euro-dollar markets are likely to be undone in London, in the same way as in the foreign exchange market, which can easily absorb large-scale buying or selling of dollars from other centres.

### (15) IS THERE A LENDER OF LAST RESORT?

We saw in Chapter 6 that the inter-bank sterling market is at a grave disadvantage because it has no lender of last resort. Technically the position is the same in respect of the Euro-dollar market because, as far as the Bank of England is concerned, it is left to its own devices. Only on major occasions is there official intervention in the form of operations by the Bank for International Settlements, usually on the initiative of the Federal Reserve. Unlike the Bank of England in the traditional money market, the B.I.S. cannot be depended upon by dealers to mop up surpluses or cover deficiencies, unless this happens to be in accordance with its policy. Thus when the Federal Reserve wanted to check a rise in Euro-dollar rates it provided the B.I.S. with the means for lending Euro-dollars.

But the London branches of American banks can always depend on their head offices in an emergency, and their head offices can fall back upon the Federal Reserve, so that in practice the Euro-dollar market is not exposed to the caprices of changing trends to the same extent as the inter-bank sterling market.

During inactive periods the spread between buying and selling rates allows for a very narrow profit margin for banks, especially if the transaction is concluded through the intermediary of brokers. But banks with a large clientèle outside the market are often able to 'marry' two orders from customers without having to undo the commitment in the market. It is such transactions that are the most profitable without involving much risk unless there is a time lag.

### (16) LIMITS FOR NAME

The difficulties arising from the possibility of refusal of certain names and from the existence of limits for all names were discussed in detail in Chapter 6. The only difference in this respect between Euro-dollar and inter-bank sterling transactions is that in respect of the former there may be some degree of delivery risk that does not exist in respect of inter-bank sterling deposits which are payable and repayable in London. The lender of Euro-dollars has to depend on the borrower for the repayment of the deposit on maturity in New York and it is a bad habit of many American banks to delay repayment till the very last minute. This means that if the depositor is depending on the repayment of his deposit for meeting a maturing liability of his own, he may not receive his dollars in time to complete the repayment on the same day. For this reason dealers in Euro-dollars – as indeed do foreign dealers in dollars – have to keep a substantial unprofitable balance with their New York correspondents to meet a payment which might not be met in time out of the proceeds of the payment of maturing Euro-dollar deposits that are due to be received. Some banks aim to avoid lending too large amounts of Euro-dollars which mature on the same day, just in case their current account balances might not be sufficient to bridge an awkward gap that might be caused by last-minute repayment of their deposits.

Transactions with foreign clients are often concluded through the intermediary of international brokers. There are a number of such brokers in Germany, in Switzerland, in France and other continental countries. It often happens that the ultimate borrower and the ultimate lender are residents in the same country, but the latter prefers to borrow through the intermediary of a London bank for the sake of the additional security of repayment.

## (17) TECHNIQUE OF EURO-DOLLAR DEALING

While in respect of dollar CDs interest is reckoned on the basis of a 360-day year, in respect of Euro-dollar deposits transacted in London according to the British practice a 365-day year is applied.

As soon as a transaction has been concluded both parties send a confirmatory note, the borrower instructing the lender to pay the amount of the deposit to the New York bank named by him. The lender cables to his New York correspondent instructing it to make the payment to that bank. The borrower also notifies his correspondent that such a payment is to be expected on such and such a date. If the deal is concluded through a broker the latter confirms it by sending copies of the contract to both parties. If it is done directly the parties exchange contracts.

All dealings in Euro-dollars and in other Euro-currencies are spot transactions unless otherwise stipulated. The deals have to be implemented by both parties on the third clear day after their conclusion. But it is possible to stipulate delivery on the same day ('value today') or delivery on the following clear day ('value tomorrow' or whichever day the next clear day happens to be). Arrangements for delivery of the dollars later than on the third clear day are not unusual, up to seven days.

## (18) FORWARD TRANSACTIONS

There is a certain amount of activity for longer periods, but the turnover is not sufficiently large for rates to be quoted as a matter of routine, and each transaction is a matter for negotiation. A lender of Euro-dollars for two months to be delivered in, say, one month covers himself against the risk of an increase in the Euro-dollar rate during that month by a long–short transaction. He can easily borrow Euro-dollars for, say, three months and re-lend them for one. He thus gains possession of the dollars in a month's time and can deliver them to the borrower of forward dollars. The latter repays the deposit two months later, enabling the lender to repay the deposit he borrowed for three months.

Such forward-forward transactions are becoming more frequent and it is now even possible to arrange them in a single transaction instead of having to arrange them in two separate transactions. Such operations are apt to be costly, however, for the party that takes the initiative, as they are rather involved and not many dealers and brokers are engaged in providing the counterparts, so that competition in the form of quoting fine rates is not very keen. It is keener, however, than in the narrower inter-bank sterling forward market.

As mentioned earlier, business in Euro-dollars is transacted in large amounts. The standard amount between big banks is $1 million, so that if a dealer, in response to a quotation, answers 'I take three' it means that he is borrowing $3 million at the rate quoted.

Many active dealers in Euro-dollars who run books of graded maturities are authorised by their managements to create and maintain discrepancies between the maturities of deposits borrowed and lent, so long as the total of deposits borrowed and lent is equal. Profit margins in a highly sophisticated market such as the Euro-dollar market are usually narrow unless dealers are prepared to take a risk on changes in interest rates. There are of course much wider profit margins in transactions with outside customers.

From the very outset I predicted an expansion of the Euro-dollar market and I am convinced that its long-term prospects favour continued expansion, even if it was interrupted in 1969. American influence on the volume and trend of the turnover and on interest rates, having become firmly established, is likely to remain, although from time to time other influences are likely to assert themselves. The market is likely to be increasingly sophisticated and before many years it will be possible to carry out forward-forward transactions as a matter of routine with long–short swap rates regularly quoted. The market in long maturities is also likely to improve.

All this presupposes the continued absence of major crises. Like all other money markets, the future of the Euro-dollar market depends on the maintenance of confidence. Major failures might cause a sharp setback but they would only interrupt its expansion temporarily.

# CHAPTER TWELVE

# Other Euro-Currency Deposits

## (1) LONDON'S LIMITED SHARE

COMPARED with the Euro-dollar market in London, the markets in other Euro-currencies, whether in London or in continental centres, are of modest dimensions. Nevertheless, a book on parallel money markets in London would not be complete without containing a brief chapter on these markets. Apart from other reasons, it is quite conceivable that the market in one or other of the Euro-currencies might expand considerably some day.

Of the estimated total Euro-currencies of $45,000 m. in 1969 $37,500 m. constituted Euro-dollars according to the B.I.S. The bulk of the remaining $7,500 m. of other Euro-currencies – mainly Euro-sterling, Euro-Swiss francs, Euro-D. marks and Euro-guilders – is divided mostly between the markets of London, Paris, Frankfurt, Zürich and the other Swiss markets, Amsterdam and Brussels. London's share in them is not likely to be more than between $1,000 million and $2,000 million, probably much nearer to the lower figure. For this reason, London is not nearly as good a market in any of these Euro-currencies as in Euro-dollars.

Nevertheless, owing to the low interest rates that prevailed in Switzerland and in Germany until 1969, and even more to the measures adopted by the Swiss and German Governments to discourage the influx of foreign money, the London market came to be used to a fairly large extent for dealing in both Euro-Swiss francs and in Euro-D. marks. The market in the latter became particularly active during the flight to the D. mark in 1968 and again in 1969, but owing to the expectations of a revaluation it was at times difficult to find borrowers in D. marks, and D. mark deposits offered in London only found takers at very low rates.

## (2) D. MARKS, SWISS FRANCS AND FRENCH FRANCS

After the revaluation conditions became more normal and next to the Euro-dollar market the market in Euro-D. marks became the most important Euro-currency market in London. Deposits of 10 and 20 million D. marks change hands as a matter of routine, but it is possible to find counterparts for much larger amounts. The market is very active on some days. The standard amount in which business is transacted is 5 million D. marks. There is dealing in smaller amounts, but the standard rate quoted applies to 5 million D. marks or over. For smaller deposits less favourable rates are allowed to lenders and higher rates are quoted to borrowers.

The same rule applies to Euro-Swiss francs, which have a fairly active market in London. The standard amount is 5 million, but dealing is possible in amounts from 1 million. Much of the foreign moneys that seek refuge in Switzerland and whose owners prefer to hold Swiss francs is re-lent by the Swiss banks in London.

An active market developed in Euro-French francs early in 1968 after the removal of exchange control by the French Government. But this market proved to be short-lived, because the troubles in May and June 1968 compelled the Government to reimpose exchange restrictions. They were relaxed, however, in July 1970. Although at the time of writing the market in London is small, the relaxation of controls opens up interesting possibilities for its expansion and also for the expansion of the Euro-currency market in Paris.

Euro-guilders have a fair market, the standard amount being 5 million. There was at one time a fairly active forward-forward market in all Euro-currencies, but the uncertainty of interest rate prospects discouraged it, so that now such transactions, though possible, are few and far between.

Interest arbitrage also created a regular if limited market in other Euro-currencies. The interest parities on which dealers operate in their arbitrage transactions are those relating to the various Euro-currencies. From time to time it becomes profitable for U.K. residents to borrow in one of the Euro-currencies other than Euro-dollars. Licences authorising them to do so were fairly freely forthcoming during 1969. In particular, borrowing in D. marks became popular after their revaluation.

## (3) LIMITED MARKET IN EURO-STERLING

There is also a very limited volume of dealing in London in Euro-sterling, even though most of it is transacted in Paris, Zürich and Frankfurt. The term is an absurdity, considering that London and the rest of the U.K. forms part of Europe, so that all sterling is, literally speaking, Euro-sterling unless it is held by residents outside Europe. The same is of course true for other Euro-currencies other than Euro-dollars. What is meant by 'Euro-sterling' is sterling held by residents outside the U.K. and the Sterling Area, not necessarily within Europe, and re-lent in the Euro-sterling deposit market. Since the term is generally accepted we may as well use it for want of a better.

London banks are not permitted to deal in Euro-sterling. They may hold Euro-sterling deposits on account of non-residents and may execute the latter's instructions about transferring these deposits to other non-resident accounts or to resident accounts. If they are transferred to non-resident accounts they retain their original status and can be converted into foreign currencies. The borrowers are entitled to re-lend the deposits. If they are transferred to a resident account they assume the status of ordinary resident sterling for the duration of the deposit.

London brokers are authorised to act as intermediaries between two non-resident holders of Euro-sterling. For this reason many non-residents lend or borrow their Euro-sterling deposits through the intermediary of London brokers. U.K. banks are not entitled to perform that function, so that the London market is confined to the transactions concluded between non-residents by London brokers. The bulk of the transactions in Euro-sterling take place in continental financial centres. Euro-sterling markets in those centres will be dealt with in Volume 2 dealing with parallel money markets outside Britain.

A number of clearing banks, merchant banks and overseas banks with head offices in London have branches or affiliates outside the Sterling Area and the sterling deposits of these branches with their parent institutions have the status of non-resident sterling for the purposes of exchange control. Likewise the sterling balances of foreign banks with their London branches or affiliates are non-resident sterling. It is at times difficult to draw a rigid dividing line between transactions in such balances in London or in other centres.

Moreover, there is nothing to prevent U.K. banks from quoting simultaneously a Euro-currency rate and a swap and deposit rate for the conversion of the Euro-currencies into sterling. This is in substance if not in form equivalent to quoting a Euro-sterling rate. But since it is a form of interest arbitrage it belongs to the sphere of the foreign exchange market rather than to that of the money market.

# CHAPTER THIRTEEN

# Dollar Certificates of Deposits

## (1) EMERGENCE OF THE MARKET IN THE UNITED STATES

ONE of the reasons why the creation of a market in dollar CDs in London was an important development from the point of view of London's position as a multiple money market was that it prepared the way for the development of a market in sterling CDs, dealt with in Chapter 8. Such a market might have developed in any case sooner or later, but it would have been later rather than sooner – indeed probably much later – had it not been for the example of the London dollar CD market and the experience gained from it. London dollar CDs assisted in the adoption of sterling CDs both by making London banks realise the advantages they could gain through issuing CDs and by enabling them to acquire the necessary specialised know-how which could be applied later to issuing sterling CDs and to creating a market for them.

Of course there could not have been a London market in dollar CDs – at any rate not in the middle 'sixties – if it had not been for the prior development and spectacular expansion of a market in CDs in the United States. This, together with the development and expansion of the Euro-dollar market in London, paved the way for the issue of CDs in London, first in terms of dollars only and later also in terms of sterling. The major institutional change represented by the emergence of the dollar market in CDs in America will be dealt with in detail in Volume 2 of this book, describing parallel money markets in New York and other centres. Between them, the Euro-dollar market initiated in Britain by British banks and the CD market in the United States initiated by American banks made it possible for American banks and later also for British and foreign banks in London to create an important market in London in dollar CDs.

The adoption of the device of CDs created a money market of first-rate importance in the United States at the beginning of the 'sixties, almost simultaneously with the creation of another money market of first-rate importance through the gradual expansion of the market in inter-bank dollar deposits in London and, to a much less extent, in other financial centres outside the United States. The main object of American banks in issuing marketable CDs and in organising a secondary market in them in New York was to attract more time deposits by enabling depositors to regain possession of their money if and when they should want it before the deposit matures. The same reason why this appeared to be advantageous both for depositors and for takers of deposits in the United States seemed to be perfectly valid also in respect of dollar deposits outside the United States. But it took a number of years before the emergence of the Euro-dollar market in London and of CDs in New York was followed by the advent of dollar CDs in London.

## (2) HOW REGULATION Q HELPED

Long before the development of the inter-bank market in dollar deposits in London, banks in London and in other centres outside the United States readily accepted time deposits in terms of dollars. But depositors, like those resident in the United States, had to renounce the use of their dollars for a definite period. With the development of the Euro-dollar market their number increased, and so presumably did the average size of individual time deposits. Their maturities tended to be longer, anything up to five years by the middle 'sixties. This made it all the more important to apply to dollar deposits of non-residents in the United States the solution successfully applied to those of depositors resident in the United States.

There was an additional reason. Regulation Q did not apply to non-resident depositors of dollar deposits held by banks outside the United States. In view of the advantages to these banks in obtaining time deposits for longer periods, they were prepared to pay much higher rates for such deposits than those permitted under Regulation Q, especially for long maturities.

## (3) ADVANTAGES OF CERTIFICATES

Euro-dollar rates were most of the time higher for long periods than for short periods. It was tempting for holders of liquid funds who did not expect that they would require their money for some time, and who did not expect a rise in interest rates, to take advantage of the higher long-term Euro-dollar deposit rates. On the other hand, those who were not certain that they would not require their funds at any moment or were undecided about the probable trend of interest rates, needed facilities which would give them the best of both worlds. They wanted high yields on deposits without relinquishing their right to regain possession of their money for a period of years. Indeed they wanted to be able to get their money back at any time whenever they needed it or whenever they changed their opinion about the prospects of interest rates.

For holders of dollar deposits who were not resident in the United States there was the additional consideration that they might want to realise their holdings if they expected a depreciation of the dollar. Admittedly that problem was capable of solution by means of a forward exchange transaction – selling forward the amount of their dollars, to be delivered on the date when the deposit matured. But in situations in which many holders would deem it to their advantage to resort to that solution they would only be able to sell their forward dollars at a costly discount. Moreover, it would not safeguard holders against the possibility of exchange restrictions which might prevent the sale of their dollars – a risk which, however remote it may appear at the time of writing, could not be ignored altogether. A widespread anticipation of that contingency would not prevent the sale of spot dollars but would greatly increase the cost of selling dollar deposits for forward delivery.

We saw in Chapter 8 that the solution of the problem by means of option clauses under which holders of time deposits are entitled to reclaim their money at any time after a certain date, raises as many problems as it solves. There is also the formula of the penalty clauses under which it would be possible to recover the funds in return for a pre-arranged charge to be deducted from the deposit. This has never been popular and has not been adopted on a large scale. Both formulas have their disadvantages and neither banks nor depositors in general have ever been very keen on them. Penalty clauses are concessions which are usually only available for favoured clients and their terms have usually to be negotiated on each occasion. One of the great advantages of the Euro-dollar market is the speed with which business can be transacted as a matter of routine, which would be impossible if clumsy and cumbersome clauses had to be negotiated. Moreover, from the banks' point of view, widespread application of penalty clauses, and to some extent also of option clauses, would deprive them of the main advantage of time deposits, which is to ensure possession of the dollars for definite periods.

Yet another reason why the application of the CD system to the Euro-dollar market was bound to come sooner or later was the unduly large size of individual transactions in the Euro-dollar market from the point of view of all but the biggest non-banking depositors. The standard amount is $1,000,000 and there are few transactions under $250,000. Rates for smaller amounts are a matter for negotiation between banker and client, and they are usually distinctly less favourable to depositors, precisely because one of the objects of the Euro-dollar market or of any other inter-bank deposit market is the segregation of wholesale banking from retail banking.

## (4) SOLUTION OF THE PROBLEMS

The answer to all these problems was the issue of London dollar Certificates of Deposits. Dollar CDs issued in the United States could not solve the problem: the CDs had to be issued in the U.K. They enabled depositors to regain possession of their dollars by selling their certificates in the secondary market at any moment at current market rates. As a result, their dollar CDs could be treated as liquid assets. It also enabled them to obtain deposit rates on medium-sized deposits which were only slightly lower than the current Euro-dollar rates quoted solely for the benefit of large deposits. Thus they could get the best – or nearly the best – of both worlds. They could benefit by higher long-term rates without being firmly committed to tying down their deposits for the full period. They could benefit by relatively high deposit rates that had hitherto been the privilege of large depositors.

During the late 'sixties interest rates in the United States rose above the deposit rates which banks were permitted to pay on time deposits under Regulation Q. The advantage of issuing dollar CDs in London bearing interest rates in accordance with prevailing market conditions then became evident. Although American residents were able to obtain in other New York markets higher rates than those American bankers were permitted to pay on deposits under Regulation Q, if they preferred to keep their money in the form of marketable deposits they were able, in given circumstances, to acquire London dollar CDs. The institution was adopted primarily for the benefit of the depositors outside the United States. Under President Johnson's guidelines residents were not supposed to export capital. There were, however, means for evading this restriction, and it is believed to have been evaded on an extensive scale.

## (5) DEVELOPMENT OF THE LONDON MARKET

The device of London dollar CDs was first adopted in 1966 and soon most American bank branches in London came to apply it. British and other non-American banks, too, came to issue such CDs. The Bank of England adopted a very liberal attitude towards the new device, in accordance with its policy favouring the expansion of the Euro-dollar market in London. Any bank, British or non-British, provided that it was an authorised dealer in foreign exchanges, was able to obtain a licence for the issue of dollar CDs. In fact a number of licences were issued, though many banks did not make actual use of their rights, or only made use of them sparingly. At the time of writing, the number of banks liable to issue dollar CDs is about 100. But in given circumstances the number of banks actually issuing them is liable to increase.

Limitations on dealing in dollar CDs arising from British exchange restrictions are identical with those applied to dealings in Euro-dollar deposits. There are no restrictions whatever on non-residents acquiring dollar CDs issued in London, with the aid of dollars or other foreign currencies or with the aid of sterling on external account. Which means that banks in the U.K. are able to acquire them against payment with the aid of Euro-sterling held on account of non-resident clients.

From a fiscal point of view dollar CDs are favourably treated. Holders of certificates can receive their interest free of any U.K. withholding tax for maturities up to five years. This is the result of a new fiscal concession granted specially for the benefit of London dollar CDs in 1968, even though later it came to be applied also to sterling CDs as we saw in Chapter 8. Until 1968 interest on dollar CDs for maturities exceeding 364 days had to be deducted at source, as it still has to be deducted for ordinary Euro-dollar deposits and for deposits of every kind. This virtually prevented the acquisition of medium-term CDs by non-residents. We saw in Chapter 8 that the need for non-residents to reclaim income tax involves considerable inconvenience, delay, uncertainty and loss of interest. The removal of this disincentive to demand for medium-term deposits was a great victory for common sense.

## (6) RESTRICTIONS ON U.K. RESIDENTS' HOLDINGS

U.K. residents are not permitted to acquire dollar CDs, unless they are authorised foreign exchange dealers, who can acquire them in the same way as they can acquire Euro-dollar deposits. To some extent discount houses are in a position to acquire dollar CDs and finance them with the aid of borrowed Euro-dollar deposits. This concession was granted to enable discount houses to participate in the creation of the market in dollar CDs.

Of course U.K. residents are theoretically in a position to acquire dollar CDs with the aid of investment dollars and might actually do so if the premium on investment dollars should ever disappear or become reduced to a sufficient extent to make the transaction profitable. If dollar CDs are bought with investment dollars and are re-sold before maturity the proceeds, and also the interest earned on them after the last interest date, are treated as investment dollars. But if they are held to maturity the interest is treated as ordinary dollars held by U.K. residents. This is just another of the inconsistencies in the British exchange regulations which are so difficult to explain. Any future changes in U.K. or U.S.A. exchange control regulations would apply probably to all dollar CDs already in circulation.

As a result of the restrictions on the acquisition of dollar CDs by U.K. residents the issue of dollar CDs could not increase pressure on sterling and could not even tend to widen the premium on investment dollars. There was therefore no reason for the Bank of England to discourage the new device, not even in the difficult year of 1968 when exchange control had to be tightened in some respect in order to defend sterling at its devalued rate.

Beyond doubt the choice of London for the issue of dollar CDs has increased London's importance as an international financial centre, which largely explains the benevolent attitude of the authorities towards the adoption of the new device. It must have contributed to some extent to the escalation of the 'invasion' of London by American bank branches, even if the main reason was the desire of gaining direct access to the London Euro-dollar market.

## (7) METHOD OF ISSUES

London dollar CDs are issued in multiples of $1,000 with a minimum of $25,000, though some banks fix the minimum at a higher figure. For medium-term deposits the minimum is fixed by some banks at $100,000. A great many certificates of between $25,000 and $100,000 are in circulation, and units of $500,000 and $1,000,000 are also frequent. Certificates for much larger amounts are also known to have been issued. The standard maturities are 30, 60, 90 and 180 days, one year and two years, though certificates for other maturities are also issued at the depositors' request. Most banks are willing to replace the certificates originally issued by certificates of smaller amounts, provided that each is a multiple of $1,000 and not less than $25,000.

Short-term dollar CDs are due to be delivered on the third clear business day, but it is possible to obtain delivery on the same day or next day under special arrangement. Delivery of medium-term CDs is normally in four days. Medium-term CDs are sometimes issued through special placement and quotation on the Stock Exchange is arranged. Such CDs can also be transacted in the secondary market, in the same way as CDs issued to dealers in that market or direct to depositors.

Certificates are issued against the payment of their dollar amount in clearing house funds in New York to the bank in the United States prescribed by the issuing bank – in the case of London branches of American banks to their head offices, in the case of other London banks to one of their New York correspondents. Payment is for value on the same date on which the CD is issued. When the issuing bank receives advice that the payment has been effected it issues the certificate to the bank prescribed by the depositor or to some other authorised depositary. Frequently the certificates are kept on deposit with the issuing bank itself.

On maturity the deposits are repaid in New York, upon the surrender of the certificates to the issuing bank in London. Repayment in clearing house funds is for value on the same day on which the CD is presented in London. All payments of interest and principal are made to a bank nominated by the depositor. Dealers in the secondary market make no charges for these services. Certificates are bearer certificates and change hands without endorsement. Under exchange control regulations they must be held by an authorised depositary.

## (8) LEGAL POSITION

Neither the issuing bank nor the depositor is subject to any U.K. tax for deposits up to five years unless the depositor is a U.K. resident, in which case the interest is subject to income tax, but this is not deducted at source. If the certificates are physically held in the U.K. at the time of the holder's death they are treated as part of his U.K. estate for the purpose of death duties. For this reason certificates of non-residents are often deposited abroad. The certificates are not subject to any U.S. taxes unless holders are citizens of the U.S. or are resident in the U.S.

It is made clear in the text of the certificates that the obligations they represent are subject to the laws of the U.K. This provision might become important to non-resident holders in the unlikely event of the adoption of new British exchange control measures that forbade the repayment of these dollar liabilities to non-residents. The ban would then apply in theory to CDs issued by London branches of American banks in the same way as to those issued by other London banks, although in practice the head offices of the American banks would be in a position to pay to holders should they wish to do so.

London dollar CDs do not come under the provisions of Regulation Q which effectively prevent American banks from issuing in the United States CDs at rates above those fixed by that Regulation. Nor do they come under the provisions of Federal Deposit Insurance. Usually the CDs are issued at par, but they can be issued at a discount instead of interest being paid.

## (9) THE PRIMARY MARKET

In the primary market interest rates are fixed every morning in the same way as sterling CD interest rates are fixed, as described in Chapter 8. There is no cartel among issuing banks, the market is entirely competitive. Some banks are in the habit of maintaining for some time the rates they have fixed in the morning in their dealings with customers outside the market – at any rate on quiet days when rates do not fluctuate unduly – so as to give less sophisticated clients who are not used to following market fluctuations closely the chance to decide whether to accept the terms. Other banks whose clients are more sophisticated, or which deal mainly within the market, change their rates in accordance with the fluctuation of Euro-dollar rates for the corresponding maturities. But the differentials between Euro-dollar rates and dollar CD rates are also subject to fluctuation according to the specific requirements of the issuing banks for particular maturities and according to whether or not they are keen to increase their issues.

In inter-bank transactions the issuing bank is not bound by the rate it quotes unless this is accepted by the depositing bank immediately. For maturities up to twelve months there are usually regular quotations readily obtainable but the rate for longer maturities is a matter for negotiation. On hectic days the spread between buying and selling rates is apt to be widened to such an extent that each deal is in practice a matter for negotiation. While interest on sterling CDs is reckoned in accordance with British practice on the basis of a 365-day year, interest on dollar CDs is reckoned in accordance with American practice on the basis of a 360-day year.

Quotations on the secondary market discount dollar CDs to maturity in the same way as they do sterling CDs, allowing for the addition of interest on various interest dates. This means that if the current interest rates on which the quotations are based are higher than the CD interest rate the price paid is below the CDs' nominal amount, while if current rates are lower, the price paid is above the CDs' nominal amount – allowing for the difference between interest deducted in advance and interest paid subsequently.

## (10) HOW INTEREST RATES ARE FIXED

Very generally speaking, interest rates on dollar CDs tend to be about $\frac{1}{8}$ per cent below the current Euro-dollar rates for corresponding maturities. This is justified by the deposits' advantage of marketability. The differentials tend to vary, however, in accordance with the supply–demand relationship, and they tend to widen for longer maturities. Neither of these textbook rules apply in all circumstances. Towards the close of 1969 and during part of 1970 the expectation of a general fall in interest rates tended to lower rates for longer maturities, and for a time in

April 1970 dollar CD rates were actually somewhat higher than the rates for Euro-dollar deposits for corresponding maturities.

Rates at which various banks issue CDs need not be uniform at any given moment. If a bank finds that it has lent too large an amount of Euro-dollars it may find it convenient to re-borrow some of it by issuing dollar CDs rather than borrowing in the Euro-dollar market. To that end it would narrow the differential to attract demand for CDs. Conversely, if it has borrowed too much in the Euro-dollar market it may find it more convenient to dis-courage demand for its dollar CDs by widening the differentials.

Apart from the factors applying to dollar CDs specifically, their rates in the primary market are subject to all the influences affecting interest rates in general, whether seasonal, technical, or fundamental. Issuing banks are keen to issue CDs on Thursdays and Fridays owing to the high yield on Federal Funds in New York on those days, and also on the eve of window-dressing dates. For such purposes the differential may be temporarily reduced. In normal conditions it may be said to fluctuate broadly between $\frac{1}{16}$ and $\frac{3}{16}$ per cent.

### (ii) THE SECONDARY MARKET

Learning from the lesson taught by the initial failure of the first attempt to issue CDs in the United States – failure caused by the lack of an adequate secondary market – the American banks and other banks issuing London dollar CDs made arrangements with a number of financial houses to act as dealers in the certificates. In the absence of such arrangements it might have taken too long for a natural secondary market to develop on its own initiative. But the existence of houses of importance which were willing from the very outset to buy and hold certificates gave depositors the necessary degree of assurance that they would have no difficulty in disposing of their dollar CDs at rates that would follow the current Euro-dollar rates reasonably closely.

The houses operating in the secondary market play a part similar to the one in the secondary market for sterling CDs described in Chapter 8. Dealers may buy dollar CDs for various maturities either from issuing banks or from the market or from depositors outside the market or from abroad, and hold them in their portfolios in order to be able to meet demand for particular maturities by would-be depositors. They are willing buyers of

CDs from depositors wanting to recover possession of their money, though the degree of their willingness affects the buying rates they quote. It depends on the amount there is already in their portfolios; on the maturity date for which they may or may not want to increase their holdings; on the liquid resources that are available or can be made available profitably; and last but not least on the amount of CDs of the individual issuing banks concerned that they already hold. Each house has a maximum limit for each name. To the extent to which dollar CDs have to be financed with sterling resources or credits the dealer's willingness to buy is also influenced by the view he takes on the dollar rate and on the cost of, or profit on, covering the exchange risk.

A number of bill brokers and foreign exchange brokers were given permission by the Bank of England to act as brokers in dollar CDs. Banks, too, are active operators in the secondary market, dealing either directly with each other or with dealers, or through brokers, or directly with their customers. As in respect of sterling CDs, it is a self-imposed rule that they do not buy back their own CDs. Some banks do not buy CDs issued by rival banks because in doing so they would tend to lower the rate at which their rivals can issue new CDs. But what is even more important is that if banks buy medium-term CDs from their rivals they make it easier for the latter to grant medium-term credits to their customers. As a result they might lose business, or they might have to concede lower interest rates.

## (12) TECHNIQUE OF OPERATIONS

The technique of operations in dollar CDs is similar in most respects to the technique of operations in sterling CDs. An essential difference is that while sterling CDs are always delivered on the same day on which the deal is concluded, in the absence of arrangements to the contrary dollar CDs, as we saw above, are treated as foreign exchange in the same way as Euro-dollars, and are delivered on the third clear business day following the transaction. An even more important difference pointed out above is that payment for dollar CDs has to be made in clearing house funds in New York.

As in the secondary market for sterling CDs, the spread between buying and selling rates quoted varies between $\frac{1}{8}$ and $\frac{3}{16}$ for maturities up to twelve months and fluctuates around $\frac{1}{4}$ or over for longer maturities. Fluctuations in the secondary market are influenced by the same factors as those in the primary market. Foremost among these factors are the fluctuations of Euro-dollar rates, which also affect sterling CD rates but not to a corresponding extent. Once removed, the fluctuations of interest rates in New York are of considerable importance, namely through their effect on Euro-dollar rates.

## (13) DEMAND FOR CERTIFICATES

There is a larger demand by non-residents for dollar CDs than for sterling CDs. The former are more attractive investments for Middle East oil millionaires and such-like. Their demands run into millions in a single transaction and if the bank receiving such large deposits covers itself by re-lending the amount received either in the Euro-dollar market or in the secondary market for dollar CDs, the bank that sells to it the CDs or the Euro-dollar deposits has no means of knowing whether this is purely a market transaction or the undoing of a commitment entered into outside the market. In addition to the Middle East, Switzerland is a frequent buyer of dollar CDs, the Swiss banks usually acting for their foreign customers. But generally speaking it is true to say that a very high proportion of the dollar CDs never leaves the London market, no matter how often it may change hands within the market.

There is a certain amount of forward-forward dealing in dollar CDs as in sterling CDs. There are operations of short dollar CDs against long Euro-dollar deposits or *vice versa*. But there is no regular market in such involved transactions, and the rates are always a matter for negotiation. Highly sophisticated dealers and brokers even engage in borrowing dollar CDs against lending inter-bank sterling, or in borrowing sterling CDs against lending Euro-dollars, etc.

Although the volume of dollar CDs rose to about $4,000 million in less than four years, in many quarters this progress is considered disappointing because a more spectacular expansion had been expected. But once the existing ban on the acquisition of London dollar CDs by American residents is removed there is bound to be an accelerated expansion in the demand for them. The Bank for International Settlements is believed to have held a certain amount acquired in connection with its intervention – especially in 1969 –

to keep down the sharply rising Euro-dollar rates. Central Banks hold most of their dollar reserves in U.S. Treasury bills, but some of them are believed to hold dollar CDs also.

The issues of dollar CDs, like those of sterling CDs, have to be declared by issuing banks in the weekly returns they submit to the Bank of England. Houses in the secondary market, too, have to enter their turnover in dollar CDs in their weekly returns. The grand totals of the amounts outstanding at the end of each quarter are published in the *Bank of England Quarterly Bulletin*. The Bank of England is watching the position closely in order to discourage any excessive issuing by individual banks or by the issuing banks as a whole. But just as its concern about Euro-dollars is believed to be less acute than its concern about inter-bank sterling, so its concern about dollar CDs is assumed to be less acute than that about sterling CDs.

# CHAPTER FOURTEEN

# Dollar Commercial Paper

## (1) A NEW MARKET

THE latest of the parallel money markets is the London market in dollar commercial paper – that is, in promissory notes bearing one signature only. There has been for many years a similar market in New York in which promissory notes of high-class industrial firms and finance paper by bank affiliates or bank holding companies are placed and dealt in. The outstanding total was estimated at nearly $40 million in 1970. In London it was until recently a firmly established rule that any credit instrument, in order to be marketable, must bear two signatures. Promissory notes played an active part in transactions between banks and their customers, or between business firms, but there was no inter-bank market in them and they were not eligible as securities against loans.

In June 1970 a leading London merchant banking firm in collaboration with the London branch of a New York issuing house initiated the issue of commercial paper for several leading American industrial firms. This was done with the consent of the British and American authorities. The declared purpose of the transactions is to provide funds for the American firms to finance their operations outside the United States. The commercial papers issued in London are in dollar denominations, but they will not be sold to U.S. residents. The minimum unit amount is $50,000. They are called Euro-commercial paper, or briefly ECP.

These ECPs are for maturities of three months and six months. The initial issue was $15 million for three leading American corporations with extensive international connections. The issuing financial houses have undertaken to provide a secondary market for them. They were issued at a rate $\frac{1}{4}$ per cent above the rates for London dollar CDs for corresponding maturities. A number of other London issuing houses and American firms wanting to borrow are likely to follow this lead. It is expected that the new market will assume considerable dimensions if and when the deeply rooted prejudice of the London market against one-name paper can be overcome. Conceivably by the time this book appears the market will have a turnover running into hundreds of millions of dollars.

## (2) PROSPECT OF STERLING COMMERCIAL PAPER

There is no reason to suppose that the new facilities will be reserved for American borrowers alone. First-rate firms all over the world will be in a position to benefit by them. Even U.K. firms, provided that they obtain licences, will be able to borrow, especially for the requirements of their external financing, once the ban on short-term and medium-term borrowing in foreign currencies is removed.

Nor is there any reason to assume that the commercial paper market will necessarily remain confined to issues in terms of dollars. Just as the Euro-dollar market was followed by the emergence of the inter-bank sterling market and the London dollar CD market was followed by the emergence of the sterling CD market, the dollar ECP market is likely to be followed sooner or later by the emergence of a sterling ECP market.

This would be contrary to all tradition, but in recent years we have witnessed many changes which were considered inconceivable until they actually materialised. The argument in favour of sterling commercial papers is that, even though they have only one signature, they are in no way less secure than a bank overdraft, which, unless guaranteed, also depends on the solvency of one debtor. So long as the notes are issued by first-class industrial and commercial firms they are probably self-liquidating to the same extent as overdrafts. If they should come to be issued by bank affiliates or holding companies as in the United States they would be finance papers, but they would not be any less secure than inter-bank deposits or CDs.

# CHAPTER FIFTEEN

# Inter-relations Between Parallel Markets

## (1) PARALLEL MARKETS ARE NOT REALLY PARALLEL

As we pointed out in the introductory chapter, the collective term 'parallel money markets' under which the new money markets discussed in this book have come to be known is strictly speaking a misnomer. 'Parallel' is a geometrical term and the geometrical definition is lines which never meet and which may continue indefinitely without coming into contact with each other. But rates quoted in parallel markets are seldom precisely equidistant from each other for any length of time. The differentials between interest rates for the same maturities in various 'parallel markets' are liable to fluctuate, albeit within a narrow range in normal conditions.

However, 'parallel money markets' is the best term we have, better than 'multiple money market', and it is near enough to economic reality to be acceptable notwithstanding any conceivable purist objections to its use. After all, economics is not geometry, even though mathematical economists pretend that it is and are doing their best to convert it into just that. Even if differentials between rates quoted in the various parallel money markets are not rigidly fixed, they tend to remain steady although they are subject to changes, and even in between changes they oscillate.

## (2) BASIC INFLUENCES AND SPECIAL INFLUENCES

To a very large degree rates in parallel money markets react to the same influences in the same way, even if not necessarily to exactly the same extent. They are apt to diverge from their parallel lines by departing from each other and converging towards each other. This is partly because they react differently to the same general influences and partly because each market is subject to special influences. Indeed once in a while their lines actually cross – rates of sterling CDs, for instance, which are normally lower than inter-bank deposit rates, rose for a short time above them in April 1970.

Major influences are liable to affect the whole structure of interest rates quoted in London, in traditional markets and parallel markets alike. They all respond to changes in the Bank rate, to major changes in the international trend of interest rates as represented by Euro-dollar rates, to devaluations or revaluations of important currencies, to sharp movements of the forward margins of sterling, etc. But the rates in the various markets do not necessarily respond to these influences to exactly the same extent, and occasionally they do not even respond to approximately the same extent. Differences in the degree of respective responses are liable to arise even within the same markets, in which rates for different maturities are apt to be affected to a different degree.

### (3) MARKETS IN DOLLAR DEPOSITS

Of course the response is apt to be quite different in the parallel markets in deposits in dollar denominations, and in the lesser markets in various other Euro-currencies. They are all subject to world trends. But if a world trend is caused by a flight from or to a particular currency then rates in the Euro-market in that currency may react in the opposite direction to those quoted in other parallel markets.

For instance, when there was a flight into D. marks in anticipation of the German revaluation in 1969, the flood of Euro-D. marks offered in London and other Euro-currency markets, as a result of German steps to discourage the influx, reduced their rate, while the rate of Euro-dollars rose sharply because of heavy borrowing for the purpose of switching them into D. marks. But even in the absence of such abnormal pressures the difference between trends in the domestic money markets of various currencies is apt to affect their quotations in the Euro-markets to a varying degree. In the case of the dollar the extent of the influence of money rates in New York on Euro-dollar rates in London is very considerable, even though the influence is reciprocal.

### (4) IMPACT OF SWAP RATES

In theory Euro-dollar rates should not affect interest rates in parallel money markets dealing in sterling deposits. For changes in interest parities resulting from changes in Euro-dollar rates are supposed to be offset by corresponding adjustments of forward margins. But this oversimplified version of the theory of interest parities of forward exchange does not allow for the multiplicity of interest parities. There can only be one swap rate between two currencies for the same maturity at any given moment, so that the swap rate can only adapt itself to one particular interest parity. In the 'fifties the parity that mattered from the point of view of arbitrage was the one between U.K. and U.S. Treasury bill rates. Since the early 'sixties it has been the parities between Euro-dollar and Euro-sterling rates that have tended to be the equilibrium rate towards which the swap sterling–dollar rates for various maturities have tended to gravitate. Any discrepancy between those parities and the actual swap rates has given rise to arbitrage operations which readjust the swap rates to their Euro-dollar–Euro-sterling interest parities. Or, as is very frequently the case, it readjusts Euro-sterling rates to Euro-dollar rates, allowing for the swap margin.

But since rates in the various parallel money markets are different from Euro-sterling rates, the discrepancies tend to give rise to arbitrage. For instance, since LA deposit rates are usually higher than Euro-sterling rates, when the sterling–dollar swap rate is at its interest parities between Euro-sterling and Euro-dollars it is profitable to engage in inward arbitrage by switching from Euro-dollars into sterling and employ the sterling in the LA deposit market.

## (5) INFLUENCE OF FEDERAL FUNDS MARKET

Simultaneously it may be profitable to engage in outward arbitrage by switching from sterling into dollars on certain days of the week to take advantage of the high rates in the New York market for Federal Funds, the rates in which market are well above Euro-dollar rates. We propose to return to this subject in Volume 2 in the chapter on Federal Funds. It is mentioned here briefly to indicate one of the reasons why rates in parallel market deposits in foreign currency denominations are apt to diverge from their parallel lines with rates in markets for deposits in sterling denominations.

There is undoubtedly a tendency for rates in various parallel markets to oscillate around standard differentials between the rates for identical maturities. Those differentials are apt to vary over a period of time, and even at any given moment they are subject to influences that are liable to move them from what are regarded as the standard differentials at that particular moment. After all, each market is subject to a set of special influences affecting the supply–demand relationship, and a single large transaction for a particular date is liable to cause the differentials to change, at any rate for a few minutes until time arbitrage removes the differential by restoring the rate for the maturity concerned to the yield curve.

## (6) INFLUENCE OF INTER-BANK STERLING MARKET

Among the parallel markets in deposits in sterling denominations the inter-bank sterling market is the most important, and its rates influence those of other parallel markets to a considerable degree. We saw in the chapters dealing with the other parallel markets that the opening rates in them are largely determined by the opening rates in the inter-bank market. All brokers, dealers of banks, discount houses and finance houses, and Municipal treasurers take their cue from the opening inter-bank sterling rates in deciding on the rates they are to quote for sterling CDs, LA deposits and finance house deposits. Apart from other reasons, the purchase of such deposits is to a very large extent financed by deposits borrowed in the inter-bank sterling market, and lenders in that market compare the interest rates they obtain with those obtainable in the alternative markets. Tight conditions in the inter-bank sterling market react on rates in the other markets, though not necessarily to the exact extent to which they affect the inter-bank sterling rates. We saw earlier that when in the spring of 1970 the rates for overnight inter-bank deposits rose to 35 per cent the rates for overnight LA deposits only rose to 18 per cent.

There is of course a particularly close relationship between the inter-bank sterling market and the market for sterling CDs. As far as the primary market is concerned the direct link is confined to maturities of at least three months. But changes in shorter inter-bank sterling rates are also liable to influence indirectly CD rates for three months and for much longer maturities, because probably as often as not acquisitions of CDs are not financed by inter-bank deposits for offsetting maturities but by inter-bank deposits for shorter maturities. To the extent to which buyers of CDs want to buy them against inter-bank deposits for offsetting maturities, and sellers of CDs want to employ the proceeds in the inter-bank market in deposits for offsetting maturities, CD rates depend very considerably in both the primary and the secondary market on inter-bank deposit rates for corresponding maturities.

### (7) NON-TRANSFERABILITY OF LA AND FINANCE HOUSE DEPOSITS

Relationships between the inter-bank deposit market and the markets for LA deposits and finance house deposits are not quite so close, because those deposits have no secondary markets. This means that while an increase in the differentials tends to attract funds from the inter-bank deposit market to the markets in LA deposits and in finance house deposits, a reduction of the differential cannot induce holders of fixed deposits with Local Authorities or finance houses to switch immediately into the inter-bank market, unless they are overnight deposits or deposits at call. Otherwise depositors have to wait until their deposits mature. They can of course give notice for deposits subject to notice, but the pattern of interest rates is liable to change even during the two days which is the shortest notice that is required in order to regain possession of the deposits.

Even so, owing to the large size of the outstanding amount of LA and finance house deposits, substantial amounts mature every day, so that their owners are in a position to switch into inter-bank deposits if they consider the differential inadequate. And CDs can be bought for forward delivery for the period of the notice that is required for the recovery of moneys lent to Local Authorities or finance houses.

### (8) EFFECT OF DIFFERENTIALS

Needless to say, if LA and finance house deposits were transferable, so that there could be a secondary market in them, the extent to which the impact they have on the inter-bank sterling market and *vice versa* is reciprocal would be considerably greater. As it is, while a widening of differentials is liable in normal circumstances to bring about an immediate flow of funds from the inter-bank market to the LA and finance house deposit markets, when the differential becomes narrower it tends to take a little longer before a reflux of funds to the inter-bank market restores them to their standard figures.

The importance of this point should not be exaggerated, however. For very often the differentials do not change for the whole range of maturities, only for certain maturities, as a result of some substantial transactions for those particular maturities, whose amounts, however, may be but an insignificant fraction of the grand total of LA and finance house deposits maturing on that particular day. A large proportion of the amount of funds released from the two markets on that day may be reinvested in sterling CDs for the maturities concerned if their differential in relation to inter-bank rates for the particular maturities becomes narrower compared with the standard differential in relation to LA and finance house deposit rates.

If the amount involved is relatively large, the change in the differentials in relation to the LA and finance house deposit rates is liable to spread over a wide range of maturities, as a result of time arbitrage. In any case the material and psychological effect of the discrepancies on CD rates for the corresponding range of maturities might in given circumstances affect inter-bank deposit rates for those maturities through the operation of the tendency towards restoring standard differentials between CD rates and inter-bank deposit rates. But persistent pressure is liable to alter the standard differentials themselves.

## (9) WHEN THE TAIL WAGS THE DOG

It is true that the volume of transactions in inter-bank deposits is much larger than the volume of transactions in sterling CDs, so that the chances are that the effect triggered off in the market in CDs by a distortion of differentials originating in the LA and finance house deposit markets on inter-bank rates will be negligible, if perceptible at all. But on inactive days, or on days when the inter-bank rate is very sensitive, the tail is liable to wag the dog.

Any noteworthy specific rise in CD rates that widens the differentials is liable to attract funds from maturing LA and finance house deposits. Such a rise is apt to occur if, for instance, some of the larger issuing banks expand their CD issues. If smaller banks tried to borrow heavily by such methods the rates for their CDs would rise above the standard rates and if this aroused distrust it might discourage the demand for their CDs even at higher rates. But if banks such as affiliates of clearing banks which are absolutely above suspicion increase their issues substantially – as two of them did in the spring of 1970 – the resulting rise in their CD rates tends to set the pace for an all-round rise in CD rates in consequence of the increase in the total supply of CDs. In given circumstances this might raise CD rates to par, or even above par, with inter-bank rates. The differential between them and LA and finance house deposit rates would then narrow and the result would be a flow of funds to the market in CDs not only from the inter-bank market but also from the LA and finance house deposit markets as and when LA and finance house deposits could be withdrawn.

### (10) ARBITRAGE BETWEEN PARALLEL MARKETS

There is very keen arbitrage between the various parallel markets. Scores of dealers and brokers are always on the lookout for discrepancies between standard differentials and actual differentials. They are not slow in taking advantage of such discrepancies, so that in normal conditions their operations restore the rates to the close vicinity of their standard differentials in a very short time.

Differentials between LA deposit rates or finance house deposit rates and CD rates are apt to be influenced by seasonal and other specific influences affecting the first two. Having no secondary markets, they are more exposed to such specific influences. Differentials between sterling and dollar CDs are subject to the interplay of differentials between Euro-dollar and inter-bank sterling rates with sterling–dollar swap rates.

# CHAPTER SIXTEEN

# The Volume of credit

## (1) EFFECT OF PARALLEL MARKETS

HAVING described in some detail the individual parallel money markets that have come into existence in London, our next task is to examine some of the broader implications of their existence and of their expansion. Foremost among the problems to be examined is the effect of their emergence and expansion, both actual and potential, on the volume of credit facilities available to industry and trade, and the extent to which any credit expansion resulting from the operation of the new system makes for inflation or is liable to make for inflation.

In this inquiry we must distinguish between the effects of the parallel money markets amidst conditions created by credit restrictions and their normal effects in the absence of credit restrictions. We shall have to try to answer the following questions:

1. How far is the availability of credit facilities in various parallel markets affected by credit restrictions?
2. Does the provision of additional credit facilities by these markets result in an overall increase of credit facilities for industry and trade or does it merely result in a re-allocation of credit facilities while leaving their grand total substantially unchanged?
3. To the extent to which the new system increases total credit facilities, does this tend to produce an inflationary effect in existing circumstances?
4. Would the operation of the parallel money markets tend to produce an inflationary effect after the removal of credit restrictions?

The answers to the above questions are apt to differ in respect of the various parallel markets. Generalisations which are sometimes encountered are liable to be misleading.

## (2) INTER-BANK DEPOSITS AND CREDIT RESTRICTIONS

In examining the operation of parallel markets under credit restrictions I do not include under that term the restrictive effects of orthodox measures such as the operation of statutory or traditional reserve ratios, liquidity ratios, etc., which exist in some form in every country. We are only concerned here with measures that are referred to at times as quantitative restrictions, such as credit ceilings, increases in reserve requirements, special deposits, hire-purchase credit restrictions, selective credit restrictions, etc.

The expansion in the volume of inter-bank deposits does add to the grand total of credit facilities. While deposits with clearing banks remained more or less stationary during 1966–69, deposits with non-clearing banks approximately trebled. This does not mean that while non-clearing banks were forging ahead clearing banks stagnated. For the heading 'non-clearing banks' includes affiliates of clearing banks which had their full share in the expansion of credit through the operation of the parallel markets in general and of the inter-bank deposit market in particular.

The expansion of non-clearing bank deposits with U.K. banks in recent years gives a vague idea of the extent to which the operation of the inter-bank market has assisted in the increase of credit facilities at their disposal, although I must repeat my earlier warning that it is unsafe to rely on these figures as an indicator of the extent of the expansion of inter-bank deposits. It is also necessary to stress – and it cannot be stressed sufficiently – that there is an essential difference between deposits lent and re-lent over and over again within the market and deposits lent outside the market. More will be said later about this aspect of the subject.

To the extent to which higher rates obtainable on inter-bank sterling deposits – or, for that matter, deposits in any of the parallel markets – attract foreign deposits, they undoubtedly tend to increase the volume of credit. But if this is contrary to official policy the authorities are in a position to mop up the additional funds in the traditional market or to reinforce credit restrictions. Above all, they are normally in a position to discourage any unwanted influx of foreign funds.

### (3) INFLUX OF FOREIGN DEPOSITS

Sterling CDs tend to attract additional deposits to non-clearing banks. Even though a large part of these deposits is diverted from inter-bank deposits or from ordinary deposits, the banking system as a whole is also liable to benefit to the extent to which CDs attract deposits from abroad or from investments in securities by the public sector. The markets in LA deposits and in other Local Authorities issues, too, attract additional deposits from abroad. Apart from the direct effect of the additional credits thus made available, the beneficial effect of such an influx of capital on sterling – as indeed of similar imports of capital induced by other parallel markets – enables the Government to relax the credit squeeze.

The market in finance house deposits is prevented from producing its full effect on the volume of credits not only by the special credit restrictions imposed on finance house borrowing but also by the measures to keep down the demand for instalment credits as a result of hire-purchase restrictions.

The Euro-dollar market and the market in dollar CDs tends to increase credit facilities to the extent to which funds are switched from dollars into sterling through interest arbitrage, and especially to the extent to which U.K. residents are permitted to borrow in terms of foreign currencies.

### (4) RE-ALLOCATION OF CREDIT FACILITIES

To the extent to which inter-bank deposits and other resources of the parallel market remain within the market their expansion is not handicapped by credit limits if they can only be raised at the rate of, say, 5 per cent. Because of these limits the increase in the liquid resources of a bank through borrowing in a parallel market does not by itself enable it to increase its lendings to industry and trade, or personal credits, if the amount of those lendings has approached the authorised limits.

It is true that clearing banks may transfer some of their customers to their affiliates, so that more resources become available within the credit limits to the customers they have retained. But the affiliates, too, are subject to credit limitations. The way in which borrowing in the inter-bank market tends to increase the volume of bank lendings outside the market is mainly through providing additional liquid resources to banks which have not reached their

ceiling but are short of liquid resources. In circumstances prevailing at the time of writing this effect may be moderate, but in
different circumstances it might become important.

The operation of the parallel markets does tend to cause a
re-allocation of credit facilities. It has increased the resources of
the non-clearing banks both in absolute terms and in relative
terms and since they are, generally speaking, not concerned with
personal loans or loans to small firms, the trend is towards a
re-allocation of credit facilities in favour of large borrowers. It also
tends to divert banking resources from the private sector to the
public sector, inasmuch as LA deposits lent to Municipalities
do not come under the credit ceiling. Banks with liquid resources to spare but which have reached their ceiling for lending
to the private sector gladly employ their resources profitably by
lending them to Municipalities. The market for finance house
deposits tends to attract funds for financing hire-purchase business but, as already pointed out, the ceiling imposed on such
lending and the limitations imposed on hire-purchase transactions
handicap the expansion of this form of credit.

## (5) EFFECT ON NON-CLEARING BANKS

Non-clearing banks benefit by the operation of the inter-bank
market and the markets in CDs, and also by the expansion of the
Euro-dollar market, because of the increase in their relative
importance compared with clearing banks. As they are more
willing to take risks than clearing banks, the result of their
expansion is that more risk-capital has become available. It
benefits larger business firms dealing with non-clearing banks.
Many of them are in need of medium-term credit facilities which
have become more easily available thanks to the availability of
offsetting medium-term inter-bank deposits and Euro-dollar
deposits for banks and to their facilities for issuing medium-term
sterling and dollar CDs. Although the extent to which the volume
of medium-term CDs is increasing is disappointingly slow they
have considerable potential. It may be said without hesitation
that the parallel money markets are very helpful, actually or
potentially, from the point of view of the growth of capital goods
industries depending largely on medium-term credits.

The easier availability of medium-term credits reduces the
requirements of business firms for long-term capital, which was

hitherto virtually the only alternative to depending on their banks to renew their short-term loans again and again.

## (6) HOW SMALL CUSTOMERS BENEFIT

It may be suggested that the types of borrowers that are liable to suffer by the segregation of wholesale banking from retail banking are private customers and small business firms, for whom the parallel money markets do not cater. But even these types of borrowers might benefit indirectly to the extent to which clearing banks relinquish big customers in favour of their affiliates, so that more of their own resources become available for their smaller customers.

So long as the credit restrictions that exist at the time of writing continue to exist, and if and when they are restored at any time in the future, the extent to which parallel money markets actually produce an inflationary effect will remain moderate. But given the high degree of employment and its effect on the balance of power between employers and employees, even a moderate additional dose of inflation is liable to produce a disproportionately substantial effect on wage demands. Moreover, the illusion of easier availability of credit in various forms is liable to exert a psychological influence on the attitudes of bankers, producers, merchants, employees and consumers alike. The operation of the parallel money markets and their rapid expansion conveys the impression that the credit squeeze need not be taken too seriously, and it is perhaps this psychological effect which is largely responsible for the inadequate extent to which the credit squeeze has been effective in checking inflation.

## (7) EFFECT AFTER RELAXATION OF THE CREDIT SQUEEZE

As soon as credit restrictions are relaxed the material effect of the expansion of parallel money markets, in addition to the increase in its psychological effect, will tend to step up inflationary expansion. It may appear at first sight that the rule about conventional liquidity ratios would then be the only restraining influence on the increase in the volume of credit as a result of increasing borrowing through the parallel markets, and that the Bank of England's control over the volume of credit would then weaken considerably. This is, however, a mistaken notion. For the Bank would remain in a position to control the overall volume of lendings by banks to customers by means of orthodox devices. It can mop up surplus funds in the traditional markets to an extent that would react on the parallel markets. It can reduce the volume of liquid assets available to banks, thereby preventing them from expanding credit without reducing their liquidity ratio below the conventional minimum.

In any case the banks themselves are likely to practise self-restraint by abstaining from financing borrowers of doubtful standing or firms which are obviously over-trading. It is true that the fact that banks are now in a position to borrow in the inter-bank market without any security or for any purpose whatsoever might conceivably tend to relax their resistance to temptations to over-lend. In theory such over-lending tends to carry its own penalty through grievous losses as a result of failures. But so long as the inflationary trend continues important business failures leading to bank failures are likely to be relatively few, for in most cases amidst the increasing demand and increasing profits the penalty for bad judgement will only be smaller profits and slower turnover. So long as this state of affairs continues, in the absence of strict credit control at least by orthodox means the self-discipline exercised by sound banks may not be sufficient to offset the inflationary effect of the lack of self-discipline exercised by less sound banks.

## (8) TRADITIONAL CREDIT CONTROL

It is difficult to form a very definite opinion about the extent to which discipline imposed from above would be effective after the removal of credit restrictions. It is true that before the war credit control applied by the Bank was virtually watertight. Sometime in the 'twenties McKenna, who was then chairman of the Midland Bank, told me that his bank would be unable to grant a credit of £100,000 even to a customer who could put up Gilt-edged securities to the value of £200,000. But then at that time there were no parallel money markets. Of course it is risky to theorise about the extent to which these markets would merely mean an increase in the lending capacity of some banks at the expense of a more or less corresponding reduction in the lending capacity of other banks, and to which, in the absence of restrictions, there would be a net increase. Only practical experience could provide a reliable answer.

One thing may safely be taken for granted. In so far as in the absence of credit restrictions the expansion of the parallel markets would produce an inflationary effect, the relaxation of those restrictions will be slowed down and their removal delayed. Their existence, and their rapid development during the late 'sixties, increases the risks attached to the return to freedom – in the sense of confining restrictive policies to the conventional devices.

## (9) MODERATE INFLATIONARY EFFECT

Meanwhile some parallel markets actually make for credit expansion that contributes to some extent to the inflationary trend prevailing at the time of writing. The inter-corporation deposit market, described in Chapter 7, enables business firms to circumvent the credit ceiling by lending to each other their liquid surpluses. So far this practice has not developed to any considerable extent, but the possibility of its expansion is there, especially if banks are willing to guarantee the deposits lent by one corporation to another. The inflationary character of this practice is enhanced by the fact that the banking system as a whole need not lose the deposits lent by one of their customers to another of their customers. The transaction which provides the borrowing business firm with additional financial resources does not reduce the volume of deposits held by banks, for it merely transfers the deposits from one account to another. Banks may continue to lend to their credit ceilings, so that the amount of inter-corporation deposits is additional to the volume allowed under the credit ceilings.

At present the total of such deposits is moderate, so that it does not constitute a problem. But a prolonged credit squeeze is likely to increase the amount considerably. And once the practice is well established it is likely to continue even after the removal of credit restrictions. If a firm were unable to obtain bank credit owing to the orthodox limitation of lending resulting from liquidity requirements, it would be able to resort to the device developed during the period of credit ceilings. To that extent the Bank of England's control over the volume would be circumvented – unless the Bank applied the orthodox devices on a large enough scale to offset the credit expansion resulting from inter-corporation deposit transactions by reducing the banks' liquid resources.

## (10) CREDIT SQUEEZE CIRCUMVENTED

But the credit squeeze was circumvented up to 1971 on a large and increasing scale with the knowledge and approval of the authorities, with the aid of money borrowed through the largest of the parallel markets – the Euro-dollar market. The borrowing of dollars or other foreign currencies is only possible for U.K. residents if the Bank grants them a licence. Such licences were forthcoming in large numbers during 1969–70, even though the restrictions on forward covering of the exchange risk tended to reduce the extent of borrowing in terms of revaluation-prone currencies. The authorities were no doubt aware that by granting licences on a large scale the effect of their credit squeeze was neutralised to that extent. In this respect the policy pursued by the British authorities was similar to the one pursued by the United States authorities (criticised in Chapter 11), permitting large-scale borrowing of Euro-dollars by American banks and thereby reducing the effect of the restraints on credit. In both instances the misgivings of those concerned with the supply of credit were overruled by those primarily concerned with the size of the foreign exchange reserve and of the external short-term debts.

What both authorities seem to have failed to realise is that the relaxation of the credit squeeze through borrowing abroad is bound to affect the balance of payments unfavourably. In Britain this effect was not evident, because the escalation of inflation abroad enabled her to achieve an export surplus. But the United States was less favourably placed in this respect.

The parallel money markets had enabled Britain to attract foreign funds, thereby converting official external short-term debts into private external short-term debts. They had also enabled the Government to relax the credit squeeze to some extent, or at any rate to abstain from reinforcing it.

The basic policy that determines the extent to which the inflationary effects of the parallel money markets are likely to be prevented is the policy under which a high degree of employment must be maintained regardless of cost. So long as this principle is upheld – and there is no reason to expect its abandonment – it will remain necessary for the Government of the day to turn a blind eye towards a certain degree of inflation, necessitated by the increased requirements for credit to finance the greatly increased wage payments in addition to financing economic growth. Rigid resistance to expansion of credit would force employers to resist excessive wage demands for lack of increased credit facilities to finance the higher costs, in so far as it would become difficult to pass these on to consumers in the form of higher prices. So while the Labour Government went through the gestures of upholding strict credit squeeze they tolerated the circumvention of that squeeze with the aid of parallel money market facilities.

In January 1971 the Conservative Government, in an effort to make the credit squeeze more effective, greatly reduced the extent to which U.K. residents were permitted to borrow short-term and medium-term Euro-currencies. The repayment of the outstanding Euro-currency debts as and when they matured tended to reduce the volume of credits.

# CHAPTER SEVENTEEN

# Velocity of Deposits

### (1) TRANSACTIONS VELOCITY

IN the last chapter, dealing with the way in which the emergence and expansion of parallel markets tends to affect, or is liable to affect in different circumstances, the volume of credit, it was pointed out that apart from an increase in its volume, they might produce an expansionary effect through an increase in the velocity of credit. Such is the importance of this aspect of the subject that it calls for more detailed examination.

In his book on *Deposit Velocity and its Significance*, published by the Federal Reserve Bank of New York in 1959, Mr George Gary states that one of the most important facets of economic analysis is the rate of spending from monetary balances. For a varying volume of monetary spending may be supported by a constant stock of money, while, on the other hand, a change in the money supply need not necessarily change the volume of spending. The explanation of this paradox lies in changes in the velocity of deposits. 'Transactions velocity', Mr Gary states, 'is an important element in assessing changes in the credit situation and in business conditions.'

Although his analysis is confined to payments made with the aid of demand deposits – in Britain mainly current account balances – his analysis could be applied with certain reservations to time deposits, even though they must be converted into current account balances before they can be spent. Many economists other than those of the Money School doubtless share his view that changes in the rate of deposit turnover may be as important for monetary policy as the quantity of money itself.

### (2) TIME DEPOSITS ARE POTENTIAL MONEY

Time deposits are excluded by most analysists from their calculations of money supply, on the ground that they must be converted into actual money before they can be spent. Even so they are potential money which can easily be converted into cash, for a high proportion of time deposits matures every day. The concept of graded liquidity, introduced by the Radcliffe Report, has not yet become an integral part of the corpus of monetary theory, or, for that matter, of the guiding principle of monetary policy. Most of those concerned with the subject can still only think of liquidity in terms of black and white and disregard the various shades of grey between the two extremes.

Even from a strictly purist point of view, a very high proportion of deposits traded in the parallel money markets may safely be included among demand deposits. There is in practice very little difference between current account balances and overnight inter-bank deposits or inter-bank deposits at call. But some economists would draw the line at including under money supply even money at call lent by banks in the discount market, even though the borrowing and discounting facilities of discount houses with the Bank of England ensure beyond any shadow of doubt that such deposits can be converted into cash at any time during normal banking hours. As for overnight deposits, in the absence of renewal they are automatically repayable on the following day.

Admittedly, since the corresponding short deposits in the inter-bank market do not benefit by the existence of a lender of last resort and are not backed by collateral securities to an extent of 105 per cent, in theory they may not appear to be quite as liquid as the loans to the traditional market. In reality demand deposits and current account balances with banks are no more secure than demand deposits lent to them in the inter-bank market. Their repayment may be depended upon because of the confidence the banks' standing inspires.

Likewise LA overnight deposits can be converted into cash as easily as demand deposits with banks. Even time deposits held in the form of sterling CDs or dollar CDs are easily convertible into cash at any moment, although the amount of their proceeds depends on the prevailing rates quoted for sterling CDs and, in the case of dollar CDs, also on the prevailing sterling–dollar exchange rates. The only reservation in this respect is that in so far as the buyer's balance with his bank is reduced as a result of the transaction, the conversion of CDs into cash does not affect the total amount of money.

## (3) VELOCITY OF DEPOSITS IN PARALLEL MARKETS

The frequency with which deposits in the parallel markets change hands does not necessarily affect the volume of demand for goods, whether by producers or consumers. It depends on who is borrowing and for what purpose. From this point of view the maturity of deposits, whether or not they are marketable, is of small consequence. If a medium-term deposit is re-lent to a firm which promptly spends the proceeds in such a way as to give rise to a multiplier process this affects demand for goods and services to a very high degree, while a deposit at call which changes hands in the market several times a day does not affect it at all. Deposits lent to Local Authorities are not marketable, but their proceeds are spent by the Municipalities and are re-spent by the recipients and are re-spent again and again, until one recipient uses them for tax payment, for buying a newly issued Government security, for repayment of bank debt or, which is much less likely in Britain than in many other countries, until he hoards it.

The spending of the proceeds of deposits by a chain of recipients means their transfer from one bank to another, or at any rate from one bank account to another with the same bank. Even the latter means an increase in the velocity of the deposit, not in the technical sense as an operation within one of the money markets, but in the meaningful sense that each transfer is linked with additional demand for goods or services by producers, merchants or consumers. It is by such means that deposits originating in parallel markets give rise to a multiplier process or, in so far as they are used for capital spending or in so far as increased consumer spending leads to more capital spending, stimulate the accelerator process. That again is a circular process, for increased capital spending leads to more consumer spending.

## (4) MULTIPLIER AND ACCELERATOR EFFECTS

To the extent to which the parallel money markets provide funds for Municipal spending, hire-purchase financing, short-term credits for business firms, etc., they influence demand through their multiplier effect. To the extent to which they facilitate the granting of medium-term credits to producers they contribute directly towards capital spending – in addition to their indirect contribution towards it through stimulating increased production in consequence of higher consumer demand – through their accelerator effect.

On the other hand, in so far as an increase in medium-term credits to producers resulting from the expansion of non-clearing banks takes the place of clearing bank credits financing consumer spending, the increase in the accelerator effect tends to be offset by a reduction in the multiplier effect, at any rate until more capital spending in turn leads to more consumer spending.

The direct and indirect use of deposits originating in parallel markets leads to an increase in their velocity in a meaningful way. But operations within the market which do not lead to operations outside the market merely amount to an increase in velocity in a purely technical sense. In the inter-bank sterling market, the Euro-currency markets and the CD markets – though not in the LA deposit market, the finance house deposit market and the inter-corporation deposit market – deposits are apt to change hands very frequently, without adding anything to the demand for goods and services – unless and until a transaction places the borrowing bank in a more favourable position to lend outside the market than the lending bank had been in. Otherwise the frequent change of ownership of deposits within the market produces no effect on production or consumption. Such an increase in the velocity of deposits can have no inflationary effect.

## (5) COMPARISON WITH MONTE CARLO CASINO

The frequent change of deposits within the market may best be compared with the frequent change of ownership of gaming counters in the Monte Carlo Casino, as a result of which the Principality of Monaco has easily the highest velocity of circulation of money without any apparent inflationary effects. If banks job in and out of the parallel markets or engage in time arbitrage operations this does not add to demand. For this reason the Bank of England is right in abstaining from adopting any measures to check the expansion of the parallel markets, and confines its intervention to limiting the re-lending of deposits to industry and trade.

Admittedly, thanks to the parallel markets in a great many instances 'idle' deposits are converted into active deposits. But the influence of such developments should not be overrated. For the fact that the owner of a deposit leaves it lying idle in his bank for years on end does not mean that the velocity of that deposit is nil. The bank may lend the deposit in such a way that its velocity of circulation increases. No deposit could be much more 'idle' than the deposits of the Imperial Russian Government, which have been left unclaimed with one of the London banks ever since November 1917 when diplomatic relations between the British Government and the newly formed Soviet Government were interrupted. The Soviet Government could not claim it without acknowledging its liability for the much larger amounts lent to the Imperial Government by the Treasury, of which the deposit constitutes the unspent balance. The Treasury has no legal right to reclaim that balance, so that it has been completely 'frozen' for over half a century. Nevertheless, it would be a mistake to imagine that for over half a century the velocity of circulation of that deposit has been nil. In whichever way the bank concerned employs the funds in its custody – unless it keeps them invested in Government loans – it must have initiated multiplier and accelerator processes. From the point of view of the velocity of circulation the only difference between a so-called idle deposit and an active deposit is that the former is kept idle from the point of view of its owner, but it is activated by the bank with which the deposit is held.

## (6) VELOCITY AND EXPANSIONARY EFFECT

Any import of deposits from abroad resulting from the more attractive terms that parallel markets are able to offer produces its multiplier effect and its accelerator effect. To the extent to which British firms borrow Euro-dollars, or to which the proceeds of Euro-dollar bank borrowed are re-lent to them, these deposits too trigger off multiplier and accelerator effects. But there is no reason why their velocity should be any higher than that of domestic deposits re-lent to customers outside the market. The total amount of deposits may increase but their average velocity of circulation is unaffected.

It is therefore reasonable to assume that such expansionary or inflationary effects as parallel markets produce come about mainly as a result of the increase in the volume of credits rather than as a result of any increase in the velocity of circulation of the total deposits caused by the operation of the parallel markets.

# CHAPTER EIGHTEEN

# The Trend of Interest Rates

## (1) UPWARD SURGE OF RATES

A QUESTION second in importance only to the effect of parallel markets on the volume and velocity of credit is their effect on the trend of interest rates. In so far as they are influenced by basic economic factors, their trend tends to be in the same direction as that of interest rates in the traditional markets, though they do not necessarily follow them all the way. What we shall try to examine in this chapter is whether the existence, operation and expansion of the parallel markets does itself tend to create influences affecting interest rates independently of the basic influences.

In the course of the late 'sixties we witnessed an almost unprecedented world-wide upward surge of the entire structure of interest rates for short-term, medium-term and long-term loans alike. Simultaneously with this movement we also witnessed the emergence of some new parallel markets and the spectacular expansion of some existing ones. Was this sheer coincidence or, if not, what was the causal relationship? Was the expansion of parallel markets the cause or the effect of the sharp and persistent rise in interest rates? Would interest rates in advanced countries have been quoted in 1970 in the vicinity of 10 per cent if the Euro-dollar market and the other parallel money markets had never come into existence or if they had never expanded into their multi-billion size? Or again, would these markets have come into existence, or at any rate would they have gained such prominence, if it had not been for basic forces raising interest rates to such a high level?

## (2) IMPACT OF PARALLEL MARKETS

There is undoubtedly room for more than one opinion about the nature of the interaction between the two phenomena, about the causal relationship between them. It is arguable that the rise in interest rates was due to fundamental influences that were independent of the expansion of parallel money markets, an expansion which was merely an accessory cause or even merely an effect. Such fundamental causes were the growing demand for credit caused by economic growth, by wage inflation, by the effect of the decline in the purchasing power of money on real interest rates as distinct from interest rates in terms of money, and by the policies in Britain and in most other countries aiming at keeping down the volume of credit in face of the effect of growing consumer demand on the balance of payments.

It is equally arguable that the parallel money markets emerged and expanded as a result of the efforts of banks and others to find ways and means to raise the necessary credits through new channels, and as a result of the high interest rates which were needed in order to attract money into the new markets. On the basis of this theory the conclusion to emerge would be that the expansion of the parallel money markets was the effect and not the cause of the rise in interest rates.

## (3) EFFECT OF LARGE VOLUME OF CREDIT

It is also arguable that the new markets created an additional volume of credit, or alternatively that they increased the velocity of circulation of credit so that the same amount of credit could do more work, and it is this credit expansion which gave rise to inflation or accentuated it, or made inflation caused by other influences possible, so therefore it is the expansion of the parallel money market that caused interest rates to rise.

On the face of it this argument may appear paradoxical, for surely an increase in the volume of credit should make for lower and not higher interest rates. But amidst prevailing circumstances we do encounter similar paradoxes in our present-day economic system. For instance it is contrary to all textbook rules that an increase in unemployment should be accompanied by an accelerated rise in wages. Yet this is precisely what was happening in the United States and in Britain in 1968–70. On the basis of textbook rules as well as on the basis of common-sense rules, the change in the supply–demand relationship in the labour market resulting from an increase in unemployment should make for lower wages. Yet in both Anglo-Saxon countries the increase in unemployment even failed to prevent an escalation of wage inflation.

This paradox appears of course to be unrelated to the paradox of the rise in interest rates that takes place in spite of the expansion of the volume or velocity of credit resulting from the expansion of the parallel money markets. It has, nevertheless, one connecting link – the basically inflationary economic trends tolerated by both British and United States Governments – by British Governments in order to maintain a high level of employment, by the United States Government to maintain the continuity of business expansion. To that end 'stop-go' was abandoned or was reduced to an extent that made it ineffective.

## (4) CREDIT EXPANSION TOLERATED

The result of this policy was to prevent higher unemployment from checking wage increases. It also prevented high interest rates from producing their normal effects on production and consumption. Unemployment did increase, especially in the United States, during 1969–70, but it would have increased much more if the volume of credit had been effectively kept down, or if the rise in interest rates had been allowed to produce its natural effect on the volume of credit and on employment.

The conclusion from the above argument is that the British and American authorities permitted or at any rate tolerated an expansion of credit through the development of the new markets, but they did not permit a sufficient degree of expansion to keep interest rates low. Alternatively, the permitted degree of expansion has produced such a fall in the purchasing power of money that interest rates, in order to stand still, had to run upwards very fast. A considerable increase in nominal interest rates became necessary in order to maintain real interest rates at an acceptable level from the lender's point of view.

The two lines of argument are not mutually exclusive: there is some degree of truth in both and there must be a fairly high degree of truth in a combination of the two.

## (5) INFLUENCE OF DEMAND FOR EURO-DOLLARS

The most striking example of the impact of one of the parallel markets on interest rates was provided by the role played by the Euro-dollar market in connection with the rise in interest rates during the late 'sixties. It was accompanied by a spectacular increase in the volume of Euro-dollars. Would the increase in interest rates have taken place if the Euro-dollar market had not been invented? To answer this question the reader is referred to Chapter 11 on the Euro-dollar market, which describes the way in which misguided American monetary policy led to a sharp increase in American borrowing of Euro-dollars, leaving a loophole through which banks sought to evade the credit squeeze with official approval, thereby pushing up Euro-dollar rates and with them the entire structure of international interest rates. Had there been no Euro-dollar market the credit squeeze in the United States might not have been mitigated sufficiently to avoid too sharp a setback to business expansion. As it was, the United States monetary authorities felt they could afford to go through the motions of being truly tough on the domestic front because the effect of their toughness could be lessened by American borrowing in the Euro-dollar market.

In reality, as I tried to explain in Chapter 11, the borrowing of Euro-dollars by London branches of American banks for the purpose of lending them to their head offices affected only marginally the credit squeeze in the United States. Its main effect is that American banks siphon off each other's deposits. Each Euro-dollar transaction means that the deposit with one American bank is transferred to another American bank – or is even merely transferred from one account to another within the same bank. The volume of credit in the United States only changes to the extent to which the American bank that has lost the deposit is able to maintain the volume of its credits by making fuller use of its available facilities.

## (6) RESULT OF MISTAKEN MONETARY POLICY

This means that the net result of the American borrowing of Euro-dollars was continued tightness and high interest rates in New York and higher interest rates all over the world caused by higher Euro-dollar rates. This result was not due to any fault inherent in the system of parallel markets or in the Euro-dollar system in particular, but to the ill-advised monetary policy of the United States authorities. They ought to have checked the large-scale American borrowing of Euro-dollars which was by far the most important cause of the world-wide trend towards interest rate increases in the late 'sixties and again in the late spring of 1970. But they let it proceed because, among other reasons, the borrowing of Euro-dollars brought welcome support to the American balance of payments, which was in bad need of support, especially after the contraction of facilities in the Euro-bond market. That contraction was itself largely the result of the rise in Euro-dollar rates. By permitting American banks to borrow Euro-dollars the United States authorities prevented borrowing through issuing Euro-bonds.

In the absence of such misuse of the facilities of the Euro-dollar market this would have tended to ease monetary tightness by providing additional facilities. As we saw in Chapter 16 and in Chapter 17, the lending of Euro-dollars increased slightly the volume of credit and its velocity. The normal effect of such a change should be a decline in interest rates, unless its inflationary effect reduces the real value of interest payments, thereby necessitating an increase in the nominal rate of interest to compensate lenders. But in the absence of such an effect, if credit is expanding interest rates should be declining. Instead they were increasing in New York and, through their international effects, all over the free world.

In Britain, too, the authorities actively encouraged the borrowing of Euro-dollars, not only in order to strengthen the official dollar reserve and reduce the external debt, but also in order to counteract the natural depressing effect that the domestic credit squeeze would have produced on the economy. Had the effect of the credit squeeze not been offset in part by the liberal granting of licences to borrow Euro-dollars and other foreign currencies, tight credit conditions might have kept down the rises in wages and prices, or at any rate their extent might have been mitigated. The resulting appreciation of forward sterling would have attracted dollars through inward arbitrage and would have kept sterling interest rates well under dollar interest rates.

## (7) IMPACT OF INTER-BANK STERLING MARKET

The effect of the expansion of the inter-bank sterling market is that short-term interest rates in London have become less easy to control. This does not mean that the Bank of England has lost control over the money market. As we saw in Chapter 3, its near-perfect control over the traditional markets affects the parallel markets indirectly to a considerable, if inadequate, extent. It is unable to prevent the wild antics of short-term inter-bank sterling rates, but Bank rate decisions and intervention in Lombard Street do affect the trend in the inter-bank sterling market as in other parallel markets.

In the absence of a market in inter-bank sterling deposits it might have been easier to keep interest rates down, because banks with surpluses, having no alternative use for their liquid resources, would have employed much of them in the traditional market. But judging by the wide differentials between Treasury bill rates and corresponding rates in the inter-bank sterling market or in other parallel markets, the attraction of the latter was unable to prevent Treasury bill rates from remaining low as a result of their eligibility and of the reduction in their volume.

### (8) OTHER PARALLEL MARKETS

The market in sterling CDs is at the time of writing still in its infancy and its rates merely reflect those of the inter-bank deposit market, allowing for the differentials due to the advantage of being able to recover the deposit by selling the CD in the secondary market. But there is no reason why Certificates of Deposits should not become as important in Britain as they were in the United States until Regulation Q made it impossible to issue them at attractive rates. More was said about the prospects of sterling CDs in Chapter 8.

In theory the possibility for finance houses to borrow deposits at current market rates – again allowing for the differentials in relation to rival short-term investments – should have brought hire-purchase terms down from the level they were at when minor finance houses advertised for deposits at twice the current market rates. But in practice there is very little relationship between the rates paid by finance houses and the incomparably higher rates charged by firms selling on deferred payments.

If LA deposits had a secondary market their rates might be a factor of considerable importance affecting inter-bank sterling rates. As it is, they do influence sterling CD rates and finance house deposit rates to some extent and are in turn influenced by those rates. But in relation to inter-bank sterling rates they usually play an essentially passive role.

## (9) EFFECT ON CAPITAL MOVEMENTS

One of the effects of the higher rates obtainable in various parallel money markets is that these markets divert some capital from short Government bonds and from the Gilt-edged market in general, indeed from the Stock Exchange as a whole. As the parallel markets offer high yields on short-term deposits it has become less urgent for investors to reinvest their capital. More of them prefer to keep their funds in a liquid form with a relatively high yield until some good long-term investment opportunity arises. They can better afford to wait instead of rushing into re-investment in order not to lose interest. As there is always a fair amount of capital awaiting reinvestment this must make some difference to the volume of demand for short-term investments and may tend to raise long-term rates. Some Stock Exchange firms specialise in the use of such funds in the parallel markets, not only for their own clients but also for investors in general.

As already pointed out in Chapter 16, parallel money markets are apt to attract foreign capital, and to the extent to which sterling benefits by this the influx tends to lower or keep down interest rates in the receiving country. Needless to say, it produces the opposite effect when a change in the interest differentials or in forward margins reverses the flow of foreign funds invested in parallel money markets. LA deposits often offer tempting rates for non-residents. Until the Mersey Docks default the deposits came to be considered to be virtually gilt-edged, in the United States and other countries, thanks to the persuasive arguments advanced by foreign bank branches in London.

Altogether the advent of a large number of foreign branches, attracted in the first instance by the Euro-dollar market, tends to lower interest rates in the parallel money markets. Most of them do not confine themselves to the Euro-dollar market but are more or less active in other parallel markets. Since American banks came over here mainly for the purpose of borrowing Euro-dollars, in order not to be one-sided borrowers they often appeared as lenders in other parallel markets. Owing to their large numbers, between them they are liable to affect occasionally the trend of interest rates in those markets.

# APPENDIX ONE

# Assets and Borrowed Funds of the Discount Market

THE following table, published by the *Bank of England Quarterly Review*, specifies the assets in which the discount market invested its funds and the sources from which it borrowed them between the end of 1966 and the end of the first quarter of 1970.

£ millions

| End of: | Total | British Government stocks | British Government Treasury bills | Assets — Other sterling bills | Assets — Local Authority securities | Negotiable Certificates of Deposit — Sterling | Negotiable Certificates of Deposit — U.S. dollars | Other |
|---|---|---|---|---|---|---|---|---|
| 1966 | 1,565 | 542 | 424 | 404 | 101 | | | 95 |
| 1967 | 1,747 | 544 | 548 | 437 | 115 | | 14 | 89 |
| 1968 Mar. | 1,459 | 573 | 255 | 414 | 131 | | 14 | 73 |
| June | 1,383 | 378 | 287 | 509 | 130 | | 17 | 61 |
| Sep. | 1,563 | 521 | 261 | 500 | 157 | | 43 | 82 |
| Dec. | 1,663 | 306 | 471 | 560 | 148 | 56 | 39 | 83 |
| 1969 Mar. | 1,357 | 254 | 261 | 520 | 140 | 60 | 24 | 99 |
| June | 1,424 | 259 | 280 | 555 | 155 | 72 | 19 | 83 |
| Sep. | 1,398 | 256 | 212 | 561 | 180 | 79 | 20 | 90 |
| Dec. | 1,817 | 364 | 399 | 629 | 192 | 97 | 31 | 104 |
| 1970 Mar. | 1,417 | 330 | 198 | 510 | 121 | 95 | 25 | 139 |
| June | 1,643 | 196 | 360 | 613 | 162 | 156 | 20 | 136 |
| Sep. | 1,985 | 197 | 514 | 671 | 183 | 264 | 31 | 123 |

| End of: | Total | Bank of England, Banking Department | Borrowed funds | | | Accepting houses, overseas banks and other banks | Other sources |
| | | | London clearing banks | Scottish banks | Other deposit banks | | |
|---|---|---|---|---|---|---|---|
| 1966 | 1,484 | 82 | 978 | 94 | 11 | 201 | 119 |
| 1967 | 1,662 | 116 | 1,076 | 102 | 21 | 218 | 130 |
| | | | | | | | |
| 1968 Mar. | 1,368 | 210 | 817 | 67 | 21 | 154 | 98 |
| June | 1,297 | 161 | 762 | 75 | 17 | 158 | 124 |
| Sep. | 1,466 | 31 | 1,044 | 95 | 12 | 161 | 123 |
| Dec. | 1,573 | — | 1,132 | 100 | 15 | 204 | 121 |
| | | | | | | | |
| 1969 Mar. | 1,270 | — | 913 | 52 | 15 | 166 | 125 |
| June | 1,336 | 17 | 1,001 | 47 | 7 | 159 | 106 |
| Sep. | 1,311 | — | 974 | 62 | 9 | 166 | 99 |
| Dec. | 1,725 | — | 1,304 | 98 | 12 | 202 | 109 |
| | | | | | | | |
| 1970 Mar. | 1,320 | 28 | 912 | 50 | 15 | 214 | 102 |
| June | 1,551 | 67 | 961 | 52 | 16 | 298 | 157 |
| Sep. | 1,886 | — | 1,281 | 75 | 9 | 355 | 165 |

## APPENDIX TWO

# Bank of England Intervention in the Money Market

THE following figures indicate the number of occasions on which the Bank of England intervened in the money market during the year ended 18 March 1970, the total amounts involved in the intervention and the form which the assistance given to the market assumed. These figures were published in the *Bank of England Quarterly Review*.

| | Frequency of intervention | | | | Amount of intervention (£ millions) | | | | |
| | | Assistance given | | | | Assistance given | | | |
| | No intervention | At or above Bank rate | Other | Surpluses absorbed by sales of bills | Advances at or above Bank rate | Other advances | Purchases of bills Treasury bills | Other | Surpluses absorbed by sales of bills |
|---|---|---|---|---|---|---|---|---|---|
| **1969** | | | | | | | | | |
| 20 Mar.–16 Apr. | 5 | — | 12 | 5 | — | — | 193·1 | — | 160·3 |
| 17 Apr. –21 May | 5 | — | 19 | 6 | — | — | 476·5 | 103·6 | 110·8 |
| 22 May–18 June | 3 | — | 7 | 13 | — | — | 92·9 | — | 165·8 |
| 19 June–16 July | 5 | — | 13 | 4 | — | 17·0 | 409·4 | 3·0 | 47·0 |
| 17 July –20 Aug. | 3 | — | 15 | 7 | — | 102·5 | 403·0 | 54·1 | 96·0 |
| 21 Aug.–17 Sep. | 4 | — | 11 | 4 | — | — | 157·4 | 5·7 | 43·5 |
| 18 Sep. –15 Oct. | 1 | — | 17 | 2 | — | — | 450·3 | 35·0 | 16·5 |
| 16 Oct. –19 Nov. | 10 | — | 8 | 7 | — | — | 236·9 | — | 169·5 |
| 20 Nov.–10 Dec. | 6 | — | 6 | 3 | — | 65·5 | 99·5 | — | 61·0 |
| **1970** 11 Dec.1969–21 Jan. | 2 | — | 14 | 12 | — | 140·0 | 396·8 | 13·0 | 190·5 |
| 22 Jan. –18 Feb. | 4 | 5 | 16 | 4 | — | 36·0 | 265·6 | 52·1 | 107·0 |
| 19 Feb. –18 Mar. | 5 | 1 | 13 | 3 | 139·3 | — | 235·8 | 61·5 | 45·5 |
| 19 Mar.–15 Apr. | 5 | 1 | 8 | 5 | 28·5 | — | 182·4 | 4·0 | 107·3 |
| 16 Apr. –20 May | 2 | 1 | 13 | 9 | 12·0 | — | 284·5 | 12·5 | 251·8 |
| 21 May –17 June | 2 | 3 | 14 | 3 | 16·5 | — | 259·4 | 9·5 | 87·0 |
| 18 June –15 July | 2 | 3 | 15 | 1 | 172·0 | — | 475·8 | 8·6 | 2·0 |
| 16 July –19 Aug. | 3 | 3 | 14 | 7 | 50·0 | — | 266·5 | 3·9 | 221·3 |
| 20 Aug.–16 Sep. | 3 | 6 | 8 | 2 | 307·0 | — | 270·8 | — | 15·8 |

# Deposits with U.K. Banks and Discount Houses

THE following table, published in the *Bank of England Quarterly Review*, shows the amount of deposits held by various categories of depositors with deposit banks (mainly clearing banks), accepting houses, overseas banks and other banks, and discount houses between the end of the third quarter of 1968 and the end of the first quarter of 1970.

£ millions

| End of: | Total | U.K. residents | | | | | | Negotiable sterling Certificates of Deposit | Overseas residents |
|---|---|---|---|---|---|---|---|---|---|
| | | Government | Local Authorities | Public corporations | Financial institutions | Companies | Other | | |
| **Deposit banks** | | | | | | | | | |
| 1968 Sep. | 11,304 | 179 | 120 | 51 | 345 | 1,944 | 8,185 | | 480 |
| Dec. | 11,667 | 175 | 125 | 53 | 375 | 2,146 | 8,313 | | 480 |
| 1969 Mar. | 11,270 | 212 | 120 | 69 | 350 | 1,818 | 8,258 | | 443 |
| June | 11,160 | 195 | 109 | 53 | 327 | 1,679 | 8,332 | | 465 |
| Sep. | 11,136 | 194 | 103 | 56 | 330 | 1,730 | 8,305 | | 418 |
| Dec. | 11,814 | 179 | 143 | 61 | 389 | 1,945 | 8,638 | | 459 |
| 1970 Mar. | 11,574 | 224 | 132 | 83 | 326 | 1,800 | 8,525 | | 484 |
| **Accepting houses, overseas banks, and other banks** | | | | | | | | | |
| 1968 Sep. | 9,600 | 8 | 4 | 17 | 346 | 1,269 | 512 | | 7,444 |
| Dec. | 10,349 | 4 | 7 | 16 | 367 | 1,301 | 521 | 83 | 8,050 |
| 1969 Mar. | 11,487 | 3 | 5 | 15 | 386 | 1,353 | 561 | 115 | 9,049 |
| June | 13,894 | 9 | 4 | 40 | 496 | 1,280 | 562 | 110 | 11,393 |
| Sep. | 15,185 | 7 | 8 | 49 | 531 | 1,329 | 602 | 135 | 12,524 |
| Dec. | 15,558 | 6 | 13 | 25 | 513 | 1,338 | 604 | 176 | 12,883 |
| 1970 Mar. | 15,874 | 7 | 8 | 23 | 478 | 1,314 | 568 | 214 | 13,262 |
| **Discount market** | | | | | | | | | |
| 1968 Sep. | 123 | — | — | — | 7 | 42 | 37 | | 37 |
| Dec. | 121 | — | — | — | 9 | 57 | 36 | | 19 |
| 1969 Mar. | 125 | — | — | — | 17 | 61 | 33 | | 14 |
| June | 106 | — | — | — | 24 | 42 | 26 | | 14 |
| Sep. | 99 | — | — | — | 32 | 30 | 23 | | 14 |
| Dec. | 109 | — | — | — | 39 | 32 | 22 | | 16 |
| 1970 Mar. | 102 | — | — | — | 38 | 24 | 23 | | 17 |

# APPENDIX FOUR

# Deposits of Non-Clearing Banks

THE following table, published by the *Bank of England Quarterly Review*, shows the amounts of deposits held with non-clearing banks, those held by non-clearing banks with other U.K. banks, the amounts of sterling and dollar Certificates of Deposits issued by them, and the amounts of their liquid assets.

£ millions

| End of: | Current and deposit accounts | | | | | | Negotiable Certificates of Deposits | |
| | U.K. banks | | Other U.K. residents | | Overseas residents | | | |
| | Sterling | Other currencies | Sterling | Other currencies | Sterling | Other currencies | Sterling | U.S. dollars |
|---|---|---|---|---|---|---|---|---|
| 1966 | 483·7 | 919·5 | 1,159·3 | 121·6 | 1,250·1 | 2,792·5 | | 80·5 |
| 1967 | 703·6 | 1,541·7 | 1,398·5 | 210·6 | 1,166·9 | 4,029·8 | | 248·8 |
| | 736·3 | 1,575·4 | 1,570·5 | 219·4 | 1,185·9 | 4,060·8 | | 248·8 |
| 1968 Sep. | 838·8 | 2,022·1 | 1,912·8 | 243·0 | 1,178·4 | 5,863·9 | | 567·9 |
| Dec. | 1,058·7 | 1,946·5 | 1,939·1 | 276·8 | 1,083·8 | 6,523·4 | 165·3 | 597·0 |
| 1969 Mar. | 1,201·6 | 2,726·9 | 2,041·0 | 282·4 | 1,059·9 | 7,394·7 | 261·3 | 754·6 |
| June | 1,190·9 | 3,640·9 | 2,060·5 | 345·6 | 1,068·5 | 9,480·0 | 280·8 | 1,025·6 |
| Sep. | 1,355·9 | 4,107·1 | 2,129·8 | 396·8 | 1,013·8 | 10,399·2 | 322·8 | 1,305·7 |
| Dec. | 1,483·0 | 4,116·2 | 2,103·3 | 396·8 | 1,079·8 | 10,484·3 | 442·5 | 1,541·2 |
| 1970 Mar. | 1,499·7 | 4,590·5 | 1,989·1 | 407·7 | 1,173·9 | 10,621·2 | 545·3 | 1,684·4 |

| End of: | Balances with U.K. banks other than Bank of England | | Money at call and short notice | | Sterling bills discounted | | | |
|---|---|---|---|---|---|---|---|---|
| | Sterling | Other currencies | To discount market | To other borrowers | Total | British Government Treasury bills | Other U.K. bills | Other |
| 1966 | 510·1 | 834·6 | 197·5 | 44·0 | 193·9 | 60·5 | 83·8 | 49·6 |
| 1967 { | 683·6 | 1,445·4 | 209·0 | 37·9 | 190·8 | 78·1 | 68·0 | 44·7 |
| | 760·2 | 1,475·3 | 209·8 | 39·0 | 197·5 | 80·0 | 70·1 | 47·4 |
| 1968 Sep. | 899·7 | 1,858·1 | 143·4 | 69·0 | 164·4 | 47·1 | 73·7 | 43·6 |
| Dec. | 1,122·6 | 1,848·4 | 181·8 | 73·1 | 171·3 | 47·2 | 79·9 | 44·2 |
| 1969 Mar. | 1,261·7 | 2,563·3 | 152·2 | 62·7 | 186·7 | 68·6 | 72·1 | 46·0 |
| June | 1,280·6 | 3,520·3 | 143·0 | 71·5 | 164·8 | 47·4 | 65·1 | 52·3 |
| Sep. | 1,457·2 | 4,176·5 | 142·7 | 81·5 | 174·0 | 49·6 | 69·2 | 55·2 |
| Dec. | 1,566·9 | 4,150·5 | 167·2 | 81·6 | 154·0 | 36·6 | 62·7 | 54·8 |
| 1970 Mar. | 1,483·9 | 4,590·5 | 177·2 | 70·8 | 161·2 | 50·0 | 63·9 | 47·2 |

# APPENDIX FIVE

# Local Authority Short-term Debts

THE following table, based on figures compiled by the Central Statistical Office, shows the changes in the outstanding amount of Local Authority short-term debts between 1963 and 1969.

£ millions

| End of period: | Total, excluding inter-Authority debt | Banks | | Other financial institutions | Industrial and commercial companies | Personal sector | Other | Total, including inter-Authority debt | Up to seven days | Over seven days and up to three months | Over three months and up to twelve months |
|---|---|---|---|---|---|---|---|---|---|---|---|
| | | Over-drafts | Other loans | | | | | | | | |
| 1963 1st quarter | 1,241 | 72 | 304 | 197 | 346 | 165 | 157 | 1,268 | 693 | 284 | 291 |
| 1964 1st quarter | 1,483 | 71 | 348 | 225 | 458 | 195 | 186 | 1,518 | 878 | 289 | 351 |
| 1965 1st quarter | 1,809 | 147 | 404 | 212 | 506 | 314 | 226 | 1,847 | 1,239 | 315 | 293 |
| 1966 1st quarter | 1,674 | 56 | 332 | 372 | 384 | 325 | 205 | 1,728 | 1,188 | 329 | 211 |
| 1967 1st quarter | 1,644 | 54 | 382 | 326 | 334 | 303 | 245 | 1,720 | 1,238 | 229 | 253 |
| 2nd quarter | 1,708 | 33 | 362 | 386 | 378 | 305 | 244 | 1,761 | 1,369 | 156 | 236 |
| 3rd quarter | 1,778 | 46 | 384 | 422 | 395 | 295 | 236 | 1,840 | 1,409 | 185 | 246 |
| 4th quarter | 1,854 | 115 | 387 | 404 | 422 | 309 | 217 | 1,918 | 1,468 | 253 | 197 |
| 1968 1st quarter | 2,007 | 174 | 491 | 353 | 410 | 334 | 245 | 2,073 | 1,545 | 311 | 217 |
| 2nd quarter | 2,151 | 141 | 617 | 386 | 422 | 349 | 236 | 2,228 | 1,836 | 186 | 206 |
| 3rd quarter | 2,063 | 117 | 631 | 362 | 411 | 338 | 204 | 2,138 | 1,722 | 195 | 221 |
| 4th quarter | 1,870 | 107 | 438 | 419 | 363 | 314 | 229 | 1,952 | 1,496 | 192 | 264 |
| 1969 1st quarter | 1,959 | 133 | 501 | 438 | 312 | 330 | 245 | 2,023 | 1,467 | 211 | 345 |
| 2nd quarter | 2,048 | 169 | 527 | 474 | 315 | 343 | 220 | 2,122 | 1,649 | 171 | 302 |
| 3rd quarter | 2,046 | 177 | 430 | 513 | 321 | 334 | 271 | 2,128 | 1,645 | 166 | 317 |
| 4th quarter | 1,896 | 102 | 404 | 527 | 285 | 327 | 251 | 1,982 | 1,429 | 215 | 338 |

# Assets and Liabilities of Finance Houses

THE following table gives the totals of selected assets and liabilities of all finance houses and compares them with the corresponding figures of members of the Finance Houses Association. It shows that some 95 per cent of deposits borrowed by finance houses at the end of 1969 was borrowed by members of the F.H.A. It also shows that during the last three years the amount of deposits borrowed by finance houses was virtually static.

£ millions

| | Dec. 31 1966 All | Dec. 31 1966 F.H.A. | Dec. 31 1967 All | Dec. 31 1967 F.H.A. | June 30 1968 All | June 30 1968 F.H. |
|---|---|---|---|---|---|---|
| *Selected assets* | | | | | | |
| Assets with United Kingdom financial institutions other than banks | 12 | 7 | 9 | 7 | 8 | 7 |
| Trade investments and investments in unconsolidated subsidiaries | 48 | 43 | 63 | 59 | 65 | 61 |
| Other securities | 35 | 33 | 24 | 13 | 17 | 13 |
| Hire-purchase, credit sale and other instalment credit outstanding* | 842 | 674 | 824 | 674 | 854 | 704 |
| Other advances and loans | 127 | 113 | 133 | 116 | 122 | 108 |
| Leasing | 52 | 47 | 64 | 56 | 75 | 65 |
| TOTAL | 1,116 | 917 | 1,117 | 925 | 1,141 | 958 |
| *Selected liabilities* | | | | | | |
| Bills discounted with United Kingdom banks and discount houses | 106 | 99 | 98 | 90 | 130 | 120 |
| Deposits by: | | | | | | |
| (a) United Kingdom banks | 81 | 80 | 85 | 83 | 104 | 103 |
| (b) Other United Kingdom financial institutions | 68 | 65 | 66 | 61 | 60 | 56 |
| (c) United Kingdom non-financial companies | 255 | 252 | 248 | 246 | 254 | 252 |
| (d) Other United Kingdom residents | 114 | 109 | 104 | 100 | 107 | 104 |
| (e) Overseas residents | 130 | 127 | 88 | 88 | 71 | 71 |
| Total deposits | 648 | 633 | 591 | 578 | 596 | 586 |
| Other borrowing: | | | | | | |
| (a) United Kingdom banks (net)† | 43 | 10 | 77 | 48 | 55 | 34 |
| (b) Other United Kingdom financial institutions | 5 | — | 9 | 7 | 7 | 5 |
| (c) United Kingdom non-financial companies | 1 | — | 1 | — | 1 | — |
| (d) Other United Kingdom residents | 6 | 5 | 8 | 7 | 8 | 6 |
| (e) Overseas residents | — | — | — | — | 1 | — |
| Total other borrowing | 55 | 15 | 95 | 62 | 72 | 45 |
| Unearned finance charges | 86 | 68 | 93 | 76 | 101 | 82 |
| Issued capital and reserves‡ | 180 | 153 | 191 | 172 | 197 | 177 |
| TOTAL | 1,075 | 968 | 1,068 | 978 | 1,096 | 1,010 |

\* Including agreements block discounted with finance houses by retailers.
† Cash and balances with United Kingdom banks have been deducted from this item.

Holdings at

| | Sep. 30 1968 | | Dec. 31 1968 | | Mar. 31 1969 | | June 30 1969 | | Sep. 30 1969 | | Dec. 31 1969 | |
|---|---|---|---|---|---|---|---|---|---|---|---|---|
| | | F.H.A. | All | F.H.A. | All | F.H.A. | All | F.H.A. | All | F.H.A. | All | F.H.A. |
| 8 | 7 | 7 | 7 | 7 | 8 | 7 | 7 | 7 | 8 | 7 | 10 | 8 |
| 1 | 58 | 48 | 45 | 48 | 45 | 47 | 43 | 51 | 47 | 55 | 50 | |
| 4 | 20 | 18 | 11 | 28 | 21 | 22 | 14 | 26 | 20 | 23 | 17 | |
| 0 | 707 | 843 | 703 | 834 | 696 | 843 | 701 | 842 | 697 | 819 | 678 | |
| 2 | 102 | 115 | 105 | 108 | 100 | 104 | 98 | 104 | 98 | 107 | 99 | |
| 1 | 69 | 95 | 78 | 103 | 82 | 109 | 88 | 119 | 95 | 127 | 101 | |
| 6 | 963 | 1,126 | 949 | 1,129 | 951 | 1,132 | 951 | 1,150 | 964 | 1,141 | 953 | |
| 2 | 102 | 109 | 102 | 105 | 97 | 102 | 93 | 102 | 93 | 97 | 90 | |
| 2 | 99 | 109 | 105 | 99 | 98 | 106 | 104 | 115 | 112 | 104 | 100 | |
| 77 | 73 | 88 | 85 | 102 | 96 | 95 | 91 | 88 | 85 | 83 | 81 | |
| 52 | 256 | 269 | 261 | 277 | 267 | 293 | 285 | 313 | 301 | 322 | 306 | |
| 05 | 103 | 103 | 100 | 111 | 108 | 110 | 107 | 101 | 99 | 101 | 98 | |
| 54 | 54 | 43 | 43 | 38 | 38 | 33 | 33 | 26 | 26 | 26 | 24 | |
| 00 | 585 | 612 | 594 | 627 | 607 | 637 | 620 | 643 | 623 | 636 | 609 | |
| 87 | 56 | 72 | 39 | 70 | 46 | 66 | 39 | 57 | 32 | 37 | 21 | |
| 7 | 5 | 7 | 5 | 7 | 5 | 7 | 5 | 7 | 5 | 8 | 5 | |
| 1 | — | 1 | — | 1 | — | 1 | — | 1 | — | 18 | — | |
| 8 | 6 | 7 | 6 | 5 | 4 | 5 | 4 | 5 | 4 | 5 | 3 | |
| — | — | — | — | — | — | — | — | — | — | — | — | |
| 03 | 67 | 87 | 50 | 83 | 55 | 79 | 48 | 70 | 41 | 68 | 29 | |
| 03 | 83 | 102 | 86 | 100 | 85 | 101 | 85 | 102 | 86 | 99 | 84 | |
| 98 | 177 | 198 | 175 | 200 | 180 | 196 | 175 | 196 | 174 | 201 | 179 | |
| 11 | 1,014 | 1,108 | 1,007 | 1,129 | 1,024 | 1,115 | 1,021 | 1,113 | 1,017 | 1,101 | 1,091 | |

‡ As shown on each company's last balance sheet.
— Indicates less than £0·5 million.

Source: Board of Trade.

# Self-Liquidating Character of Hire-Purchase Credits

THE following table, published in the *Board of Trade Journal*, indicates the essentially self-liquidating character of credits granted for the financing of hire-purchase transactions. It shows that repayments of such credits, whether extended by shops or by finance houses, run very close to newly granted credits. These figures confirm the contention that deposits borrowed by finance houses are based on essentially self-liquidating credits, even though the process of self-liquidation is necessarily longer than for ordinary commercial transactions financed by commercial bills.

£ millions — Seasonally adjusted

| | | Total | By shops* | By finance houses | Repayments | Increase in debt |
|---|---|---|---|---|---|---|
| | | | | *New credit extended* | | |
| 1966 | | 904 | 235 | 669 | 1,041 | − 137 |
| 1967 | | 981 | 235 | 746 | 1,027 | − 46 |
| 1968 | | 1,027 | 258 | 769 | 996 | 31 |
| 1969 | | 930 | 229 | 701 | 956 | − 26 |
| 1966 | 1st quarter | 270 | 69 | 201 | 274 | − 4 |
| | 2nd quarter | 251 | 61 | 190 | 268 | − 17 |
| | 3rd quarter | 202 | 55 | 147 | 251 | − 49 |
| | 4th quarter | 181 | 50 | 131 | 248 | − 67 |
| 1967 | 1st quarter | 198 | 53 | 145 | 254 | − 56 |
| | 2nd quarter | 215 | 53 | 162 | 254 | − 39 |
| | 3rd quarter | 274 | 61 | 213 | 261 | 13 |
| | 4th quarter | 294 | 68 | 226 | 258 | 36 |
| 1968 | 1st quarter | 292 | 77 | 215 | 264 | 28 |
| | 2nd quarter | 227 | 59 | 168 | 249 | − 22 |
| | 3rd quarter | 251 | 64 | 187 | 243 | 8 |
| | 4th quarter | 257 | 58 | 199 | 240 | 17 |
| 1969 | 1st quarter | 225 | 56 | 169 | 242 | − 17 |
| | 2nd quarter | 223 | 57 | 166 | 239 | − 16 |
| | 3rd quarter | 234 | 58 | 176 | 235 | − 1 |
| | 4th quarter | 248 | 58 | 190 | 240 | 8 |

* Durable goods shops and department stores; not including other instalment credit retailers.

# APPENDIX EIGHT

## Interest Rates in Traditional and Parallel Markets

THE following table, published by the *Midland Bank Review,* shows the changes in interest rates in traditional money markets and some parallel money markets between 1964 and 1969.

Per cent per annum – end of period

| | 1964 | 1965 | 1966 | 1967 | 1968 Mar. | June | Sep. | Dec. | 1969 Mar. | June | Sep. | Dec. |
|---|---|---|---|---|---|---|---|---|---|---|---|---|
| Bank rate | 7·00 | 6·00 | 7·00 | 8·00 | 7·50 | 7·50 | 7·00 | 7·00 | 8·00 | 8·00 | 8·00 | 8·00 |
| Clearing banks: | | | | | | | | | | | | |
| Deposit rate | 5·00 | 4·00 | 5·00 | 6·00 | 5·50 | 5·50 | 5·00 | 5·00 | 6·00 | 6·00 | 6·00 | 6·00 |
| Call money rate* | 5·375 | 4·375 | 5·375 | 6·25 | 5·875 | 5·375 | 5·375 | 5·375 | 6·25 | 6·375 | 6·375 | 6·375 |
| Treasury bills (yield) | 6·74 | 5·60 | 6·64 | 7·62 | 7·24 | 7·37 | 6·69 | 6·90 | 7·93 | 8·04 | 7·97 | 7·80 |
| Bank bills (three months) | 6·84 | 5·91 | 6·91 | 7·78 | 7·41 | 7·66 | 6·97 | 7·28 | 8·41 | 8·88 | 8·88 | 8·88 |
| Deposits with Local Authorities: | | | | | | | | | | | | |
| (seven days) | 8·00 | 6·25 | 7·38 | 8·44 | 9·00 | 8·13 | 7·44 | 7·25 | 8·69 | 8·69 | 9·63 | 8·88 |
| (three months) | 7·69 | 6·38 | 7·28 | 7·63 | 8·06 | 8·13 | 7·40 | 7·75 | 8·88 | 9·38 | 9·88 | 9·03 |
| Deposits with finance houses: | | | | | | | | | | | | |
| (three months) | 7·69 | 6·56 | 7·38 | 8·19 | 8·75 | 8·50 | 7·56 | 8·00 | 9·13 | 9·81 | 10·38 | 10·38 |
| (six months) | 7·63 | 6·75 | 7·44 | 8·25 | 8·00 | 8·50 | 7·56 | 8·13 | 9·19 | 9·94 | 9·56 | 9·63 |
| Euro-dollar deposits (three months) | 4·50 | 5·25 | 7·75 | 6·31 | 6·38 | 6·38 | 6·25 | 7·13 | 8·53 | 10·56 | 11·25 | 10·06 |

* Minimum.

# Index

## DATE DUE

| 6/19 | | | |
|------|------|------|------|
| | | | |
| | | | |
| | | | |
| | | | |
| | | | |
| | | | |
| | | | |
| | | | |
| | | | |
| | | | |
| | | | |
| | | | |
| | | | |
| | | | |
| | | | |
| | | | |

GAYLORD | | | PRINTED IN U.S.A.